Women of Color in STEM

A volume in
Research on Women and Education
Janice Koch and Beverly Irby, *Series Editors*

Women of Color in STEM

Navigating the Workforce

edited by

Julia Ballenger
Texas A&M University–Commerce

Barbara Polnick
Sam Houston State University

Beverly Irby
Texas A&M University

INFORMATION AGE PUBLISHING, INC.
Charlotte, NC • www.infoagepub.com

Library of Congress Cataloging-in-Publication Data

A CIP record for this book is available from the Library of Congress
http://www.loc.gov

ISBN: 978-1-68123-706-0 (Paperback)
        978-1-68123-707-7 (Hardcover)
        978-1-68123-708-4 (ebook)

CONTENTS

Foreword vii

Introduction.. xi

PART I

WOMEN OF COLOR IN STEM: RESILIENCE AND OPPORTUNITY

1 What Plato Took for Granted: An Examination of the First Five
African Female Mathematicians and What That Says About
Resistance to the Western Epistemological Canon............................ 3
Nicole M. Joseph

2 Women of Color in the STEM Academic Workplace........................ 39
Lindsay Johnson, Kecia M. Thomas, and Lindsay Brown

3 Breaking Barriers: Inspiring Stories About NASA
Women of Color 57
Lisa Brown, Andrea Foster, and Barbara Polnick

4 Mathematics Literacy, Identity Resilience, and Opportunity
Sixty Years Since *Brown v. Board:* Counternarratives of a Five-
Generation Family.. 79
*Jacqueline Leonard, Erica N. Walker, Victoria R. Cloud
and Nicole M. Joseph*

PART II

WOMEN OF COLOR IN STEM:
STORIES OF STRUGGLES AND SUCCESS

5 The Fulfillment of a Mother's Dream: An African Woman's
Story of Struggle and Success in Science...111
Cailisha L. Petty and Catherine Dinitra White

6 Navigating the STEM Landscape: Examining the Role
of Spatial Reasoning for Women of Color...................................... 135
Samina Hadi-Tabassum

7 Diversity in STEM? Challenges Influencing the Experiences
of African American Female Engineers 157
Delores Rice

8 Present But Not Accounted For: Examining How
Intersectional Identities Create a Double Bind for and Affect
Leadership of Women of Color in Educational Settings................ 181
*Adrienne R. Carter-Sowell, Danielle D. Dickens, Gabe H. Miller,
and Carla A. Zimmerman*

About the Editors 203

About the Contributors.. 205

FOREWORD

Mary Alfred

The current state of affairs regarding people of color in STEM disciplines has become one of the thorniest issues of contemporary focus, according to Bonner, Alfred, Lewis, Nave, and Fryzel (2009). These authors, along with many other critical scholars, lament on what started as a national concern in STEM has now escalated to crisis point. The crisis is more pronounced when we peel away the layers and examine participation in STEM by race and gender, and explore how these two identity dimensions shape the experiences of those who are bold enough to enter the pipeline. Such glaring underrepresentation starts during the early school years and continues within institutions of higher education and the workplace. Noting the global competitiveness of this nation lies in growing its talent pool in the STEM fields—a talent pool that is inclusive of racial minorities—then it is imperative we make visible and take action to address the crisis of representation that many scholars speak.

There are different perspectives regarding the STEM talent pool deficit to include the poor quality of public school education, the small number of students majoring in STEM at the undergraduate and graduate levels, the high rate of attrition among undergraduate STEM majors, and poor quality

Women of Color in STEM, pages vii–ix
Copyright © 2017 by Information Age Publishing
All rights of reproduction in any form reserved.

programs that inadequately prepare students to perform successfully in the workplace. While each of these perspectives has merit, the question that remains unanswered is the following: Why are males, particularly White males, in both academic settings and work organizations navigating the pipeline more successfully than women, particularly women of color? For example, Hurtado, Egan, and Hughes (2012) found that although undergraduate women of color are more likely to complete their degree within 6 years, those aspiring to major in STEM fields at the entry point were less likely than their racial minority male counterparts to be retained in STEM. For those who complete the baccalaureate degree, persevere through graduate school, and earn a master's and/or doctoral degree, the current literature is replete with evidence of the challenges they endure both in academia and in the workplace.

The plight of women of color in STEM work environments was first brought to national attention by Shirley Malcolm, Paula Hall, and Janet Brown in 1976 with their book, *The Double Bind: The Price of Being a Minority Woman in Science.* To accentuate the continued invisibility of women of color in social science literature, the editors of *Harvard Educational Review* (2011) in their column "Unraveling the Double Bind: Women of Color in STEM" reported that their journal, from 1976 when the book was published to 2010 (36 years), had published only 16 articles that related specifically to women of color in higher education or minority participation in STEM. They noted,

> None of these articles addressed this unique intersection—the "double oppression of sex and race or ethnicity plus the third oppression in the chosen career, science." This intersection of race and gender in STEM highlights the disparity in levels of achievement of women of color when compared to white women or to men of color, especially at the most advanced level. (Harvard, 2011, p. 2)

This book, *Women of Color in STEM: Navigating the Workforce,* is a timely contribution that calls attention to the double oppression of race and gender and the additional oppression of the STEM discipline. It comes at a unique time during which the national dialogue on STEM and its role in promoting global competitiveness of a nation take center stage. Central to this conversation is the dire need to find solutions to include and promote success among those who have been overlooked. Indeed, the fastest growing population groups are among racial minorities, thus making the long-term economic growth of the United States dependent upon its racial minority population.

We are now at a crisis point with threats of losing ground because the nation lags behind in recruiting and retaining members of the fastest growing population into the STEM fields. Women of color as a neglected group must publicize their experiences within the workplace so that organizational leaders can use their data to inform solutions that would enhance their recruitment and retention within an inclusive and empowering environment.

Women of Color in STEM: Navigating the Workforce is an opportunity for making public the life stories of racial minority women who have persevered in STEM workplace settings. The authors used various critical theories to situate and make visible the lives of women of color in such disciplines and workplace contexts like mathematics, science, engineering, NASA, academia, government agencies, and others. They skillfully centered women and their experiences at the intersection of their identity dimensions of race, gender, and the respective discipline. While the disciplines and career contexts vary, the oppression, alienation, and social inequities were common realities for all. Despite the challenges, the women were resilient and persevered with tenacity, a strong sense of self as a person of color, and reliance on family and community. While we celebrated the success, it is critical that organizational leaders, whether in education or other workplace settings, draw from narratives and counternarratives of these women to improve the organizational climate where individuals can thrive, despite their racial and gender identity.

REFERENCES

Bonner, F. A., II, Alfred, M. V., Lewis, C. W., Nave, F. M., & Fryzel, S. S. (2009). Historically Black colleges and universities (HBCUs) and academically gifted Black students in science, technology, engineering, and mathematics (STEM): Discovering the alchemy for success. *Journal of Urban Education: Focus on Enrichment, 6*(1), 122–136.

Harvard Educational Review. (2011). Unraveling the double bind: Women of color in STEM. *Harvard Educational Review, 81*(2), 1–5.

Hurtado, S., Egan, K., & Hughes, B. (2012, June). *Priming the pump or the sieve: Institutional contexts and URM STEM degree attainments.* Paper presented at the annual forum of the Association for Institutional Research, New Orleans, LA.

Malcolm, S., Hall, P., & Brown, J. (1976). *The double bind: The price of being a minority woman in science.* Washington, DC: American Association for the Advancement of Science.

INTRODUCTION

Julia Ballenger

Women comprise nearly half of the workforce, but are underrepresented in the science, technology, engineering, and mathematics (STEM) occupations. Landivar (2013) noted that 26% of STEM workers were women, and 74% were men. However, disparities in STEM employment by sex, race, and ethnicity exist. African Americans, Hispanics, American Indians, and Alaska Native workers remain underrepresented in the STEM workforce.

While racial and ethnic representation differs by the STEM occupation, the average distribution revealed that 11% of the workforce is African American, but their share of STEM occupations was 6% (up from 2% in 1970). While the Hispanics share of the workforce has increased significantly from 3% in 1970 to 15% in 2011, Hispanics made up 7% of the STEM workforce. American Indians and Alaska Natives held 0.4% of STEM jobs and those of some other race held 1% of STEM jobs (Landivar, 2013). These occupational statistics vividly reveal the disparities in STEM employment by race.

The authors in this book did not only focus on the underrepresentation of women of color in the workforce, but explored their unique lived experiences as they navigated the double bind of race and gender in the STEM workforce. These women's resilience and agency were inspiring as they spoke of the barriers encountered and strategies employed to overcome.

Women of Color in STEM, pages xi–xvii
Copyright © 2017 by Information Age Publishing
xi

This book, *Women of Color in STEM: Navigating the Workforce,* is part of the Research on Women and Education (RWE) SIG of the American Educational Research (AERA) scholarly book series. The RWE series editors are Beverly Irby, Texas A&M University, College Station, and Emeriti Janice Koch, Hofstra Univerity. One goal of the RWE mission is to provide a mechanism to facilitate communication between researchers and practitioners who are concerned about women in education at the intersection of race, class, gender, and culture. The aim of this book is to provide an opportunity for women of color to interrogate the dominant oppressive systems of racism, sexism, and classism with counternarratives that dismantle stereotypical, nontruths.

These authors accomplished the aim of this book by including historical, empirical, and philosophical engaging discourses through various theoretical frameworks. One such framework was intersectionality. The theory of intersectionality articulates a framework for understanding the complexities of minority women's identities and experiences (Crenshaw, 1989). It refers to ways in which social and cultural constructs interact (i.e., race and gender; Lloyd-Jones, 2009).

Before the theory of intersectionality was developed by Kimberle Crenshaw in 1989, the metaphor of "double jeopardy" was coined in the 1970s to describe the multiple disadvantages that women of color encounter. The metaphor double jeopardy refers to "minority women membership in two subordinate groups adds or multiplies their disadvantage" (Williams, 2015, p. 188). The double jeopardy metaphor was replaced by the theory of intersectionality (Crenshaw, 1989).

Parker (2005) acknowledged that social realities and the multiple dimensions of the lived experiences of African American women are shaped when the spheres of race, gender, and social class intersect. However, Stanley (2009) posited that through intersectionality "the lived experiences of African American women are not located within separate spheres of race, gender, and social class, rather these spheres intersect and shape their social and cultural beings" (p. 552). Other authors in this book utilized Black feminist thought, standpoint theory, and critical theory as theoretical frameworks to interrogate, agitate, and unpack the discourse surrounding the unique experiences of African American women who faced multiple forms of oppression in the STEM workforce. Also, critical theory (CT) was used as a frame to disrupt and challenge the status quo.

The CT theorists aimed to expose master narratives with counternarratives (Kincheloe & McLaren, 2000). Counternarratives are personal, composite stories of people of color (Bernal & Villalpando, 2002). The authors also framed their research with Black feminist thought (BFT). This theory is concerned with the consciousness and empowerment of Black women (Collins, 2000). Employing this perspective enables one to "place Black women's experiences at the center of the analysis and offers fresh insights on the epistemologies of this worldview" (Collins, 2000, p. 1).

Standpoint theory is used in this book as a lens to express the voices of these women of color. Standpoint is a location shared by a group who are experiencing outsider status within the social structure. This standpoint imparts a kind of sense-making to one's lived experiences (Hartsock, 1983). Subsequently, Collins (1989) noted that standpoint theory may be presented as a way of empowering oppressed groups by pointing toward a way of developing an "oppositional consciousness" (p. 2).

One other theory employed to frame the research in this book was critical race theory (CRT). Developed out of legal scholarship, CRT has spread to many disciplines. This theory is often used to uncover the ingrained societal disparities that support a system of privilege and oppression (DeCuir & Dixson, 2004; Ladson-Billings, 1998; Ladson-Billings & Tate, 1995). While CRT places race at the center of the paradigm, this does not mean that other identities are ignored. One cannot think of race, gender, and class independent of each other (Crenshaw, 1989). One of the tenets of CRT is counterstorytelling. Several of the authors wrote proactive counternarratives that legitimized the racial and subordinate experiences of marginalized groups (DeCuir & Dixson, 2004). Lastly, the authors spoke of issues related to barriers and successes encountered by women of color in the STEM workforce.

OVERVIEW OF CHAPTERS

In the first chapter, "What Plato Took for Granted: An Examination of the First Five African American Female Mathematicians and What That Says About Resistance to the Western Epistemological Canon," the authors challenged Plato's knowledge claims about women, whiteness, and White supremacy in regards to their access and participation in the STEM workforce. The author employed CT (Kincheloe & McLaren, 2000), feminist standpoint theory (Harding, 1993; Hartsock, 1984), and Black feminist thought (Collins, 2000; hooks, 1999) to engage in an epistemological and philosophical dialogue within the context of, access to, and participation in mathematics by women of color. The findings of this research suggest that the lives of these Black women mathematicians complement Plato's notion of an elite who have reached such levels of advanced mathematics.

In the second chapter, "Women of Color in the STEM Academic Workplace," the authors critiqued the research from the fields of industrial/organizational psychology, organizational behavior, and the career literature to interrogate the world of work for underrepresented women in the STEM workforce. These authors argued that the significant underrepresentation of women of color in the STEM workplace intensified their negative experiences. These researchers concluded their chapter with thoughts on how dominant group diverse ideologies, such as colorblindness, can disengage as well as deplete women of color from the cognitive resources needed to excel in these very demanding work environments.

Employing a holistic case study approach, the authors in the third chapter, "Breaking Barriers: Inspiring Stories About NASA Women of Color," the authors illuminate the contributions of four women of color who worked at NASA. They poignantly share the intriguing stories of these four exceptional women who grew up in four distinct decades (the 1960s, 1970s, 1980s, and 1990s). Each story is uniquely positioned by the eras in which these women grew up.

The authors in the fourth chapter, entitled "Mathematics Literacy, Identity, Resilience and Opportunity Sixty Years Since *Brown v. Board of Education*: Counternarratives of a Five-Generation Family," employed Solorzano and Yasso's (2002) three types of counterstorytelling to examine mathematics education and the educational achievement of African American females in a matrilineal line that spanned five generations. These authors found that the societal meme that women are not good in mathematics or are not confident in mathematics did not apply to these Black women. While these five generations of Black women and girls exhibited the strides Black women have made in mathematics education and professional settings, the authors caution us that there is still much to be done to ensure that all children, especially children of color, have the opportunities to determine their path.

In the fifth chapter, entitled "The Dreams and the Hope: An African American Women's Story of Struggle and Success in Science," the authors used Black feminist thought and critical race theory as theoretical positions to privilege the lived experiences of an African American woman who completed her PhD in science. In this scholarly narrative, grounded in autoethnography narrative inquiry, the author illustrated the necessity for continuous, open, and honest conversations regarding the experiences of African American women who aspire to succeed in science.

The author concluded that while this narrative is a cause for celebration among women of color, we must pause and realize that sexism and racism still present barriers that create stress and pressure that African American women must contend with and fight to overcome.

Spatial reasoning studies focus on the singular identity of gender rather than the intersection of both race and gender to examine this concept from a holistic perspective. Thus, in this fifth chapter, "Navigating the STEM Landscape: Examing the Role of Spatial Reasoning for Women of Color," the author acknowledged the troubling outcome of STEM research in which race, ethnicity, class, and gender are collapsed together and argues for more intersectionality research. Through a critical synthesis of the literature on spatial reasoning, the author examined gender differences and concluded the chapter with recommendations for curricular interventions that may help improve spatial reasoning in female minority students and give them leverage in science achievement.

In the sixth chapter, "Diversity in Stem? Challenges Influencing the Experiences of African American Female Engineers," the author employed an interpretive inquiry qualitative method to examine the career experiences of African American female engineers to identify the personal and structural factors that served as challenges for their career progression. Additionally, the author addressed the interaction between the macro and micro subsystems to examine the career experiences of African American female engineers. In summing up the chapter, the author acknowledged the difficulty in analyzing the microsystem components, which served as challenges for the women without considering the larger context (i.e., macrosystem), and concluded that the influence of the macro system served as an umbrella for the experiences that occurred in the microsystem.

In the last chapter, "Present But Not Accounted For: Examining How Intersectional Identities Create a Double Bind For and Affect Leadership of Women of Color in Educational Settings," the authors employed an intersectionality approach to explore how Black women negotiate dual identities to prevail as leaders in the workforce. Findings from this study provide insight into factors that may influence Black women's participation in the negotiation of their race and gender identities, and the unique experiences of early career Black women in the United States. The researchers concluded that identity negotiation could take a psychological toll on the psyche of Black women because it can be a stressful process to engage in. Therefore, devoting research to understanding the complexities of identity negotiation for women of color is critical in today's colleges and universities.

CONCLUSION

To remain globally and economically competitive, the United States must continue to grow its science, technology, engineering, and mathematics' (STEM) workforce. Given the increase in the enrollment of students of color and women in United States colleges and universities, women and students of color represent a growing source of domestic talent to meet the needs of the nation (Ong, Wright, Espinosa, & Orfield, 2011).

Women of color from African American, Asian, American/Pacific Islander, Chicana/Latina, and Native American groups represent untapped human capital. These women can provide a much-needed force for sustaining American's economic vitality (Community on Equal Opportunities in Science and Engineering, 2009; National Academies 2010a, 2010b). However, statistics show that these groups are consistently underrepresented in most STEM fields as compared to White women and men of color (National Science Foundation, 2011).

REFERENCES

Bernard, D. V., & Villalpando, O. (2002). Apartheid of knowledge in academia: The struggle over the legitimate knowledge of faculty of color. *Equity & Excellence in Education, 35*(2), 169–180. doi 10.1080/713845282

Collins, P. H. (1989). The social construction of Black feminist thought: Signs. *Journal of Women in Culture and Society, 14*(4), 745–773.

Collins, P. H. (2000). *Black feminist thought: Knowledge, consciousness, and the politics of empowerment.* New York, NY: Routledge.

Committee on Equal Opportunities in Science and Engineering (CEOSE). (2009). *2007–2008 biennial report to Congress.* Arlington, VA: National Science Foundation. Retrieved from https://www.nsf.gov/od/oia/activities/ceose/Agenda/CEOSE_Agenda2June29_30_2009_Meeting.pdf

Crenshaw, K. (1989). Demarginalizing the intersection of race and sex: A Black feminist critique of antidiscrimination doctrine, feminist theory and antiracist policies, *University of Chicago Legal Forum, 139,* 143.

DeCuir, J., & Dixson, A. (2004). So when it comes out, they aren't that surprised that it is there: Using critical race theory as a tool of analysis of race and racism in education. *Educational Researcher, 33,* 26–31

Harding, S. (1993). Rethinking standpoint epistemology: What is strong objectivity? In L. Alcoff & E. Potter, (Eds.), *Feminist epistemologies,* New York, NY: Routledge.

Hartsock, C. M. (1983). The feminist standpoint: Developing the ground for a specifically feminist historical materialism. In S. Harding & M. Hintikka (Eds.), *Discovering reality: Feminist perspectives on epistemology, metaphysics, methodology and philosophy of science* (pp. 283–310). Dordrecht, the Netherlands: Kluwer.

hooks, b. (1999). Excerpts from feminist theory: From margin to center. In K. Foss, S. Foss, & C. Griffin, (Eds.), *Feminist rhetorical theories.* Thousand Oaks, CA: Sage.

Kincheloe, J. L., & McLaren, P. L. (2000). Rethinking critical theory and qualitative research. In N. K. Denzin & Y. S. Lincoln (Eds.), *Handbook of qualitative research* (2nd ed.; pp. 279–313). Thousand Oaks, CA: Sage.

Ladson-Billings, G. (1998). Just what is critical race theory and what's it doing in a nice field like education? *International Journal of Qualitative Studies in Education, 11*(1), 7–24.

Ladson-Billings, G., & Tate, W. (1995). Toward a critical race theory of education. *Teachers College Record, 97*(1), 47–68.

Landivar, L. C. (2013). Disparities in STEM employment by sex, race, and Hispanic origin, *American Community Survey Reports,* ACS-24, U.S. Census Bureau, Washington, DC.

Lloyd-Jones, B. (2009). Implications of race and gender in higher education administration: An African American woman's perspective. *Advances in Developing Human Resources, 11*, 606–618. doi: 10.1177/1523422309351820

National Academies. (2010a). *Rising above the gathering storm, revisited: Rapidly approaching category 5.* Washington, DC: National Academies Press.

National Academies. (2010b). *Expanding underrepresented minority participation: America's science and technology talent at the crossroads.* Washington, DC: National Academies Press.

National Science Foundation, Division of Science Resources Statistics. (2011). *Women, minorities, and persons with disabilities in science and engineering.* Special Report NSF 11-309, Arlington, VA. Retrieved from http://www.nsf.gov/statistics/wmpd/

Ong, M., Wright, C., Espinosa, L., Orfield, G. (2011). Inside the double bind: A synthesis of empirical research on women of color in science, technology, engineering, and mathematics. *Harvard Educational Review, 18*(2), 172–208.

Parker, P. S. (2005). *Race, gender, and leadership: Re-envisioning organizational leadership from the perspectives of African American executives.* Mahwah, NJ: Erlbaum.

Solorzano, D. G., & Yasso, T. J. (2002). Critical race methodology: Counter-storytelling as an analytical framework for education research. *Qualitative Inquiry, 8*(1), 23–44.

Stanley, C. A. (2009). Giving voice from the perspectives of African American women leaders. *Advances in Developing Human Resources, 11*(5), 551–561.

Williams, J. C. (2015). Double jeopardy: An empirical study with implications for the debates over implicit bias and intersectionality. *Harvard Journal of Law & Gender, 37*, 186–242.

PART I

WOMEN OF COLOR IN STEM:
RESILIENCE AND OPPORTUNITY

CHAPTER 1

WHAT PLATO TOOK FOR GRANTED

An Examination of the First Five African Female Mathematicians and What That Says About Resistance to the Western Epistemological Canon

Nicole M. Joseph

Drs. Haynes, Granville, Brown, Hewitt, and Malone-Mayes are the first five African American females in the United States to earn PhDs in pure mathematics during the Jim Crow era (1940s to mid-1960s). African American females earning doctorates in pure mathematics or doctorates in any discipline for that matter from a United States higher education institution during this era represented a signal achievement—personally, socially, epistemologically, and politically. The social context of this era, particularly in the South, was a dejure system of structural and social racism that privileged Whites over non-Whites. To this end, Whites had overwhelming control over power and material resources. White supremacy was and still is a master narrative that was created, maintained, and sustained for hundreds of centuries

Women of Color in STEM, pages 3–38
Copyright © 2017 by Information Age Publishing
All rights of reproduction in any form reserved.

before not just in the United States, but globally. In the South, there were two educational systems: one for Blacks and one for Whites (Anderson, 1988).

Southern states maintained separate education for Blacks and Whites. Therefore, they provided subsidies to Black college graduates who would agree to attend institutions outside of the southern region (Jordan-Taylor, 2011). These programs allowed states to "circumvent the law by supposedly providing equal educational opportunities, while avoiding the expense of creating a separate system of graduate education for Blacks" (Jordan-Taylor, 2011, p. 2). Drs. Haynes, Granville, Brown, Hewitt, and Malone-Mayes had two choices when they decided to go to graduate school. They could "challenge deeply entrenched southern norms by pursuing admission to the regions' historically White universities" (Jordan-Taylor, 2011, p. 2). Some African Americans did this, but they also understood that the legal pathways would involve long delays and threats of physical violence. The second choice was to pursue their academic goals immediately through out-of-state study (Jordan-Taylor, 2011, p. 2). Dr. Euphemia Haynes earned her doctorate in 1943 from Catholic University in Washington, DC. Twenty years later, Dr. Gloria Conyers Hewitt finished in 1963 at the University of Washington, located in Seattle. Only three Black women earned doctorates in mathematics in between that time frame (see methodology section for their profiles).

The 2013 National Science Foundation report entitled *Women, Minorities, and Persons With Disabilities in Science and Engineering* reveals that out of 863 doctorates awarded in 2010 in mathematics and statistics to all United States citizens and permanent residents, only nine or 1% went to African American females. By comparison, 168 or 19% of the 863 doctorates went to White women, and 466 or more than half of the doctorates in mathematics went to White males. The National Science Foundation has been reporting statistics about awarded doctorates in STEM fields since 2001.

Table 1.1 shows a historical trend of few African American females earning doctorate degrees in mathematics. These numbers are similar to other STEM areas including engineering and science (NSF, 2013). I include these statistics as evidence to begin a different type of conversation about the complexities of this phenomenon. This distinct dialogue examines a

TABLE 1.1 Mathematics Doctorates Awarded to Black and White Females and White Males: 2001–2010

	2001	2002	2003	2004	2005	2006	2007	2008	2009	2010
Total	525	438	513	508	540	583	645	671	788	863
Black Females	7	7	4	1	9	5	5	11	16	9
White females	108	102	108	118	101	102	132	161	154	168
White males	292	258	281	270	297	326	326	329	405	466

broader contextual story about African American females' access and participation in mathematics from a historical and philosophical perspective.

Addressing access and participation of females in STEM fields has become a national effort. For instance, President Obama earmarked $5 million (supported by the Bill and Melinda Gates Foundation and the Carnegie Corporation of New York) for the Change the Equation campaign led by Ursula Burns, head of the White House national program on STEM. Additionally, high-profile nonprofit organizations like the American Association of University Women (AAUW) support research, policy, and programs that empower women and girls in STEM education. Despite these efforts, none include conversations about investigating the historical and canonical philosophical influences, ideas, and assumptions that undergird the long-standing *organizing principles of mathematics access and participation* (i.e., tracking)[1]. These organizing principles are based upon, in part, innate ability, a conceptualization espoused by Plato and adopted by Western traditionalists in mathematics (Oakes, 1990a; Plato, 1987). In the United States, organizing access to and participation in mathematics by native ability has resulted in a distribution of individuals along racial, class, and gender lines (Henrion, 1997; Kenschaft, 2005a; Martin, 2009; Woodson, 1933) and perpetuated the construct of whiteness—a valued social identity by Whites that means "a right to exclude" (Harris, 1993, p. 1714). Organizing mathematics learning based on so-called native ability has reinforced and perpetuated subliminal and intended messages that only White males do mathematics and are mathematicians. The messaging has discouraged all women, but especially many African American women from "seeing" themselves as mathematicians and pursuing advanced degrees in mathematics or other math-related disciplines (Herzog, 2004).

Mainstream mathematics communities, mathematics professors, and mathematics teachers as well as the general society often subscribe to the idea that mathematics is reserved for the select few. Within this mainstream idea, a student either does or does not have a mathematical mind, even though Dweck (2008) has shown that students' mindsets are flexible and can change. The discourse of mathematics being only for those individuals who have a gift, talent, or knack for mathematics has been sustained for hundreds of years. Native ability is an important conceptualization that has influenced the historical and contemporary organization of mathematics participation, which I argue in this paper can be linked in part to the philosophical views of Plato, particularly his theories regarding women and the assumptions that underlie his theories. I also argue that the roots of Plato's theories are embedded in whiteness and White supremacy (Harris, 1993; Mills, 1997).

I focus on Plato because ancient Greek philosophy has had a major influence on the Western philosophical tradition and undergirds historical and modern issues of White supremacy, normativity, and privilege (Harris, 1993).

The scholarship of great philosophers such as Plato and Socrates dominates the mainstream academic knowledge that is taught and constructed in most secondary schools, colleges, and universities. Plato's *The Republic* is a prototype of the kind of text Western traditionalists, such as Ravitch and Finn (1987) or Bloom (1987) consider a part of the Western-oriented canon. It is understood that Plato stands with Socrates and Aristotle as one of the shapers of the whole intellectual tradition of the West (Plato, 1987).

British philosopher Alfred North Whitehead (1970) poignantly stated that "the history of philosophy is but a series of footnotes to Plato" (p. 39). Because Plato's ideas are rooted in whiteness and White supremacy, and White supremacy has origins that are hegemonic with tenants of patriarchy, both racial and gender dimensions are present. Consequently, the field should pay close attention to his ideas and ways in which his philosophy illuminates whiteness. This preeminence of whiteness also leads to gender and racial oppression in mathematics access and participation, and shapes various inequities and outcomes. In this chapter, I illustrate this critique and demonstrate how these ideas affected Black women many centuries later in higher education. Higher education is a space that preserves White self-interests; and because White self-interests cultivate White supremacy (i.e., normalcy, advantage, privilege, and innocence), it can be argued that *by design* White faculty are afforded more opportunities (Haynes, 2013). Dr. Haynes, Granville, Brown, Hewitt, and Malone-Mayes's narratives reveal important lessons in this space—at the intersection of Plato's ideas and their lived experiences as mathematicians both inside and outside of the academy.

In an effort to problematize issues of access and participation that are informed by Plato's assumptions of gender and race, this study explores the lived experiences of the first five Black women mathematicians in the Jim Crow era. To date, no other scholar has offered an analysis of the intersection of Plato's theories about women, whiteness and White supremacy, as well as the lived experiences and perspectives of the first five African American female mathematicians. The focus of this chapter on Black women mathematicians presents a unique contribution to the contemporary discourse on access and participation. The analysis and discussion represent a historical, philosophical, and epistemological perspective and conversation. It is a historical dialogue because it interrogates ways in which access and participation in mathematics for African American females have developed and stagnated over time. It is a philosophical conversation in part because it seeks principles that explain the phenomenon of limited access and participation of African American females in mathematics. It is an epistemological conversation because epistemology is concerned with what conditions are necessary to have knowledge and to know what individuals know. Traditionally, ways of knowing have been supported through scientific methodologies that are objective and neutral (Harding, 1993).

I position the first five African American female mathematicians' experiences and perspectives as legitimate and valued ways of knowing that represent strong objectivity (Harding, 1993). Their ways of knowing are objective because their experiences and perspectives represent a unique standpoint and provide insightful accounts of the world of African American females pursuing advanced degrees in mathematics during a time when racial and gender discrimination was legal, overt, and oppressive—a social context that should have radically deterred them from studying mathematics. Their stories are rich reservoirs of places to study mathematics' pipelines: the process of an individuals' continued participation in mathematics, achievement in mathematics, and the development of attitudes and interests that lead people, particularly women and racial minorities, to continue to pursue mathematics (Berryman, 1983; Herzig, 2004; Oakes, 1990b; Stage & Maple, 1996). Rooted within a complex theoretical framework of critical theory, feminist standpoint theory, and Black feminist thought (BFT), this study asked and answered the following research questions:

1. How might a perspective informed by an analysis of Plato's views of women and the lived perspectives of the first five Black females to earn PhDs in mathematics help us understand contemporary issues of access and participation as illustrative of White supremacy?
2. What can we learn from this analysis that can inform contemporary conversations about mathematics educational reform and policy related to African American females?

PHILOSOPHICAL INFLUENCE ON THE ORGANIZATION OF MATHEMATICS ACCESS AND PARTICIPATION: GENDER AND RACIAL OPPRESSION

To support the claim that Plato's philosophy of education has influenced the organization of modern mathematics access and participation, a brief discussion of an important theme of his *Republic* is necessary. One significant theme of *The Republic* is justice and how it should operate in society. The concept of justice was important to Plato because he thought it would bring order and happiness to society. *The Republic* offers Plato's process for creating this ideal society by examining questions regarding conceptions of human nature (the soul), the relationships between individuals and the world, the nature of the mind, and the relative value of different kinds of knowledge. For Plato, the soul has three parts: a part is ruled by *reason*, another by *spirit*, and the third part is ruled by *appetite*. This is parallel to Plato's polis caste system: philosophers (reason), guardians (spirit), and merchants (appetite; Plato, 1987).

Plato sought a cure for the ills of society through philosophy and arrived at his final conviction that those ills would never cease until philosophers gained political power, or politicians become true philosophers. However, philosophers were only a third of the class system that Plato created. His ideal society also included guardians and merchants. Merchants were the lowest class and included the majority of society: slaves (men and women) and most Athenian women. Plato argued that the knowledge constructed by these individuals was unreliable because, by nature, their appetites trumped reason. Plato thought that the merchants' reality was changeable, and merchants processed their connections and interactions with the world only through feelings (sense) experience (Plato, 1987). Guardians were the protectors of the state. Plato suggested that these individuals had spirit and should possess the innate dispositions of a philosopher. The text states, "and so our properly good Guardian will have the following characteristics: a philosophic disposition, high spirits, speed, and strength" (p. 66). The guardians' reality was conceived as stable and orderly. Plato asserted that the kind of knowledge guardians produced was theoretical, and their interpretation of the world was constructed through logic and reasoning. Finally, the highest class was the philosopher. Plato thought that only philosophers could serve as kings because this select group of individuals had knowledge of absolute truth. Plato defined a philosopher as a man who loves "wisdom, learning, knowledge, and truth" (p. 192). In his thinking, philosophers were the only individuals capable of reaching the transcendent form of perfect beauty, truth, order, and stability.

The terms truth, order, and stability can be associated with characteristics of pure mathematics. Mathematicians Davis and Hersh (1982) stated that "mathematicians see their work as containing truths, which not only are valid forever, but also apply to the most remote corner of the universe" (p. 34). This statement suggests that the discipline of mathematics, particularly pure mathematics, seeks eternal knowledge, objectivity, and purity— all of the important qualities Plato sought in his philosophers. Feminist philosopher Code (1991) would challenge this belief by contending that all knowledge, including mathematical knowledge, is socially constructed and reflects human interests and values, and thereby includes elements of both subjectivity and objectivity. Moreover, the cultural experiences of the knower are epistemologically significant because factors like gender, race, and class influence knowledge construction and the way individuals interpret reality (Banks, 1996). Consequently, Plato's views on ways to organize individuals in society are problematic.

In Plato's time, individuals were educated based on their role or function (merchant, guardian, or philosopher) because he thought that individuals should be trained based on their natural proclivities. There were three *educational paths* that were also associated with three specific curriculums since "those born to play different societal roles are to be given different educational treatment" (Martin, 1985, p. 17). The mathematics curriculum in particular included arithmetic and geometry for merchants and guardians, and it was introduced and studied up through the age of 18 (Plato, 1987). However, it was only the philosophers who received training in arithmetic and geometry as well as training in astronomy, harmonics, and philosophy (Plato, 1987). Plato viewed astronomy as a mathematical science, since he thought advanced mathematics would be necessary to describe the orbit of planets; and harmonics was associated with frequency, which would have included ideas in trigonometry (Plato, 1987). In Plato's time, these perceived distinguishing characteristics of mathematical knowledge influenced who would have access to advanced mathematics, thus limiting most individuals' mathematics education, but especially impacting women. Although Plato puts forth the radical idea that women be included among the exalted guardians and philosophers in his ideal state, an examination of the explanations about private property and family (see for example Okin, 1977, 1979) suggest a paradox of sort and demonstrate implications for women that are oppressive (Pomeroy, 1974).

The mathematical sciences were very important to Plato because he thought that mathematics trained the mind to think abstractly and would get the soul to the highest ideal. The thinking that only a few individuals are capable of becoming philosophers, thus getting additional training in mathematics, is elitist; this thinking has influenced the organization of mathematics access and participation in the modern world. This organizing principle can be seen in U.S. schooling structures, especially via tracking in mathematics (Oakes, Joseph, & Muir, 2004).

THEORETICAL FRAMEWORK

Plato is considered one of the West's greatest philosophers and his theories represent canonical epistemology. To use the biographies of the first five African American female mathematicians to take up and challenge Plato's knowledge claims about women, whiteness, and White supremacy, and problematize issues of access and participation required a tripartite multilevel framework. I used critical theory (Kincheloe & McLaren, 2000), feminist standpoint theory (Harding, 1993), and Black feminist thought (Collins, 2000; hooks, 1999) to demonstrate the complex relationships and variables operating in identifying, naming, interpreting, and writing about access and participation for Black women. Consequently, it is important to identify theories that support this innovative and transformative endeavor to (a) confront mathematics education injustices, (b) use frameworks and tools that explicitly value women's ways of knowing and challenge racist canonical ideology, and (c) employ analytical tools that legitimize African American women's ideas and intellectual activism. Figure 1.1 shows the connectivity of the frameworks used as a means of viewing and understanding the epistemological significance of the perspectives and experiences of the first five African American female mathematicians, and how their perspectives and experiences can illustrate what Plato took for granted in his theories on women, their ways of knowing, and education.

Critical theory is concerned with issues of power, justice, and "the ways that the economy, matters of race, class, and gender, ideologies, discourses, education, religion and other social institutions and cultural dynamics interact to *construct a social system*" (Kincheloe & McLaren, 2000, p. 288, emphasis added). The culture of mathematics and the mathematicians that participate within this social system often reflect hegemonic images, concepts, theories, and narratives. These narratives, theories, concepts, and images rarely get challenged because pure mathematics is considered a space of established and institutional knowledge. This space of established and institutional knowledge can be viewed as emerging out of Platonist influence, since his influence can be seen in how schools arrange students by mathematics ability (or nature). Consequently, only those students who demonstrate high levels of cognitive demand, particularly in logic or reasoning, should accelerate to advance mathematics (Oakes, Joseph, & Muir, 2004). Platonist philosophy is canon, and critical theory provides tools to challenge the canon by allowing for reinterpretation of ways in which the ideas, concepts, and generalizations associated with this canon are embedded in

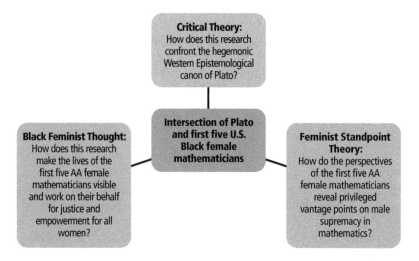

Figure 1.1 Interconnectivity of tripartite theoretical framework.

White supremacy and can impact all women, but especially African American women who aspire to become mathematicians.

Standpoint epistemology interrogates the scientific ways of knowing (objectivity) associated with the status quo representing the dominant White male position of privilege. Harding (1993) states:

> The standpoint claims that all knowledge attempts are socially situated and that some of these objective social locations are better than others as starting points for knowledge projects that challenge some of the most fundamental assumptions of the scientific world view, and the Western thought that takes science as its model of how to produce knowledge. (p. 56)

This statement suggests that science is not the only way to produce knowledge. Hartsock (1983) argues that life activity is epistemology, and that the feminist standpoint "expresses female experience at a particular time and place, located within a particular set of social relations" (p. 303). Standpoint epistemology is transformative because it seeks what Harding (1991, 1993) calls "strong objectivity" (p. 49) or the notion that the points of view of marginalized and oppressed individuals can create more objective accounts of the world. Drs. Haynes, Granville, Brown, Hewitt, and Malone-Mayes's perspectives and experiences represent a "starting off place" that can raise critical questions and insights that would not arise "in thought that begins from dominant group lives" (Harding, 1993, p. 56). Standpoint theory can further our understanding of their perspectives and experiences by going beneath the surface of appearances to reveal particular and privileged vantage points of male and White supremacy in the field of mathematics. Mining beneath the surface is significant because it broadens the participation of different groups. As a result, the canon of objectivity is interrogated and makes the values and blind spots of Plato's scholarship explicit.

Black feminist thought (BFT) is a theory concerned with the knowledge, consciousness, and political empowerment of Black women (Collins, 2000). The intellectual work of Black women in the United States has been socially constructed through various historical oppressions, including economic, political, and ideological features. Collins points out that the exploitation of Black women's labor that was and still is essential to capitalism represents the economic dimension of oppression. The political dimension of oppression has denied African American women the rights and privileges routinely extended to White male citizens. Educational institutions have fostered patterns of disenfranchisement in past practices, such as denying literacy to slaves and relegating Black women to underfunded, segregated southern schools. Mullings (1997) contended that these practices ensured that a quality education for Black women remained the exception rather than the rule. Controlling images applied to Black women (i.e., mammies, jezebels, smiling Aunt Jemimas) represent the body of ideas that reflect the interests of the dominant group. Collins (2000) argues that within U.S. culture, racist and sexist ideologies permeate the social structure "to such a degree that they become hegemonic, namely, seen as natural, normal, and inevitable" (p. 5). Dominant ideologies must be challenged.

BFT is an important framework in this study, because as a critical social theory BFT aims to empower African American women within the context of social injustice sustained by intersecting oppressions (i.e., Black and female mathematicians). BFT has six distinguishing characteristics that I summarize. BFT acknowledges that U.S. Black women are an oppressed group and as a collective they participate in a *dialectical* relationship between oppression and activism because the two entities—domination from the oppressor and liberation by the oppressed—are in disagreement and have different views about what represents truth. A second feature of BFT is that while on the one hand Black women experience common challenges, on the other hand, their individual responses to the common challenges are diverse. More specifically, although most African American women face similar challenges that result from living in a society that historically devalues them (Collins, 2000), this commonality does not mean that individual women have had all of the same experiences, or that they all agree on the importance of the diverse experiences. As a result, it is important to understand that what Black women experience in their daily lives may or may not influence their consciousness about what they think as a whole in relation to a broader collective of issues related to Black women.

Understanding that U.S. Black women's collective historical experiences with oppression can stimulate a self-defined (individual) Black women's standpoint, which can consequently foster Black women's activism, is a third feature of BFT. Collins (2000) suggests that a self- defined standpoint can stimulate resistance. She describes this notion as a *dialogical* relationship because the dialogue (internal, self-talk, misunderstandings, trust, and distrust) between individual Black women and the collective standpoint is a communicative process that is to some degree mutually orienting. On the individual and group level, a dialogical relationship suggests that changes in individual thinking may be accompanied by changed actions, which have the potential to alter experiences to stimulate a change in the consciousness (Collins, 2000). A fourth feature of BFT is that it acknowledges the need for the ongoing investigation of African American women's viewpoints for the purpose of exerting intellectual contributions.

Black feminism posits that Black women contribute to the production of knowledge in two ways: One way is through the commonplace knowledge shared by African American women "growing from our everyday thoughts and actions" (p. 34); another way is through the expert specialized knowledge that emerges out of analysis of complex thought and theories by Black women like Anna J. Cooper.

Anna J. Cooper received her PhD in history from the University of Paris-Sorbonne in 1924. One of her well known books was *A Voice From the South: By a Woman From the South.* This book is considered one of the first articulations of Black feminism because its central thesis was that the educational, moral, and spiritual progress of Black women would improve the general standing of the entire African American community. Cooper (1892/1988) argued that the violent natures of men often run counter to the goals of higher education, so it is important to foster more female intellectuals who bring more elegance to education. Black women intellectuals are central to advancing BFT for many reasons. First, their experiences provide critical insights into the condition of oppression that those outside of the structures may not understand. Second, Black women, both inside and outside of the academy, are less likely to abandon the struggles when the work seems overwhelming and the rewards are minimal. Third, Black women must continue to push the theme of self-definition because this develops empowerment. Finally, Black intellectuals foster group accord, which promotes unambiguous coalitions with other groups (Collins, 2000).

The importance of social change and the need to engage in new and current BFT analysis is the fifth distinguishing feature. More specifically, scholars who use this framework need to recognize that social conditions that confront African American women change, and these changing conditions should stimulate new analysis of the common differences that make up U.S. Black womanhood. Finally, the sixth characteristic of BFT acknowledges its relationship to other projects aiming for social justice, and has advanced the view that African American women's struggles are part of a larger struggle that promotes humanity and social justice.

METHODOLOGY

In this chapter, the findings are presented from a phenomenological study that used close readings of archival documents to problematize issues of access and participation of Black women in mathematics. Specifically, I examine the intersection at the experiences of the first five Black females to earn PhDs in mathematics during Jim Crow and Plato's assumptions about women. In this section, I discuss the type of archival data sources that I use and my process for analysis.

Data Sources

Several data sources and levels of analysis were employed. Data sources included online archives from several institutions: the *Biographies of Women in Mathematics* archives at Agnes Scott College, the *Mathematics Genealogy Project* (n.d.) archive at the Department of Mathematics at North Dakota State University, the *School of Mathematics and Statistics* archive at the University of St. Andrews in Scotland, and the *Mathematics of the African Diaspora* website created by Dr. Scott W. Williams, a retired professor of mathematics at the University of Buffalo SUNY. Other primary and secondary sources included Plato's *The Republic* (1987), the newsletters from the Association for Women in Mathematics and the American Mathematical Monthly, along with personal interviews about some of the Black women in mathematics conducted by Patricia Clark Kenschaft (1981, 2005a, 2005b), Claudia Henrion (1997), and Bettye Anne Case and Ann M. Leggett (2005).

Table 1.2 shows profiles of the first five African American female mathematicians. I focus on the first five because they represent almost a 25-year span for Black women earning doctorate degrees in pure mathematics (1943–1966). In comparison, Sofia Kovalevskaia was the first European women to earn a PhD in mathematics in the 19th century in 1874 (Kenshaft, 2005a). Therefore, it took nearly 70 years after the first White female before the first African American female was allowed to earn a PhD in mathematics. Susie Johnson McAfee (1889–1974) is 19th century African American who might have earned a doctorate in mathematics if she had not been met with blatant racism (Kenshaft, 2005a). The first five Black female mathematicians are progenitors and trailblazers in the field of mathematics, and we can learn from their perspectives and experiences.

Data Analysis

Multiple levels of analysis were used in this study. First, to carefully formulate some of Plato's assumption about women, close readings and content analysis (Neuendorf, 2002) were used to examine "Book V" (Plato's proposals concerning women and education) in *The Republic*. Additional scholarship and commentary from seminal feminist philosophers (who have written the most about Plato and female education) including Jane Roland Martin (1985), Lorraine Code (1991), Susan Moller Okin (1977, 1979), Christine Garside Allen (1975), Julia Annas (1976), and Jean Bethke Elshtain (1982) were also used. Contextualizing the roots of Plato's views as embodying White supremacy required a critical examination of Charles W. Mills's (1997) *The Racial Contract*, Paget Henry's (2000) *Calibans' Reason: Introducing Afro-Caribbean Philosophy*, Cheryl I. Harris's (1993) *Whiteness as Property*, and Audrey and Brian D. Smedleys' (2012) *Race in North America: Origin and Evolution of a Worldview*.

Content analysis (Neuendorf, 2002), in part, is the process of taking large amounts of textual information and identifying frequencies of keywords. It

TABLE 1.2	Profiles of First Five African American Female Mathematicians					
Name	Born/Died	BA	Masters	Dissertation Title	PhD	Marital Status
Dr. Martha Euphemia Haynes	Born: September 11, 1890 Died: July 25, 1980	Smith College, 1941, Psychology	University of Chicago, 1930, Education	*Determination of Sets of Independent Conditions Characterizing Certain Special Cases of Symmetric Correspondences*	1943 Catholic University	Married and no children
Dr. Evelyn Boyd Granville	Born: May 1, 1924	Smith College, 1945, Mathematics & Physics	Yale, 1946, Mathematics	*On Laguerre Series in the Complex Domain*	1949 Yale	Married twice and no children
Dr. Marjorie Lee Browne	Born: September 9, 1914 Died: October 19, 1979	Howard University, 1935, Mathematics	University of Michigan, 1939, Mathematics	*Studies of One Parameter Subgroups of Certain Topological and Matrix Groups*	1950 University of Michigan	Single and no children

TABLE 1.2 Profiles of First Five African American Female Mathematicians (Continued)

Name	Born/Died	BA	Masters	Dissertation Title	PhD	Marital Status
Dr. Gloria Conyers Hewitt	Born: October 26, 1935 Note: I tried contacting Dr. Hewitt several times with both letters and phone calls. I am not sure if she is still alive.	Fisk University, 1956, Mathematics	University of Washington, 1960, Mathematics	*Direct and Inverse Limits of Abstract Algebras*	1962 University of Washington	Single with one child
Dr. Vivienne Malone-Mayes	Born: February 10, 1932 Died: June 9, 1995	Fisk University, 1952, Mathematics	Fisk University, 1954, Mathematics	*A Structure Problem in Asymptotic Analysis*	1966 University of Texas, Austin	Married with one child

Source: Biographies of Women Mathematicians (n.d.)

is pertinent in revealing what various texts (including nonwritten materials, i.e., photos) mean, represent, highlight and exclude, encourage, or deter. These documents were read multiple times to identify underlying assumptions of Plato's theories of women and to make claims about whiteness and White supremacy. The analysis regarding women suggested two presuppositions: (a) women are feeling-driven versus logic-driven, and (b) women normally make contributions to reproductive processes of society rather than productive processes. I then used these presuppositions as a framework to critically read and analyze the biographies, interviews, newsletters, and other sources. In the analysis, I was looking for where the biographies complemented and/or contradicted Plato's two assumptions.

Simultaneously, I also applied coding schemes to the biographies that looked for emerging themes initially by identifying first level codes (words or phrases that were directly tied to the data). Next, I looked for patterns and collapsed the first level codes into larger categories. I coded to understand how the women created meaning in their lives as Black mathematicians (intersecting identities), how their experiences illuminated gender and racial patterns, and how those patterns might challenge Plato's assumptions about women. Finally, the larger categories were mined for codes that represented more theoretical meaning, which will be discussed in the findings section. Conducting analysis in these ways models education as a practice of freedom (hooks, 1994), and it allows those who have been traditionally underrepresented, marginalized, and disenfranchise a space "to challenge and question the dominant, White, male, Western research ethos in the university" (Collins, 2000, p. 5). Critical theory, feminist standpoint theory, and Black feminist thought are frameworks that provoke and promote such an analysis.

FINDINGS

The purpose of this unique and transformative study was to problematize the access and participation of Black women in mathematics by putting forth a historical and philosophical perspective. The two research questions that guided the study were: (a) How might a perspective informed by an analysis of Plato's views of women and the lived perspectives of the first five Black females to earn PhDs in mathematics help us understand contemporary issues of access and participation as illustrative of White supremacy? and (b) What can we learn from this analysis that can inform contemporary conversations about mathematics educational reform and policy related to African American females? The findings are organized by the study's research questions.

How might a perspective informed by an analysis of Plato's views of women and the lived perspectives of the first five Black females to earn PhDs in mathematics help us understand contemporary issues of access and participation as illustrative of White supremacy?

Analysis of the biographies suggests three overarching themes that spanned all five women: (a) the value of segregation, (b) logic in the face of racism and sexism, and (c) academy, industry, and community leadership. In discussing these themes, connections are made to Plato's two assumptions regarding women: they are feeling-driven versus logic-driven, and women normally make contributions to reproductive processes of society rather than productive processes. Table 1.3 shows contrasts between feeling-driven and logic-driven. It also illustrates issues of White supremacy and connects back to the complex theoretical framework.

The Value of Segregation

All five Black female mathematicians attended segregated elementary and secondary schools and their biographies reveal agential experiences. Dr. Browne attended LeMoyne High School in Memphis, Tennessee, a private school founded by the American Missionary Association to educate Blacks. The students were all Black, but the teaching staff was diverse. Dr. Browne viewed the teachers as competent and excellent, and credits much of her later success in mathematics to her excellent preparation at LeMoyne (Kenshaft, 2005b). A level of excellence was not a new concept. Other studies have shown that despite the suppression of African American teachers as a central component of the perpetuation of White supremacy in the South, Black teachers "were among the best-educated African Americans of their generation...and individually, African American teachers were superbly trained, both academically, and pedagogically" (Fultz, 1995, p. 206). Elementary and secondary teachers who taught in certain schools in College

| TABLE 1.3 Feeling and Logic Processes ||
Feeling-Driven	Logic-Driven
Emotion	Cognition
Subjectivity	Objectivity
Impulsive	Thoughtful
Intuition	Reason
Creativity	Truth
Dependent	Independent
Bias	Impartiality

Station, Texas, were required to take "improvement courses" every 2-3 years even if they already had a master's degree (Standish, 2006). Other research suggests that Black teachers who taught mathematics at historically Black colleges and universities engaged in improving their content and pedagogical knowledge by attending northern institutions during their summers for additional work in mathematics and science (Russell, 2014).

Dr. Granville attended Dunbar High School in Washington, DC, a school known for sending its graduates to Ivy League schools. She described her value of the segregated system:

> I loved school. The "colored" school system of Washington was in no way an inferior school system. The system attracted outstanding administrators and teachers; teachers at all levels were well-trained and highly dedicated to their profession. I cannot think of one teacher I had in elementary school, junior high school, or high school who did not demand excellence. *My favorite subject was mathematics, and as far back as I can recall, I set my sights on becoming a mathematics teacher* [italics added]. (Granville, 1989, p. 45)

This statement suggests a sense of pride in the segregated school system. In this context, high expectations for African American students were normative and limitations were rarely placed upon what they could become in life. There was value and positive gain in the segregated system as many teachers focused on their responsibilities and social positioning (Standish, 2006)—that is academics and racial uplift. Consistent with other studies, many Black students viewed their segregated school as a "personalized school environment" (Siddle-Walker, 1996, p. 201) where the teachers and principals were often referred to as people who cared. Drs. Haynes, Granville, Browne, Hewitt, and Malone-Mayes understood that when their teachers were "demanding excellence," it was as an indication that they cared. More pointedly, if a teacher cared about the students, then that teacher would expect them to learn (Siddle-Walker, 1996).

The nature of caring in segregated schools both resembles the contemporary scholarship (i.e., see Noddings, 2002) that documents the significance of caring in schools and exceeds it (Siddle-Walker, 1996, p. 201). Overall, despite many school boards' poor response to the educational needs of African American children compared to its response to the needs of White students, African Americans' experiences in the segregated school system received tremendous support. For instance, these schools provided role models, parental support and advocates, self-sacrificing teachers and principals, and a broader community that authentically believed in the educational abilities of its members (Anderson, 1988; Siddle-Walker, 1996).

Black role models in segregated schools played an important role in the success of the Black mathematicians. Each of the women recalls significant role models who made an impression on her during her youth and adolescence. Dr. Malone-Mayes, who attended a public school in Waco, Texas, stated: "In every Black school I've attended, there's always been at least one Black woman teacher or professor with whom I could identify and who was a model I'd like to emulate" (Malone-Mayes, 1975, p. 4). Having a role model from the same racial background can be an important feature in the development of mathematicians, and is consistent with research suggesting students benefit from working with teachers who come from similar racial and gender backgrounds (Beady & Hansell, 1981; Pigott & Cowen, 2000; Rezai-Rashti & Martino, 2010). The influence of African American teachers on the school achievement of their African American students posits positive results. Research has suggested that the "single most important factor for all forms of second generation discrimination is the proportion of Black teachers" (Meier, Stewart, & England, 1989, p. 140). This was especially true during de jure segregation, as many teachers saw it as their responsibility to focus on academic achievement (Standish, 2006).

Strong parental support and advocacy also were a part of the value of segregation. A retrospective look at the historically segregated schooling of African Americans and the parental support is noteworthy (Jones-Wilson, 1981; Sowell, 1976). The five female mathematicians' parents represented an out-of-school factor that directly influenced, shaped, and supported their elementary and secondary educational experiences. Each of the mathematicians had parents who inspired them to pursue education and mathematics, and many of their parents had college degrees. Dr. Malone-Mayes' father had a natural understanding of mathematical ideas. She recalls an important time when she and her father worked on some mathematics homework.

> He and I would sit down, and he would listen to my spelling words and my multiplication tables. I think he enjoyed learning, too. I had had 5s and then we were on the 7's, and we just took them one by one...So my daddy said, "What's after 7 times 1?" I answered, "7 times 2, 7 times 3," etc., and when we got to 7 times 5, I couldn't answer. So daddy said, "What's 5 times 7?" And I said, "35." He said "What's 7 times 5?" And I said, "I don't know." He sat there and I don't know how many times he had to say it before I caught on, but he never told me the answer of 7 times 5. He kept saying, "What's 5 times 7?" He taught me, without knowing, the commutative law of multiplication. That's how I know it now. No one else ever pointed that out. (Henrion, 1997, p. 197)

This quote reveals that some Black parents were involved in their daughters' mathematics education, coconstructing mathematical knowledge. The finding regarding the value and influence of parents is consistent with other research that examined in-school and out-of-school factors influencing the successful mathematics achievement of African American students

(Russell, 2011). During segregation, the community and the school were mutually dependent (Siddle-Walker, 1996). It was normative behavior for parents and community to be inextricably linked to the school to accomplish the overall goals of racial uplift and high academic standards. Teachers put in extra time to conduct home visits where teachers and parents communicated about the students and set goals for learning.

Dr. Hewitt's parents were both college graduates, and she pays respect to their sacrifice and uncompromising position about the benefits of education. She stated:

> My parents believed that education was the only avenue through which an African American man or women could better themselves. Therefore, they encouraged all of their children to attend college. All of my siblings did attend college, and they earned graduate degrees. (Lattimore, 2001, p. 10)

This comment suggests that some African American parents understood that education was an important way for their daughters to change the way they saw their lives and to have options for their future. Dr. Granville received powerful messages from her parents when she commented on the following:

> Fortunately for me as I was growing up, I never heard the theory that females aren't equipped mentally to succeed in mathematics...our parents and teachers preached over and over again that education is the vehicle to a productive life, and through diligent study and application we could succeed at whatever we attempted to do. I was aware that segregation placed many limitations on Negroes. However, daily one came into contact with Negroes who had made a place for themselves in society: We heard about and read about individuals whose achievements were contributing to the good of all people. These individuals, men and women, served as our role models; we looked up to them and we set our goals to be like them. We accepted education as the means to rise above the limitations that a prejudiced society endeavored to place upon us. (Granville, 1989, p. 44)

This statement suggests that psychosocial development, positive images of self, role modeling, and persistence were outcomes that Dr. Granville experienced in a segregated schooling system and society, which supported her long-term goal of being a mathematician.

Logic in the Face of Racism and Sexism

Plato's views have created a context for gender and racial oppression, particularly with mathematics (Herzig, 2004). He assumed that the majority of women were irrational, dependent, and impulsive: all qualities unfit for philosophers. I liken the position of philosophers to mathematicians because of the expectations associated with the role as well as the expectations from the members of its community. As already discussed in previous sections, philosophers were male, White, considered wise, objective, cognitively sound, and detached in ways that allowed them to fully engage in the cerebral exercise of logical reasoning. Similarly, mathematicians are characterized as engaged with their content, "loners," and as valuing protected time to think and solve problems (Kenshaft, 2005a). Alone time and quiet conversations to engage in problem solving are generally in short supply for the sex that is expected to clean the house, raise the family, and prepare the food. Subsequently, domestically comfortable and professionally successful seem to be mutually exclusive.

The theme logic in the face of racism and sexism captures the intricacies of the meaning across the five Black female mathematicians because it exemplifies the system or principles of reasoning the women lived by as they sojourned in the space of being Black, female, and a mathematician in U.S. society. We understand that logic is the set of processes that enables individuals to go beyond given information. When individuals use logic to engage with the world, they are identifying and verifying facts to draw conclusions. Drs. Haynes, Boyd-Granville, Browne, Hewitt, and Malone-Mayes illustrated logic in complicated ways. Their experiences and perspectives illustrate what I call a *transformative logic* because the interaction between emotion (feelings) and cognition (logic) intersected in important ways, and they used both types of processing mechanisms to engage with and navigate a culture and system designed to discourage them from realizing their dreams of becoming mathematicians and thriving as practicing mathematicians.

It is largely known that during the 1940s and 1950s the United States was filled with de jure and de facto salient issues around racism and sexism. These issues permeated social, educational, political, and economic life for racial minorities and many White women. Becoming a mathematician was an enterprising endeavor for anyone regardless of race or gender, because it meant dedicating one's life to the study of complex research topics such as algebra and number theory, analysis, applied mathematics, computational mathematics, or geometry/topology. These life sacrifices necessary for success as a mathematician parallel those of philosophers in Plato's setting. While mathematicians usually study a breadth of topics in their undergraduate education, they specialize in a topic of interest in their graduate work, including the qualifying exams and the doctoral dissertation. When we think about what it would have taken to become a mathematician during the Jim Crow era, when an individual was Black and female, the complexities and nuances of such an endeavor increase exponentially. The complexities increase because a Black female had to not only study challenging topics in mathematics, she also had to overcome formidable obstacles by resisting stereotypes, prejudices, and discrimination.

At a talk she made in 1975 for the Association of Women in Mathematics, Dr. Malone-Mayes discussed her experience with the intersectionality of race and gender and their influence upon her career.

> When you are both Black and female, it is difficult to distinguish which of these traits may account for the way you are received by others. I shall briefly review my career as a student and as a professor in an attempt to use hindsight as a tool in determining the influence these traits may have had on my professional growth. In many instances, it will be quite difficult to conclude whether these events happened because I am Black or because I am a woman or because I am both Black and female. (Malone-Mayes, 1975, p. 4)

This statement suggests that Dr. Malone-Mayes was unable to disaggregate what challenges in her life as a graduate student and professor were caused by race or gender. She fully understood that these two traits (Black and woman) impacted her educational goals and professional growth. This statement also demonstrates the complexities of multiple identities, and furthermore how those identities played out in her struggle of becoming a mathematician. Intersecting oppressions help us to understand that oppressions work together in producing injustice, as Black feminist thought highlights. Collins (2000) refers to this idea as the "matrix of domination" (p. 18) because regardless of the respective intersections involved, "structural, disciplinary, hegemonic, and interpersonal domains of power reappear across quite different forms of oppression" (p. 18). Therefore, although Dr. Malone-Mayes was victimized because of her race and gender, the structural barriers associated with institutions of higher education impacted her journey in very negative ways. Dr. Malone-Mayes and the other four female mathematicians engaged in these unfavorable and unsupportive environments in empowering ways, and also resisted and fought for the fruition of their dreams of becoming mathematicians, thereby illustrating transformative logic in the face of racism and sexism.

In 1961, Dr. Malone-Mayes decided to apply to Baylor University because it was in her hometown of Waco, Texas, and she wanted to study more mathematics. Dr. Malone-Mayes was confident in her abilities to do, learn, and persist in mathematics. She had already proven her mathematical talent by earning bachelor's and master's degrees in mathematics from Fisk University, one of the most prestigious institutions at the time. There at Fisk, she met and mentored young Gloria Hewitt, and took mathematics courses from Dr. Boyd Granville, (two other female mathematicians featured in this study). Dr. Granville was a graduate of Smith College for women and had earned both her master's and doctorate in mathematics from Yale University, which suggests that Dr. Malone-Mayes studied under a female professor with strong mathematics content knowledge. In a tribute to Dr. Lee Lorch, a White male mathematics professor who also taught at Fisk for five years, Dr. Malone-Mayes pointed out his 35 published articles that he used to develop Black students' interests in the "resource value of the journal literature...always questioning us about details which were omitted in the texts and articles...he required us to read mathematics" (Malone-Mayes, 1976, p. 709). In addition to her mathematics training and mentorship, Dr. Malone-Mayes also had been a faculty member and served as chair of the mathematics department at Paul Quinn College, a historically Black college that was founded and operated by the AME church (Biographies, n.d.).

These realities all suggested that Dr. Malone-Mayes was more than qualified to teach at Baylor University. She received the following letter from Alton B. Lee, the registrar and director of admissions.

Dear Mrs. Mayes:

Thank you for your letter of August 24. I have discussed it with my superiors in the office here but have nothing favorable to report. We have not yet taken down the racial barrier here, although I have been hopeful that it would be done eventually. It seems that everyone is waiting for everyone else and no one will take the initiative in such matters. I sincerely wish that it were possible for me to process your application for admission to Baylor University as a student.

Very sincerely yours,

Alton B. Lee, Registrar and Director of Admission (Henrion, 1997, p. 194)

This letter indicates that Dr. Malone-Mayes was denied admission because of racism. Denying Blacks admission to White graduate schools in the South simply because they were Black was a part of a larger context, as was discussed in the introduction. For example, in 1948 *Sipuel v. the Board of Regents at the University of Oklahoma* was a case brought all the way to the Supreme Court because Ada Lois Sipuel was

concededly qualified to receive the professional legal education offered by the State, applied for admission to the School of Law at the University of Oklahoma, the only institution for legal education supported and maintained by the taxpayers of the State of Oklahoma, and was denied for admission, solely because of her color. (*Sipuel v. Board of Regents at the U of Oklahoma*, 1948)

Other similar cases include *Sweatt v. Painter et al.* (1950) and *McLaurin v. Oklahoma Regents* (1950).

Plato's assumption that women are feeling-driven when applied to this situation should have included a concession by Dr. Malone-Mayes because of the specific details of her circumstance. First, higher education institutions within Black students home states blatantly discriminated against them and still practiced racism, sexism, and segregation. Secondly, although the conventional wisdom of the time was to deny Blacks the opportunity to further their education, Baylor administrators lacked progressive leadership because they wanted to continue to practice whiteness, the right to exclude. Having the right to exclude suggests that the leaders were afraid to relinquish power and exercise a commitment to social justice, such as was practiced at the University of Michigan and Oberlin. We know that the University of Michigan had some degree of understanding regarding the benefits of tearing down the racial barrier in higher education, and more particularly in their mathematics department, because Dr. Marjorie Lee Browne (featured in this study) graduated from the University of Michigan with both her master's and doctorate in mathematics nearly 10 years prior in 1950. DuBois's (1900) sociological study, *The College Bred Negro*, also pointed out that the University of Michigan and Oberlin were two institutions with the highest enrollment of Blacks in 1900, compared to other White institutions.

Dr. Malone-Mayes faced both racism and sexism. She had previous educational experiences at segregated elementary and secondary schools as well as had done graduate work at Fisk University, all of which prepared her for such moments in her life. She understood that while the circumstances were against her, she would not cave in and give up on her desire to become a mathematician. As it turned out, Baylor did not offer a doctorate in mathematics at that time, so she viewed the denial as beneficial because, she stated, "If they'd accepted me at Baylor, I would have just taken a few courses and not pursued a doctorate" (Mathematicians, n.d.).

Undeterred by Baylor University's segregation policy, Dr. Malone-Mays applied and was accepted at the University of Texas at Austin to pursue her PhD in mathematics. She began by taking only summer courses, and in the following she discusses the isolation and difficulty of being the only Black student, as well as the only woman, in the graduate mathematics program.

> My first recollection of my tenure as a graduate student at the University of Texas was a summer class that met at 7:00 am in which I was the only Black and the only woman. *For nine weeks, thirty or forty White men ignored me completely* [italics added]. I never initiated any conversations as there was no encouragement to do so. It seemed to me that conversations before class on mathematics between classmates quickly terminated if it appeared that I was listening. My rapport with students in the other two classes was not much better. This was my first experience attending school in a vacuum. My mathematical isolation was complete; I was not acquainted with any Blacks who had interest in these subjects. (Malone-Mayes, 1975, p. 4)

This recollection is another example of consequences faced due to the intersections of race and gender; it also illustrates transformative logic. The double jeopardy of race and gender limited her capacity to build relationships with other colleagues who were White and male to get support in studying mathematics. Combined, these factors had the potential of limiting her persistence. Other studies have pointed out that students' involvement or integration in the communities of their departments is an important factor in their persistence (Girves & Wemmerus, 1988; Herzig, 2002; Lovitts, 2001; National Science Foundation, 1998; Tinto, 1993).

The messages being sent to Dr. Malone-Mayes were that White males were superior in the mathematics domain and that it was up to her to learn mathematics in isolation. Stating that her isolation was complete further complicated her experience because not only were the White males aiming to bring about despair, she did not have any other Black students in her mathematics program with which she could communicate about advanced mathematics. In her quest to find camaraderie with her people, she still experienced segregation since the Black students she knew were not in her major. Dr. Malone-Mayes recalls further experiences at the University of Texas at Austin.

I could not become a teaching assistant. Why? Black.

I could not join my adviser and other classmates to discuss mathematics over coffee at Hilsberg's Café. Why? Because Hilsberg would not serve Blacks. Occasionally, I could get snatches of their conversation as they crossed our picket line outside the café.

I could not enroll in one professor's class. He didn't teach Blacks. *And he believed that the education of women was a waste of the taxpayers' money* [italics added]. (Malone-Mayes, 1975, p. 5)

The statement points out an interlocking system of racism and sexism. Feeling abandoned and outcast, Dr. Malone-Mayes should have dropped out of the program. However, she was determined to continue her career as a mathematics graduate student and eventually professor. The overarching values of the institution were clear: Blacks, and moreover Black females, were not supported or encouraged to study mathematics or thrive as an academic. In fact, they were denied the opportunity to access and participate in the mathematics community. The law could not protect the school in denying her, but the interpersonal and structural practices that existed within the mathematics department reinforced and perpetuated racism and sexism. Dr. Malone-Mayes graduated from the University of Texas at Austin and then went back to Baylor to become their first African American faculty member in the mathematics department, the same institution that had rejected her as a student only 5 years previously. There she spent the balance of her career teaching, and retired because of declining health in 1994.

Dr. Malone-Mayes's narrative demonstrates the nuances of a transformative logic in the face of racism and sexism, because throughout her journey she combined her faith within herself and her identity as a true mathematician to inform her decisions and her experiences. There was nothing feeling-driven about her engagement with the world, and she did rely on her truth, intuition, emotion, and personal perspective to bring her success to fruition.

Academy, Industry, and Community Leadership

The mathematicians used their feelings and intuition, along with their truth and cognition, to demonstrate a transformative logic. Moreover, they privileged the segregated school system and demonstrated leadership in the academy, industry, and their local communities. Table 1.4 shows their individual and collective scholarship and contributions to mathematics and mathematics education.

Plato was clear on the social roles of females: that they contribute to reproductive rather than productive processes in society. For example, in Plato's discussion about women becoming guardians in his state, he points out that to contribute to activities of war and philosophy (requirements of guardians), females had to give up all that was associated with the reproductive processes of society, such as divorcing their emotions and relinquishing their role to a maid to nurse their babies (Allen, 1975; Annas, 1976; Pomeroy, 1974).

Today, the social roles for women are still gendered, and to be a female mathematician can mean that one is a silo: detached, unattractive, and unable to have both family and a career. Although the mathematicians in this study did not have many children, they maintained relationships outside of the academy and were connected to their home communities in important ways. We can see some of the influences and consequences of racism and sexism on these mathematicians at the individual level. Specifically, we see that across all five women over a period of at least 50 years, their combined publications numbered 20 articles. This scholarship included publications in mathematics and mathematics education venues, newsletter commentaries, and textbooks. After she graduated with her doctorate, Dr. Granville worked as a post-doctoral researcher at New York University where she worked with Dr. Fritz John, the famous German mathematician whose work focused on partial differential equations and their applications in modeling the movement of water waves (Kolata, 1994). It is unfortunate that Dr. John had not "encouraged her to submit her research for publication" (O'Conner & Robertson, 2001, p. 2). Not being encouraged to publish could be one of the reasons why Dr. Granville, in particular, chose to seek a position in private and government arenas.

The relative dearth of publications provides only a part of the story. As a collective, their scholarship spans the same 50 years and represents incredible success given the social and political context of the time. Drs. Haynes,

TABLE 1.4 Professional Life as a Mathematician

	Haynes (1943)[a]	Granville (1949)	Brown (1950)	Hewitt (1963)	Malone-Mayes (1966)
Publications	1	2	6	3	8
External Funding/ Fellowships	None	Post-doc at NYU Institute for Mathematics; Sam A. Lindsey Chair at University of Texas at Tyler in 1990.	Faculty Fellow from Ford Foundation, NSF, and Columbia University; NSF Institute for Secondary Teachers of Mathematics; Shell grants to outstanding mathematics students; $60K IBM grant for supporting academic computing.	Visiting lecturer for the Mathematical Association of America; Raised over $500K in gifts to endow innovative new programs to support undergraduate and graduate mathematics students at U of Montana.	None
Academy Service	Mathematics Department Chair at Miner's Teacher's College for 30 years.	Professor of Mathematics at Fisk for 3 years.	Professor of Mathematics at North Carolina Central University; Mathematics Department chair for 19 years at NCCU.	Professor of Mathematics at U of Montana; Mathematics Department Chair at University of Montana for 6 years.	Professor Mathematics at Baylor University; Chair of the Mathematics Department at Paul Quinn, Bishop College for a total of 6 years. First Black to serve on Executive Committee of the Association of Women in Mathematics.

(continued)

TABLE 1.4 Professional Life as a Mathematician (continued)

	Haynes (1943)[a]	Granville (1949)	Brown (1950)	Hewitt (1963)	Malone-Mayes (1966)
Outcomes	Upon her death left a $700K endowment to establish the Euphemia Lofton Haynes Chair in the Dept. of Education at Catholic University.	Received an honorary doctorate from Smith College.	NSF-supported Marjorie Lee Browne Scholars Program at U of Michigan W.W. Rankin Memorial Award for Excellence in Mathematics Education from NCTM North Carolina.	Provided a voice for underrepresented minorities through her role as a member of the Board of Governors for the Mathematical Association of America.	Baylor Student Congress elected her Outstanding Faculty Member of the Year.
Community Service	Cofounded Catholic Interracial Council of Washington, DC; Catholic College Alumnae/Sigma Delta Epsilon.	Taught elementary school enrichment mathematics for California Miller Mathematics Improvement Program; educator at NSF Institute for Secondary Teachers of Mathematics summer program at USC.	Used her money to pay tuition for gifted Black students to pursue degrees in math.	Executive Council for Pi Mu, the mathematical honor society.	Served on board of directors for Goodwill Industries and Family Counseling and Children.
Industry/K–12	Board member and later president of the board of the District of Columbia Schools.	Worked as a mathematician for International Business Machines (IBM) working on the formulation of orbit computations and computer procedures for NASA's Project Mercury.	N/A	Served four years on Calculus Development Committee where she helped develop a syllabus for AP Calculus courses. Wrote mathematics questions for the Graduate Record Exam.	N/A

[a] Dates in parentheses refer to the year the doctorate was awarded.
Source: Black Women in Mathematics (http://www.math.buffalo.edu/mad/wmad0.html)

Granville, Brown, Hewitt, and Malone-Mayes secured funding for the advancement of mathematics education for minorities, they also served on prestigious boards, received opportunities to be fellows at respected universities, and were department chairs at their respective institutions. In addition to their commitment to the academy and industry, they served in the K-12 system in a variety of roles, as well as giving back to local organizations that were focused on the betterment of African Americans in general. Important outcomes included scholarship programs for minorities to study mathematics. Their life's work holistically is distinguished and extraordinary and reveals contributions both to public and private life.

What can we learn from this analysis that can inform contemporary conversations about mathematics educational reform and policy related to African American females?

What we learn from this analysis is that the first five Black women to earn doctorates in mathematics during the Jim Crow era provide standpoints that illuminate issues of access and participation as embedded in whiteness and White supremacy. These issues are still relevant today, given a close examination of the way school mathematics—elementary, secondary, and postsecondary—is organized around ability. These are the modern day footprints of Plato. We also learn that in seeking to understand the identity of a mathematician, it is unproductive to view feeling orientations and logic orientations as binary. Relying solely on their emotions, these Black female mathematicians would have met the gender and racial expectations society had placed upon them during the time of Jim Crow (i.e., dropping out of their doctoral programs). Instead, their tenacity, strength, and self-determination disrupted the advancement of the myth that Black females and mathematics are an oxymoron. On the one hand, Dr. Malone-Mayes's recollection about experiencing "complete isolation" in the mathematics department and "White men ignoring me completely" are chilling, yet not surprising given the time. However, what is noteworthy is her steadfastness and persistence not to let gendered and racial circumstances deter her from the endeavor of becoming a mathematician. On the other hand, Dr. Hewitt experienced more openness from her White colleagues.

> Some of my fellow graduate students did all they could to help and encourage me. They included me in most of their activities. I know this situation was not the norm for a lot of Blacks studying mathematics, but I was fortunate enough to be at the right place at the right time.

Dr. Hewitt's situation would be considered an anomaly, as she notes in her comment. She did attend graduate school at the University of Washington, an institution in Seattle where racism and sexism were still visible and real, but not so blatant like it was in some of the other universities in the

South (Douglas, 2008). Dr. Hewitt also was one of the later female mathematicians to graduate in the early 1960s, a time when African Americans all around the country were fighting for civil rights. Consequently, there was a larger social and political agenda that Dr. Hewitt was a part of and this may have positively influenced her experience.

The Black female mathematicians in this study used both feelings and logic to sustain and retain themselves in a space that was designed with the fabric of whiteness—the right to exclude. I call this transformative logic. Their logic was transformative in part because they cultivated faith within themselves via their families and larger communities, and took a courageous stance in sending a message to the world. That message was that Black females do have the knowledge, skills, and dispositions to become mathematicians. I recommend that elementary, secondary, and postsecondary institutions take notice and aim to create policies that specifically and intentionally work to create more welcoming environments and to develop Black females interested in mathematics. Above and beyond content development, I also recommend that reform policies aim to create a balance between logical reasoning and the characteristics of intuition, creativity, and subjectivity. Developing and offering courses in the mathematics departments of universities that integrate mathematics and the arts could be a strong starting point. Another recommendation includes offering courses in the mathematics departments that examine issues of race, class, and gender historically and contemporarily. Offering these types of courses in a traditional mathematics department would be innovative, transformative, and would promote these issues as critical and worthy of attention. In addition, strongly encouraging university mathematics professors to participate in book studies and faculty learning groups focused on these important issues could also stimulate positive change in higher education institutions.

Other lessons learned from this study that can inform mathematics reform research and policy include (a) establishing Black female-only mathematics classrooms and academic support across the preK-20 continuum, and (b) recruiting and developing White male allies and mentors for African American females interested in pursuing advance degrees in mathematics. White privilege and capital in the mathematics field is deeply rooted. Thus White allies can act as brokers in advancing the larger agenda of transforming Platonist thinking about who can do mathematics, just as Dr. Lorch did in the 1950s and 1960s. From the student perspective, creating STEM research groups on university campuses that focus on unpacking issues of race, class, and gender specifically related to access, participation, and achievement in mathematics is another way that policy can advance these ideas. These are important recommendations that can potentially improve the experiences of Black women in U.S. mathematics classrooms across the pipeline.

DISCUSSION

The overall findings of this study suggest that the lives and experiences of the first five female African American mathematicians both complement and counter Plato's assumptions about women. The intersection at Drs. Haynes, Brown, Granville, Hewitt, and Malone-Mayes's lives and Plato's theories about women help us understand a variety of principles. First, whiteness and White supremacy is embedded in the nature of mathematics and mathematics learning. Second, the organization of mathematics learning can be traced to Plato's philosophy and this organization of mathematics learning around ability can negatively influence access and participation of African Americans in general, and women in particular. This type of analysis is missing from dominant approaches and discussions of mathematics education reform, as are discussions around philosophical influences on the organizing of mathematics access and participation. Within a critique of Plato's views being rooted in White supremacy and gender oppression, this study aims to engage in an epistemological, historical, and philosophical dialogue about ways the experiences and perspectives of the first five African American female mathematicians illustrate contemporary issues of access and participation in mathematics.

To some degree, the lives of these Black women mathematicians complement Plato's notion of an elite few having the ability to reach such levels of advanced mathematics, particularly when considering the time in which they earned their degrees. However, Black women consistently find themselves at the intersections of contradiction;[2] more pointedly, they were outsiders within this elite community. They were practicing mathematicians within prestigious universities and governmental agencies; yet, their gendered and racial oppression often overshadowed such things as opportunities to prolifically publish or engage in a learning community of their peers. Findings also contend that the first five Black female women to earn doctorates in mathematics had perspectives and experiences that problematize Plato's assumptions that women are feeling-driven and productive only as mothers and caregivers. Plato assumes one way of being logical or making logical decisions and limits alternatives to the dominant conceptualization. Logical reasoning can be culturally or contextually bound, as demonstrated by the five Black women mathematicians who employed transformative logic in their thinking and decisions in becoming mathematicians. Through critical theory, the findings of this study are a reinterpretation of ways in which Plato's ideas and concepts can impact all women, but particularly Black women mathematicians. Critical theory is a tool that challenges Plato's assumption because he represents the Western epistemological canon.

Although any female mathematician could have been used to challenge Plato's assumptions, it was important to use the first five Black female mathematicians because they are positioned in a way that highlights the complexities and intersectional ties of race, gender, and the mathematics discipline. Their biographies clearly demonstrate evidence of privileged vantage points from White males and the White supremacy of the nature and culture of mathematics. The spaces Black female mathematicians occupy are places where one can find patterns of behavior that those immersed in the dominant culture are unable to recognize. It is unrecognizable to those in the dominant group in part because of the deeply rooted belief in meritocracy, which can emerge from hegemony, and also in part because individuals from the dominant group can be misinformed or ignorant about history and the lives of people with different backgrounds than themselves. These female mathematicians' lives should be visible as suggested by Black feminist thought. Their perspectives and experiences can advance social justice and empowerment for all women seeking to become mathematicians. These women worked to a level of empowerment and self-actualization that should be investigated for the mathematics community and the educational field broadly to better inform policy and practice regarding access and participation.

CONCLUSION

This chapter put forth a historical, epistemological, and philosophical perspective to problematize contemporary discourse about mathematics access and participation for African American females. Using important archival documents from the papers of the first five African American female mathematicians, this study investigated what mathematics education researchers might learn at the intersection of these women's journeys to becoming mathematicians and Plato's views about women. This intersection is important to study given the prominence of Plato's influence on the West and the unique insights about race and gender oppression revealed in the narratives of Drs. Haynes, Granville, Brown, Hewitt, and Malone-Mayes. The findings of a valued segregated education, the use of a transformative logic in the face of racism and sexism, and participation in the academy, industry, and their communities all suggest that these Black female mathematicians disrupted what Plato took for granted: that women are feelings-driven and only participate in productive ways through motherhood and caregiving. Additionally, the findings reveal that the pathway to becoming a mathematician is wrought with racial and gender oppression that is embedded in the nature of mathematics and the structures that are a part of the mathematics community.

Some broader implications of this study are that policymakers and mathematics educators should understand that we must be courageous, innovative, and transformative in our approach to reform. It is not enough to create programs that only focus on what Black females should do in and out of classrooms without considering the historical, epistemological, and philosophical. Important decision makers need to understand that whiteness and White supremacy is entrenched in how we organize mathematics learning that mainly benefits a few. Consequently, we need to aim to dismantle whiteness and fight collectively as a mathematics education community for the betterment of Black girls. A limitation of this work includes the focus on only five Black women. The field might benefit from conducting interviews with a larger sample of African American females who have received their doctorates in mathematics more recently to compare and contrast their experiences with those featured in this study. Overall, hearing and understanding the stories of Black females persisting in the mathematics pipeline is important work for informing policy and advancing the field.

NOTES

1. Close examination of these programs reveal that they focus on programing—creating programs that address access and participation. Creating programs are effective; however, they often do not include structural issues.
2. I want to thank my colleague, Dr. Bianca Williams, anthropologist at University of Colorado Boulder for this contribution to my study.

REFERENCES

Allen, C. G. (1975). Plato on women. *Feminist Studies, 2*(2/3), 131–138.

Anderson, J. (1988). *The education of Blacks in the South: 1860–1935.* Chapel Hill, NC: University of North Carolina Press.

Annas, J. (1976). Plato's republic and feminism. *Philosophy, 51*(197), 307–321.

Banks, J. A. (1996). The canon debate, knowledge construction, and multicultural education. In J. A. Banks (Ed.), *Multicultural education, transformative knowledge, and action: Historical and contemporary perspectives* (pp. 3–29). New York, NY: Teachers College Press.

Beady, C. H., & Hansell, S. (1981). Teacher race and expectation for student achievement. *American Educational Research Journal, 18,* 191–206.

Berryman, S. (1983). *Who will do science? Minority and female attainment of science and mathematics degrees: Trends and causes.* New York, NY: Rockefeller Foundation.

Biographies of women mathematicians. (n.d.). *Agnes Scott College.* Retrieved from http://www.agnesscott.edu/lriddle/women/alpha.htm#M

Black Women in Mathematics (n.d.). Retrieved from http://www.math.buffalo.edu/mad/wohist.html

Bloom, A. (1987). *The closing of the American mind.* New York, NY: Simon & Schuster.

Case, B. A., & Leggett, A. M. (Eds.). (2005). *Complexities: Women in mathematics.* Princeton, NJ: Princeton University Press.

Code, L. (1991). *What can she know? Feminist theory and the construction of knowledge.* Ithaca, NY: Cornell University Press.

Collins, P. (2000). *Black feminist thought: Knowledge, consciousness, and the politics of empowerment.* New York, NY: Routledge.

Cooper, A. J. (1988). *A voice from the South.* Oxford, England: Oxford University Press. Originally published in 1892.

Davis, P. J., & Hersh, R. (1982). *The mathematical experience.* Boston, MA: Houghton Mifflin Harcourt.

Douglas, D. M. (2008). *Jim Crow moves north: The battle over northern school segregation, 1865–1954.* New York, NY: Cambridge University Press.

DuBois, W. E. B. (1900). *The college bred Negro.* Atlanta, GA: Atlanta University Press.

Dweck, C. (2008). *Mindsets and math/science achievement.* Report prepared for the Carnegie Corporation of New York, Institute for Advanced Study Commission on Mathematics and Science Education. Retrieved from http://www.growthmind setmaths.com/uploads/2/3/7/7/23776169/mindset_and_math_science_achievement_-_nov_2013.pdf

Elshtain, J. B. (1982). Public man, private woman. *Political Theory, 10*(4), 616–619.

Fultz, M. (1995). Teacher training and African American education in the South, 1900–1940. *The Journal of Negro Education, 64*(2), 196–210.

Girves, J. E., & Wemmerus, V. (1988). Developing models of graduate student degree progress. *Journal of-Higher Education, 59,* 163–189.

Granville, E. B. (1989, Fall). My life as a mathematician. *Sage: A Scholarly Journal of Black Women, 6*(2), 44–46.

Harding, S. (1991). *Whose science? Whose knowledge? Thinking from women's lives.* Ithaca, NY: Cornell University Press.

Harding, S. (1993) Rethinking standpoint epistemology: What is "strong objectivity?" In L. Alcoff & E. Potter, (Eds.), *Feminist epistemologies* (pp. 49–82). New York, NY: Routledge.

Harris, C. I. (1993). Whiteness as property. *Harvard Law Review, 106*(8), 1707–1791.

Hartsock, N. (1983). The feminist standpoint: Developing the ground for a specifically feminist historical materialism. In S. Harding & M.B. Hintikka (Eds.), *Discovering reality* (pp. 283–310). Dordrecht, the Netherlands: Springer.

Haynes, C. (2013). *Restrictive and expansive views of equality: A grounded theory study that explores the influence of racial consciousness on the behaviors of White faculty in the classroom.* (Doctoral dissertation). Retrieved from ProQuest Dissertation Database. (Order No. 3597960)

Henrion, C. (1997). *Women in mathematics: The addition of difference.* Bloomington, IN: University Press.

Henry, P. (2000). *Caliban's reason: Introducing Afro-Caribbean philosophy.* New York, NY: Routledge.

Herzig, A. H. (2002). Where have all the students gone? Participation of doctoral students in authentic mathematical activity as a necessary condition for persistence toward the PhD. *Educational Studies in Mathematics, 50,* 177–212.

Herzig, A. H. (2004). Becoming mathematicians: Women and students of color choosing and leaving doctoral mathematics. *Review of Educational Research, 74*(2), 171–214.

hooks, b. (1994). *Teaching to transgress: Education as the practice of freedom.* New York, NY: Taylor & Francis.

hooks, b. (1999). Excerpts from feminist theory: From margin to center. In K. A. Foss, S. K. Foss, & C. L. Griffin's (Eds.), *Feminist rhetorical theories.* Thousand Oaks, CA: Sage.

Jones-Wilson, J. (1981). *A traditional model of educational excellence.* Washington, DC: Howard University Press.

Jordan-Taylor, D. (2011). "I'm not Autherine Lucy": The circular migration of southern Black professionals who completed graduate school in the north during Jim Crow, 1945–1970 (Doctoral dissertation). Retrieved from UMI Dissertations Publishing. (Order No. 3452746)

Kenschaft, P. C. (1981). Black women in mathematics in the United States. *The American Mathematical Monthly, 88*(8), 592–604.

Kenschaft, P.C. (2005a). *Change is possible: Stories of women and minorities in mathematics.* Providence, RI: American Mathematical Society.

Kenschaft, P. C. (2005b). Marjorie Lee Browne. In B. A. Case & A. M. Leggett (Eds.), *Complexities: Women in mathematics* (pp. 19–23). Princeton, NJ: Princeton University Press.

Kincheloe, J. L., & McLaren, P. (2000). Rethinking critical theory and qualitative research. In N. Denzin & Y. Lincoln (Eds.), *Handbook of Qualitative Research* (2nd ed., pp. 139–157). Thousand Oaks, CA: Sage.

Kolata, G. (1994). Fritz John, a master mathematician, dies at 83. *New York Times.* Retrieved from http://www.nytimes.com/1994/02/12/obituaries/fritz-john-a-master-mathematician-dies-at-83.html

Lattimore, R. (2001). Gloria Hewitt: Mathematician. *Mathematics Teacher, 94*(1), 9–13.

Lovitts, B. E. (2001). *Leaving the ivory tower: The causes and consequences of departure from doctoral study.* Lanham, MD: Rowman & Littlefield.

Malone-Mayes, V. (1975). Black and female. *Association of Women in Mathematics Newsletter, 5*(6), 1–22.

Martin, D. B. (Ed.). (2009). *Mathematics teaching, learning, and liberation in the lives of Black children.* New York, NY: Routledge.

Martin, J. (1985). *Reclaiming a conversation: The ideal of the educated woman.* New Haven, CT: Yale University Press.

Mathematicians of the African Diaspora. (n.d.). Retrieved from http://www.math.buffalo.edu/mad/

Mathematics Genealogy Project. (n.d.). Retrieved from http://genealogy.math.ndsu.nodak.edu/

Mayes, V. (1976). Lee Lorch at Fisk: A tribute. *The American Mathematical Monthly, 83*(9), 708–711.

McLaurin v. Oklahoma. 339 U.S. 637 (1950).

Meier, K. J., Stewart, J., & England, R. E. (1989). Race, class, and education: The politics of second generation discrimination. Madison, WI: University of Wisconsin Press.

Mills, C. W. (1997). *The racial contract.* New York, NY: Cornell University Press.

Mullings, L. (1997). *On our own terms: Race, class, and gender in the lives of African American women.* New York, NY: Routledge.

National Science Foundation (2013). *Women, minorities, and persons with disabilities in science and engineering.* Arlington, VA: Author.

National Science Foundation, Division of Science Resource Studies. (1998). *Summary of workshop on graduate student attrition* (NSF Publication No. 99–314). Arlington, VA: Author.

Neuendorf, K. A. (2002). *The content analysis guidebook.* Thousand Oaks, CA: Sage.

Noddings, N. (2002). *Educating moral people: A caring alternative to character education.* Williston, VT: Teachers College Press.

Oakes, J. (1990a). *Multiplying inequalities: The effects of race, social class, and tracking on opportunities to learn mathematics and science.* Santa Monica, CA: Rand Corp.

Oakes, J. (1990b). *Lost talent: The under participation of women, minorities, and disabled persons in science.* Santa Monica, CA: Rand Corp.

Oakes, J., Joseph, R., & Muir, K. (2004). Access and achievement in mathematics and science: Inequalities that endure and change. In J. A. Banks & C. A. M. Banks (Eds.), *Handbook of research on multicultural education* (2nd ed.; pp. 69–90). San Francisco, CA: Jossey-Bass.

O'Conner, J. J., & Robertson, E. F. (2001). *Evelyn Boyd Granville: MacTutor history of mathematics.* Retrieved from http://www-history.mcs.st andrews.ac.uk/Biographies/Granville.html

Okin, S. M. (1977). Philosopher queens and private wives: Plato on women and the family. *Philosophy & Public Affairs, 6*(4), 345–369.

Okin, S. M. (1979). *Women in Western political thought.* Princeton, NJ: Princeton University Press.

Pigott, R. L., & Cowen, E. L. (2000). Teacher race, child race, racial congruence, and teacher ratings of children's school adjustment. *Journal of School Psychology, 38*(2), 177–195.

Plato (1987). *The Republic.* London, England: Penguin Group.

Pomeroy, S. B. (1974). Feminism in book V of Plato's republic. *Apeiron, 8*(1), 33–35.

Ravitch, D., & Finn, C. E., Jr. (1987). *What do our 17-year-olds know? A report on the first national assessment of history and literature.* New York, NY: Harper & Row.

Rezai-Rashti, G. M & Martino, W. J. (2010). Black male teachers as role models: Resisting the homogenizing impulse of gender and racial affiliation. *American Educational Research Journal, 47*(1), 37–64.

Russell, N. M. (2011). *Black students and mathematics achievement: A mixed-method analysis of in-school and out-of-school factors shaping student success.* Retrieved from ProQuest. (Order No. 3452750).

Russell, N. M. (2014, April). *The mathematics education of African Americans, 1866–1954.* Paper presented at the American Educational Research Association, Philadelphia, PA.

Siddle-Walker, V. (1996). *Their highest potential: An African American school community in the segregated South.* Chapel Hill, NC: University of North Carolina Press.

Sipuel v. Board of Regents of University of Oklahoma, 332 U.S. 631 (1948).

Smedley, A., & Smedley, B. D. (2012). *Race in North America: Origin and evolution of a worldview* (4th ed.). Boulder, CO: Westview Press.

Sowell, T. (1976). Patterns of Black excellence. *Public Interest,* (43), 26.

Stage, F. K., & Maple, S. A. (1996). Incompatible goals: Narratives of graduate women in the mathematics pipeline. *American Educational Research Journal, 33*(1), 23–25.

Standish, H. A. (2006). *A case study of the voices of African American teachers in two Texas communities before and after desegregation, 1954–1975* (Doctoral dissertation). Retrieved from UMI Dissertations Publishing. (Order No. 3296545).

Sweatt v. Painter et al. 339 U.S. 629 (1950).

Tinto, V. (1993). *Leaving college: Rethinking the causes and cures of student attrition* (2nd ed.). Chicago, IL: University Chicago Press.

Whitehead, A. N. (1970). *Process and reality.* New York, NY: Free Press.

Woodson, C. G. (1933). *The mis-education of the Negro.* Washington, DC: Associated Publishers.

CHAPTER 2

WOMEN OF COLOR IN THE STEM ACADEMIC WORKPLACE

Lindsay N. Johnson, Kecia M. Thomas, and Lindsay Brown

Professional women of color in STEM experience unique career barriers and forms of diversity resistance (Thomas, 2008) that are not well articulated. The goal of this chapter is to frame the experiences of women of color in the STEM workplace within the context of being highly underrepresented workers. In many ways, these double minorities in the STEM world share comparable experiences to other high potential women of color in non-STEM work environments. Therefore our chapter uses research from the fields of industrial/organizational psychology, organizational behavior, and the careers literature to examine the world of work for underrepresented women in STEM.

It is first important to understand the extent to which women of color in STEM are underrepresented. Table 2.1 provides a startling snapshot. Regardless of discipline and ethnicity, women of color appear to work in STEM environments in which they are isolated culturally and probably alienated like many of their business world counterparts who are attempting to get to the executive suite. Similarly, about 3.2% of Fortune 500 boardroom

Women of Color in STEM, pages 39–56
Copyright © 2017 by Information Age Publishing
All rights of reproduction in any form reserved.

TABLE 2.1 Numbers of Tenured/Tenure Track Faculty at the Top 100 Research Institutions by Race/Ethnicity and by Gender (FY 2007)

Discipline/department	African American		Hispanic		Native American		Total number of faculty	
Chemistry	44	(8)	58	(13)	8	(1)	2,787	(383)
Mathematics and statistics	64	(7)	74	(16)	3	(0)	4,303	(554)
Computer science	23	(6)	46	(5)	1	(0)	2,531	(334)
Astronomy (top 40)	6	(2)	7	(1)	0	(0)	594	(94)
Physics	21	(2)	61	(9)	2	(0)	3,335	(304)
Biological sciences	101	(26)	190	(45)	16	(3)	7,455	(1,822)
Earth sciences	19	(4)	48	(8)	8	(1)	2,047	(338)

Note: The data are displayed as number of men followed by the number of women in parentheses.
Source: Towns (2010).

positions are held by women of color as opposed to 13.4% held by White women and 73.3% held by White men (Catalyst, 2013).

We will review literature on a number of issues found to create limitations for high potential women in general, and apply that literature to the STEM workplace. Our perception is that the significant underrepresentation of women of color in STEM workplaces exacerbates and intensifies their negative experiences. These experiences likely subsequently derail women's aspirations and interest in further career development in STEM, thus creating a sticky floor for those more junior in their career. Unfortunately, women of color who withdraw to disengage might also manifest a self-fulfilling prophecy based upon the belief that they simply aren't committed or willing to work hard enough. Therefore, after exploring these issues around how workplace diversity dynamics impact women of color in STEM, we will follow our review by offering recommendations for both women and STEM disciplines and organizations to overcome these barriers.

Our focus in this chapter relates to these women's psychological experience of underrepresentation physically, psychologically, and perhaps emotionally. We'll discuss how lacking workplace relationships, especially developmental relationships, such as those with mentors, limits these women's professional opportunities and aspirations. We will also discuss the physical environments of STEM workplaces, which can at times render women and people of color virtually invisible, thus making women of color seem valueless. We then turn to how the experience of underrepresentation for women of color leads to the very unique experience of being vulnerable to both sexual and racial harassment. Next, we'll discuss how their experience of being highly underrepresented leads to these women's treatment and subsequently identity formations as workplace *pet* and *threats* (Thomas,

Johnson-Bailey, Phelps, Tran, & Johnson, 2013). We conclude with a discussion of the larger issue of the climate for diversity in STEM, with a focus on how dominant group diversity ideologies such as colorblindness can disengage (Plaut, Thomas, & Goren, 2009) as well as deplete women of color from the cognitive resources needed to excel in these very demanding work environments (Holoien & Shelton, 2012).

LACKING DEVELOPMENTAL RELATIONSHIPS

Much of the research on the glass ceiling in for-profit organizations also applies to the experiences of women of color in STEM. Like executive women of color, STEM women of color are often locked out of informal information and developmental relationships at work, both of which are crucial in acquiring the mentoring and sponsorship needed to effectively navigate one's career (Eyring & Stead, 1998; Ragins, Townsend, & Mattis, 1998). Likewise, women of color who have "broken through" reveal that their career strategies often involve exceeding all performance expectations and making others feel comfortable with their race and gender (Giscombe & Mattis, 2002). Although these strategies work, they only open doors for individuals in ways that are somewhat oppressive. That is, they put the responsibility on women to compensate for such environments, and do little to change the organization to be more accommodating of differences that would benefit women of color collectively rather than individually. In fact, better understanding and repairing inhospitable climates for diversity in STEM and other workplaces would likely benefit the quality of work life for all workers, not just women of color.

Mentoring Relationships in STEM

Women of color in STEM face several barriers to establishing high-quality developmental relationships within the workplace, with mentoring relationships being one of the least understood. A mentoring relationship is defined as the developmental relationship between a more senior individual and a less senior individual that allows a protégé to gain the skills and abilities and the personal validation necessary to be successful in professional roles (Kram, 1985). Receiving mentoring has been shown to be an important part of organizational socialization and career development (Allen, Eby, Poteet, Lentz, & Lima, 2004; Eby, Allen, Evans, Ng, & DuBois, 2008). Unfortunately, women of color often lack access to high quality mentoring, if they are even able to acquire a mentor at all. The majority of senior-level positions within organizations are held by White men, making it more likely that mentors will also be White males. Additionally, minority employees have been found to be less likely to establish mentoring relationships with White male mentors than White male employees (Dreher & Cox, 1996). Once a mentoring relationship has been established, women of color are also less likely to be satisfied with their mentor (Giscombe, 2008). It is possible that a mentor who belongs to a majority group may not be able to adequately provide some of the more psychosocial components of mentoring to a woman of color. Psychosocial mentoring involves aspects such as personal acceptance and validation as a professional, which may be impaired due to a lack of ability to identify with one another based on groups differences (e.g., a cross-race/sex mentoring relationship; Thomas, 1989).

Matching mentors and protégés has been theorized to facilitate more successful mentoring relationships for minority protégés. Blake-Beard, Bayne, Crosby, and Muller (2011) found that undergraduate protégés in STEM departments preferred mentors of the same gender and race, especially when the students were women or ethnic minorities. These same students reported more help from demographically similar mentors, but gender and racial/ethnic similarity was not significantly related to academic outcomes (e.g., GPA, student self-efficacy). The lack of significant findings for matched mentoring relationships is a common finding in the academic mentoring literature (Smith, Smith & Markham, 2000; Turban, Dougherty, & Lee, 2002). However, some studies have found that matching on race/ethnicity can be associated with positive outcomes such as greater satisfaction and comfort with the mentor and more mentoring received (Frierson, Hargrove, & Lewis, 1994; Ortiz-Walters & Gilson, 2005). The nuances of race and gender similarity in STEM mentoring are still largely unknown. How does the history of underrepresentation with STEM as a student, graduate student, post-doc, and faculty member change the dynamic among minorities who occupy the same workspace? Is there an increased need to connect and support, or might there be a tendency to separate given the lack of familiarity of the situation? It is likely the racial identity development levels (Chrobot-Mason & Thomas, 2002) of the individuals involved might impact the drive to connect or separate as well as the larger diversity readiness of the institution in which they work.

Nonmentoring Developmental Relationships in STEM

Access to mentors can be severely limited for women of color, particularly in STEM, but some research has suggested that women of color can combat this by trying to gain job information from other sources such as formal organizationally run events (Bell & Nkomo, 2001). These authors also suggest that women of color who lack access to mentors should expand their conceptualization of developmental relationships to extend beyond traditional mentoring to focus on individuals who are willing to sponsor women of color within the organization. Sponsorship represents a more senior employee promoting (e.g., nominating for important job tasks) and protecting (e.g., advocating on behalf of the individual) a less senior employee. Ultimately all employees, but especially those who are underrepresented who might be first generation professionals, need a constellation of mentors (Bell & Nkomo, 2001) and sponsors to provide them with resources that are comparable to the cultural default (Jones, 2002) of STEM workers, namely middle-class, White men.

PHYSICAL ENVIRONMENT

Frequently, women of color study and ultimately work in physical environments that are not reinforcing of their presence. Environmental cues can occur in many forms and have negative or positive effects on individuals belonging to certain social groups. Individuals who belong to traditionally stigmatized groups often rely on social environmental cues to determine whether or not they will be discriminated against or accepted within that environment.

Women of color in STEM environments are subject to a number of cues that may make them feel unaccepted, inferior, unheard, and unseen. Emerson and Murphy (2014) offer a categorization of types of workplace situational cues related to stereotypes and prejudice. The authors suggest that environmental cues can make representation salient (e.g., whether an individual feels his or her social group is proportionately represented in the environment). Women of color in STEM are drastically underrepresented relative to other social groups and this disparity is glaringly obvious just by looking at the demographics of the classroom or academic workplace. Previous scholars have suggested that a critical mass must be reached in order for underrepresented groups to thrive (Avery, 2003; Ely, 1995; Kanter, 1997; Steele, 2010). The presence of more people of color (especially women of color) would be environmental cues that signal a more psychologically-safe work setting.

Emerson and Murphy (2014) also suggest that situational cues can make identity and stereotypes salient. Similarly, Cheryan, Plaut, Davies, and Steele (2009) examined stereotypical environmental cues as a contributor to women's lack of participation in computer science. These same cues could be examined based upon both race and gender.

The authors describe what they called *ambient identity cues*, which are objects that symbolize certain stereotypes about group members to other individuals or groups that might be evaluating the stereotyped group. Cheryan et al., found that objects placed in a computer science classroom that were considered stereotypically male (e.g., *Star Trek* posters) could communicate to female participants that computer science was a masculine field and thus unwelcoming to them. The authors suggest that *ambient belonging* is an important concept in the process of underrepresented group members feeling fully accepted or not in certain environments. Ambient belonging is comprised of an individual's sense of fit with the material (e.g., physical objects), the structural components of the environment (e.g., layout), and the people who may also be in that environment. Women of color in STEM are often exposed to different types of physical objects and artifacts that may not reflect their identities or their group's contributions to their discipline.

Another study demonstrating the impact that situational cues can have on sense of belonging asked female undergraduates to watch one of two videos: a male-dominated STEM conference video or a female-dominated STEM conference video. The female participants who watched the female-dominated video felt less stress and more belonging while attending a STEM conference than the female participants who watched the male-dominated video (Murphy, Steele, & Gross, 2007). For women of color in STEM, who have traditionally remained outside of the STEM sector, there are many symbols that represent this history of exclusion that can trigger threats to one's identity. Even when the contributions of women are celebrated, the diversity of women who exist may not be fully considered.

Situational cues often appear innocuous and of little concern, but they can symbolize and communicate stereotypes that hinder the positive experiences of women of color in STEM. Organizations and academic institutions must be aware of the impact that physical objects in the work environment can have on identity and feelings of belonging. Furthermore, it may be possible to use physical environment cues to facilitate more positive experiences and feelings of inclusion of women of color in STEM. For example, posters or promotional material for certain disciplines (e.g., chemistry) that depict more diverse people might be linked to increased feelings of inclusion among female ethnic minorities.

VULNERABILITY TO HARASSMENT

Women of color in STEM occupy a unique social position within their professional workspace. In addition, climates in science and engineering are typically described as being less "culturally competent" and less inclusive of individuals who represent marginalized groups (Silverstein, 2006). Lack of culturally competent models of inclusion, tends to create work climates that are hostile toward women of color professionals. This places women of color in unique and sometimes physically and psychologically dangerous situations.

Workers who are underrepresented are often vulnerable to harassment and discrimination (Berdahl, 2007; Cortina 2008). For example, Berdahl and Moore (2006) found that women of color were more likely to face both gender and racial harassment compared to White women and all men. Berdahl and Moore (2006) described this phenomenon as a *double jeopardy* for minority women who are "doubly" exposed to harassment in the workplace. It was later demonstrated the prevalence of harassment increases when women are in male-dominated work environments. Berdahl (2007) found occurrences of harassment intensified in work environments traditionally designated for men within which women were perceived as being "out of place." Women who violated the prescribed gender-stereotypic norms were subject to more severe (or overt) forms of gender harassment. Gender harassment in this case is one that does not stem from sex or sexual desire, but rather is employed as a means to reposition women to an appropriately prescribed field of work (Berdahl, 2007).

For women of color in fields perceived as traditionally masculine, the social, cultural, and professional penalties for being out of place are potentially just as severe if not more due to their gender as to their race (Heilman, 2001; Settles, Cortina, Stewart, & Malley, 2007). Specifically, research has used the term *double bind* to describe the duplicitous nature of discrimination or harassment for women of color in STEM (Malcom, Hall, & Brown, 1976; Ong, 2002). The term, similar to double jeopardy, refers to the idea that women of color are likely to experience oppression or discrimination based on both their race or ethnicity and gender. As a result, women of color are described as the least recognized and most undervalued among underrepresented groups in STEM (Malcom et al., 1976). Invisible and without value, women of color are at high risk for harassment in their STEM workspace, and would likely lack voice if they made a complaint.

Underrepresented workers are also vulnerable to subtle forms of interpersonal discrimination or mistreatment. Subtle forms of interpersonal mistreatment such as microaggressions have the potential to be as adverse to women of color as overt forms of discrimination. Microaggressions are described in research as subtle snubs, insults, assaults, or invalidations of people of color (Sue et al., 2007). Sue et al. (2007) suggests microaggressions as innocuous and easy-to-dismiss everyday exchanges that send denigrating messages to people of color. These exchanges are often automatic and unconsciously delivered, yet have the power to be impair the performance of minorities and people of color in their work environments. For example, many high potential women of color new-hires may experience encounters where they are told their "position came available only because an associate or colleague left," or because "the company or organization is trying to diversify its workforce." These types of snubs invalidate the expertise and presence of women of color, and are especially harmful when many of these women are the "only" in their work units. Given the incredible lack of representation of women of color in STEM workplaces, it would appear they are highly vulnerable to such types of invalidations.

In many instances, these chronic messages are not just human delivered, but they are embedded in the environment. For example, in a work setting the identities of underrepresented people of color are at times made salient by the exclusion of literature and posted displays pertinent to their racial groups (Cheryan, Plaut, Davies, & Steele, 2009; Sue, 2003). This type of exclusion can speak volumes about the culture of the work environment. In the STEM workplace, culture is still defined by notions of whiteness and masculinity (Settles, Jellison, & Pratt-Hyatt, 2009; Johnson, 2007). Maclachlan (2006) found cultural belief in the prevailing White male superiority manifested as microaggressions in everyday practices and policies in STEM departments, which led minority women to feel isolated and in some instances judged as intellectually inferior. In turn, women of color are likely to experience questions of whether or not they belong in their work unit. The cultural messages and cues received by women of color are the result of what Settles, Cortina, Malley, & Stewart (2006) refer to as the masculine worldview of science. Further, the culture of science is competitive, objective, and a perceived meritocracy; as a result, women of color become the target of incivility in their workspace.

Cortina (2008) discusses incivility as also subtle and prevails particularly in sexist work environments. In sexist environments, incivility has the potential to cause psychological and social injury to individuals who represent certain groups (Caza & Cortina, 2007; Cortina, 2008). Further, she refers to *selective incivility* as more than general incivility or prejudice, but rather prejudice based on individuals being members of socially undervalued groups, primarily gender and race. Thus, highly underrepresented and typically undervalued women of color encounter discrimination targeted directly at their own identity. Caza and Cortina (2007) demonstrated direct targets of incivility experience issues related to psychological distress, and overall decline in well-being, to a greater degree than other social groups. To that end, Lim and Cortina (2005) found the negative impacts of incivility on well-being also adversely impacted organizational outcomes such as satisfaction and withdrawal. Psychological injury caused by incivilities at work has greater implications for women of color in STEM who are particularly vulnerable due to their identity status. The nature of these hurtful experiences for women of color likely differ across career stage, such that young junior women's experiences can be very different from their more senior colleagues although both groups continue to work in environments in which they experience isolation and alienation.

WOMEN OF COLOR IN STEM AS PETS AND THREATS

Thomas, Johnson-Bailey, Phelps, Tran, and Johnson (2013) engaged in qualitative research on academic women across career stages. One noteworthy finding was that women who worked in areas in which they were underrepresented often identified with *pet* and *threat* identities. Specifically, pets provided narratives in which they explained their token status as leading to benevolent sexist behavior from their male coworkers. These pets were often overexposed for their novelty, but underutilized for their talent. They often discussed being a source of diversity capital for their coworkers, being overly protected, and not having the opportunity to fully stretch their knowledge, skills, and abilities. Those who identified as threats were similarly underrepresented and isolated, but they were more senior. In contrast to their more junior pet colleagues, they experienced more hostile sexism and felt they lacked access to the rewards and recognition that they came to expect in observing the treatment received by their male colleagues. Unfortunately for these perceived threats, the support systems they cultivated as pets had begun to erode and their family and friends began to question their success, further exasperating their isolation and alienation.

Supporting women of color in STEM therefore means that disciplines and workplaces must be sensitive to issues of race, gender, and disciplinary cultures, but also the career stage at which the woman of color finds herself. This literature seems to suggest that women of color at more junior career stages are likely to experience more benevolent forms of prejudice (Glick & Fiske, 2001). Benevolent prejudice may in fact "feel good" and provide young women of color with enhanced visibility, but it could also deprive her of opportunities to develop and stretch her talents, even acquire feedback that comes from failure that isn't necessarily available if one is not permitted the opportunity to fully engage in one's work. Instead, pets can also be overprotected, underutilized, and highlighted for the wrong reasons (Thomas et al., 2014).

In contrast, perceived threats seemed to report more experiences with more hostile forms of sexism, which involved a questioning of their credentials and career trajectories (Thomas et al., 2013). Like pets, they encounter isolation and alienation, but also as they moved up in their careers an unforeseen erosion of their support systems, as other women of color perhaps explored other career opportunities; or friends and family lacked a clear understanding of the role of their careers to their overall identities and esteem. Clearly, women at either stage are at career risk and emotional risk from working in environments in which they are not fully seen or appreciated.

POOR DIVERSITY CLIMATES

The overarching workplace diversity climate has consequences for how an institution engages in diversity practices, supports underrepresented workers, and makes visible or invisible the concerns of these employees. In organizational climates with strong demographic fault lines, the negative consequences in practice are magnified toward underrepresented workers (Avery, 2003). In this case, the workplace diversity climate also dictates strong disparities in subgroup power, resulting in a lack of social power for those who are outnumbered. Previous research suggests lack of social power and greater disparity in representation between subgroups elicits less favorable outcomes related to perceptions of fairness, commitment, and satisfaction from underrepresented employees (Riordan & Shore, 1997; Tsui & O'Reilly, 1989). A similar argument could be made for the STEM workplace.

The diversity climate in science is often criticized as "ill-equipped" to foster inclusive environments for underrepresented groups, especially women of color. For example, a multitude of evidence demonstrates that there is a lack of perceived support (both formal and informal) and access to resources for women of color scientists compared to their colleagues (Brown, 2000; Ong, 2002; Seymour & Hewitt, 1997). As a result, women of color potentially experience fewer instances of positive visibility among their peers. Therefore, poor diversity climates in the STEM workplace create legitimate concerns for engagement, support, and visibility for women of color.

Cultural ideas about certain groups and difference get inscribed into practices and inform everyday experiences and behavior (Plaut, 2010). Ideologies about difference are then reproduced into structural and cultural patterns that signal an overall diversity climate to underrepresented workers. Two common diversity ideologies are colorblindness and multiculturalism (Thomas, Plaut, & Tran, 2014). In colorblind workspaces, leaders and their followers downplay differences and silence conversations about them. In contrast, multicultural workplaces see differences as opportunities for learning, development, and enhanced competitiveness.

Employee diversity ideologies have been shown to impact employee outcomes. Plaut, Thomas, and Goren (2009) examined the role of Whites' diversity ideologies, namely colorblindness or multiculturalism, on minority workers' engagement in a STEM workplace (a hospital). Their data consisted of 5,000 hospital workers whose educational backgrounds ranged from PhDs and MDs, through GEDs. When examined at the department level and across education, these researchers found that White colorblindness was related to decreases in minority engagement, whereas the opposite occurred—increases in minority engagement—when coworkers were Whites who were more multicultural in their diversity ideology. In the STEM workplace, default understandings of diversity (those typically tied to Whiteness and colorblindness) can cause social and cultural barriers to socializing and engaging women of color as active members of their work environments.

Diversity ideologies have also been linked to individual cognitive and mathematical performance among ethnic minorities. Recent research demonstrates that White colorblindness appears to be a source of cognitive completion for ethnic minorities. In fact, in a laboratory study, Whites demonstrating more colorblindness exhibited more behavioral prejudice that subsequently depleted the cognitive performance of the ethnic minorities with whom they had interacted (Holoien & Shelton, 2011). Wilton, Good, Moss-Racusin, and Sanchez (2015) found in a series of studies that colorblind messages were especially detrimental to the performance of women of color. After exposure to colorblind messages, women of color, as compared to other demographic groups, were least likely to expect race and gender diversity in an organization, and they expected to perform poorly on a math test, which was subsequently confirmed by their data. It appears that colorblindness is not only related to disengagement, but it is a form of identity threat, especially for women of color, that threatens the performance expectations as well as their actual performance.

These issues of ideologies and climate may present an ongoing problem in STEM, as women of color frequently report experiencing social isolation and distancing from their White or male peers (Johnson, 2011; Ong, Wright, Espinosa, & Orfield, 2011). Without an adequate understanding of diversity ideologies at play, women of color are left to reconcile feelings of exclusion with their own needs for support and performance expectations.

For underrepresented women of color, lack of support from supervisors, peers, and top leadership is a persistent issue in non-STEM and STEM workplaces. In each case, women of color are likely to face challenges securing mentors and allies, and accessing informal networks to support their advancement. Finding adequate support in hostile climates that are usually less welcoming is a particularly significant barrier for high potential women of color. Answering difficult questions such as who are their allies, who can be trusted with their careers, and what type of role models do they really have within their work units becomes part of their daily work realities.

In lieu of lack of support, women of color face additional barriers to achieving positive visibility within their work units. Women of color are forced to navigate spaces where they are highly visible due to the salience of their race and gender (because they represent one of few in their units) and other spaces in which they remain highly invisible also because of their identity. Achieving a balance of positive visibility is not an endeavor that should fall on the part of women of color alone, but also on the part of leadership and the overall climates within their departments. In order to identify necessary interventions targeted toward more effective styles of leadership and culturally competent climates, a more inclusive research agenda is needed.

A MORE INCLUSIVE RESEARCH AGENDA

Future research should focus on better understanding the work and career development experiences of women of color, particularly within STEM contexts. Findings from mentoring studies have been largely inconclusive in that we are still unsure of the benefits of mentor-protégé matching based on social identity. Future research should examine the nuances of mentoring (and other developmental nonmentoring) relationships for women of color in STEM.

Research on environmental social cues can also be used to not only stop unintentional exclusionary practices, but promote more inclusive STEM environments. Because of the changing nature of treatment (i.e., pet to threat) that women of color may experience based on where they are in their career (e.g., more junior or senior), longitudinal studies may also be especially rich in unpacking the career development experiences that women of color face in STEM. More research that investigates the coping mechanisms and long-term psychological and physical well-being of women of color in STEM may help illuminate what works and what does not work.

Finally, research that engages the diversity within women of color and explores different dimensions of diversity, such as economic background and social location, can ensure interventions are comprehensive and strategically target the needs of women of color in STEM. In sum, an inclusive agenda fully embodies the unique as well as the collective realities of this underserved population. We offer the following recommendations in preliminary fulfillment of this research agenda.

RECOMMENDATIONS FOR INDIVIDUAL WOMEN

"Corner Circle" to Interpret Incivility and Mistreatment

Conversations with social group members or identity allies (those you know to be in your corner) can serve as a springboard to relate or interpret events of mistreatment and incivility. Connections made within this circle can also be used to strategize the necessary action to take, and if action should be taken. Strategies for action are likely to have different career implications for those who may be tenure versus pretenure. Nonetheless, a trust circle can prove to be critically important across career stages.

Securing Trust in Unexpected Places

Extending oneself beyond those who represent a member of your social or identity groups offers additional opportunities for outside allies and sponsors who can lobby on your behalf. Such individuals can be found in places like administration, across colleges, department heads of other units, colleagues of other social identity groups, all of which can offer support. Making an effort to extend oneself beyond an internal circle of comfort potentially creates more vulnerability for women of color to a degree. To the extent that a quality connection is made, this type of effort can prove very beneficial in the long run.

RECOMMENDATIONS FOR STEM

Climate Studies and Long-Term Commitments to Culture Change

Long-term commitments to culture change should continue with rigorous and steady investigations of persistent challenges and barriers due to poor climates in STEM. Future theory development should be explicitly framed in the context of these uniquely challenging work environments. Understanding of environmental social cues should be integrated into STEM climate studies.

Culturally Competent Models of Leadership

Multicultural models of leadership are needed at the top, unit heads. Leadership is critically responsible for being aware of complex challenges on underrepresented individuals. Efforts should be made to ensure diverse individuals occupy leadership positions. Doing so will also communicate to underrepresented groups that the workplace is a not a place that will discriminate based on social identity.

Buffer Against Underrepresentation With Organizational Support

Some organizations may be severely underrepresented in regards to women of color. Understanding the needs of these women means understanding that support must be provided by the organization in the form of affinity groups, formal mentoring programs, and opportunities to gain sponsorship (Avery, McKay, & Wilson, 2008; Chao, 1997; Kirby & Jackson, 1999; Thomas & Kram, 1988).

Integrating Diversity Science into Practice

There are potentially other ideologies yet to be identified (e.g., color-blindness) that diminish the value and identity of underrepresented groups in STEM (Plaut, 2010). As mentioned, these ideologies invalidate the experiences of women of color and other diverse groups resulting in work climates that are generally less inclusive. Recognizing problematic ideologies that alienate underrepresented workers is vitally important for developing strategic interventions targeting incivility and mistreatment in the workplace.

Building a Complexity Paradigm in STEM Research

New and future research should begin to think beyond the categories of race and gender. There are various dimensions of diversity also likely at play. A complexity paradigm allows and encourages a commitment to examining all salient features of identity, social location, inequities in power, and other cultural theories that impact unique realities of marginalized individuals (Silverstein, 2006). The STEM workplace stands to benefit from research that encompasses a broader scope of diversity dimensions.

Renewed Commitment to Social Justice

As a larger community, a renewed commitment to understanding equity or different notions and meanings of equity therein can also be beneficial to areas of science and engineering. Research should investigate questions such as: What does equity look like and how might it be defined differently across underrepresented groups? There remains a lack of theory to address impartiality in discourses related to definitions of equity in work contexts. Theory development in areas of social justice will help to bridge this gap.

REFERENCES

Allen, T. D., Eby, L. T., Poteet, M. L., Lentz, E., & Lima, L. (2004). Career benefits associated with mentoring for protégés: A meta-analysis. *Journal of Applied Psychology, 89*, 127–136.

Avery, D. (2003). Reactions to diversity in recruitment advertising: Are differences black and white? *Journal of Applied Psychology, 88*(4), 672–679.

Avery, D. R., McKay, P. F., & Wilson, D. C. (2008). What are the odds? How demographic similarity affects the prevalence of perceived employment discrimination. *Journal of Applied Psychology, 93*(2), 235.

Bell, E. L., & Nkomo, S. (2001). *Our separate ways.* Boston, MA: Harvard Business School Press.

Berdahl, J. L. (2007). The sexual harassment of uppity women. *Journal of Applied Psychology, 92*(2), 425–437.

Berdahl, J. L., & Moore, C. (2006). Sexual harassment: Double jeopardy for minority women. *Journal of Applied Psychology, 91*(2), 426–436.

Blake-Beard, S., Bayne, M. L., Crosby, F. J., & Muller, C. B. (2011). Matching by race and gender in mentoring relationships: Keeping our eyes on the prize. *Journal of Social Issues, 67,* 622–643.

Brown, S. V. (2000). The preparation of minorities for academic careers in science and engineering: How well are we doing? In G. Campbell, R. Denes, & C. Morrison (Eds.), *Access denied: Race, ethnicity, and the scientific enterprise* (pp. 239–269). New York, NY: Oxford University Press.

Catalyst Census. (2013). *Fortune 500 women board of directors.* Retrieved from http://www.catalyst.org/system/files/2013_catalyst_census_fortune_500_women_board_director.pdf

Caza, B. B., & Cortina, L. M. (2007). From insult to injury: Explaining the impact of incivility. *Basic and Applied Social Psychology, 29*(4), 335–350.

Chao, G. T. (1997). Mentoring phases and outcomes. *Journal of Vocational Behavior, 51,* 15–28.

Cheryan, S., Plaut, V. C., Davies, P. G., & Steele, C. M. (2009). Ambient belonging: How stereotypical cues impact gender participation in computer science. *Journal of Personality and Social Psychology, 97,* 1045–1055.

Chrobot-Mason, D. L., & Thomas, K. M. (2002). Minority employees in majority organizations: The intersection of individual and organizational racial identity in the workplace. *Human Resource Development Review, 1*(3), 323–344.

Cortina, L. M. (2008). Unseen injustice: Incivility as modern discrimination in organizations. *Academy of Management Review, 33*(1), 55–75.

Dreher, G. F., & Cox, T. H., Jr., (1996). Race, gender, and opportunity: A study of compensation attainment and the establishment of mentoring relationships. *Journal of Applied Psychology, 81,* 297–308.

Eby, L. T., Allen, T. D., Evans, S. C., Ng, T., & DuBois, D. L. (2008). Does mentoring matter? A multidisciplinary meta-analysis comparing mentored and nonmentored individuals. *Journal of Vocational Behavior, 72,* 254–267.

Ely, R. J. (1995). The power of demography: Women's social constructions of gender identity at work. *Academy of Management Journal, 38,* 589–634.

Emerson, K. T., & Murphy, M. C. (2014). Identity threat at work: How social identity threat and situational cues contribute to racial and ethnic disparities in the workplace. *Cultural Diversity and Ethnic Minority Psychology, 20*(4) 1–13.

Eyring, A., & Stead, B.A. (1998). Shattering the glass ceiling: Some successful corporate strategies. *Journal of Business Ethics, 17,* 245–251.

Frierson, H. T., Hargrove, B. K., & Lewis, N. R. (1994). Black summer research students' perceptions related to research mentors' race and gender. *Journal of College Student Development, 35,* 475–480.

Giscombe, K. (2008). *Women of color in accounting: Women of color in professional services series.* New York, NY: Catalyst.

Giscombe, K., & Mattis, M.C. (2002). Leveling the playing field for women of color in corporate management: Is the business case enough? *Journal of Business Ethics, 37,* 103–119.

Glick, P., Fiske, S. T. (2001). An ambivalent alliance: Hostile and benevolent sexism as complementary justifications for gender inequality. *American Psychologist, 56*(2), 109–118.

Heilman, M. E. (2001). Description and prescription: How gender stereotypes prevent women's ascent up the organizational ladder. *Journal of Social Issues, 57*, 657–674.

Holoien, D. S., & Shelton, J. N. (2011). You deplete me: The cognitive costs of colorblindness on ethnic minorities. *Journal of Experimental Social Psychology, 48*, 562–565.

Johnson, A. C. (2007). Unintended consequences: How science professors discourage women of color. *Science Education, 91*(5), 805–821.

Johnson, D. R. (2011). Women of color in science, technology, and mathematics (STEM). *New Directions for Institutional Research, 152*, 75–85.

Jones, M. (2002). *Social psychology of prejudice.* Upper Saddle River, NJ: Prentice-Hall

Kanter, R. M. (1977). *Men and women of the corporation.* New York, NY: Basic Books.

Kirby, D., & Jackson, J. S. (1999). Mitigating perceptions of racism: The importance of work group composition and supervisor's race. In Murrell, A. J., Crosby, F. J., & Ely, R. J. (Eds.), *Mentoring dilemmas: Developmental relationships within multicultural organizations.* Hillsdale, NJ: Erlbaum.

Kram, K. E. (1985). *Mentoring at work.* Glenview, IL: Scott Foresman.

MacLachlan, A. J. (2006). The graduate experience of women in STEM and how it could be improved. In J. M. Bystydzienski & S. R. Bird (Eds.), *Removing barriers: Women in academic science, technology, engineering, and mathematics* (pp. 237–253). Bloomington, IN: Indiana University Press.

Malcom, S. M., Hall, P. Q., & Brown, J. W. (1976). *The double bind: The price of being a minority woman in science.* (American Association for the Advancement of Science Report No. 76-R-3). Washington, DC: AAAS Office of Opportunities in Science.

Murphy, M. C., Steele, C. M., & Gross, J. J. (2007). Signaling threat: How situational cues affect women in math, science, and engineering settings. *Psychological Science, 18*, 879–885.

Ong, M. (2002). *Against the current: Women of color succeeding in physics.* (Doctoral dissertation.) Retrieved from ProQuest Dissertations and Theses database (No. 304803810).

Ong, M., Wright, C., Espinosa, L., & Orfield, G. (2011). Inside the double bind: A synthesis of empirical research on women of color in science, technology, engineering, and mathematics. *Harvard Educational Review, 18*(2), 172–208.

Ortiz-Walters, R., & Gilson, L. L. (2005). Mentoring in academia: An examination of the experiences of protégés of color. *Journal of Vocational Behavior, 67*, 459–475.

Plaut, V. (2010). Diversity science: Who needs it? *Psychological Inquiry, 21*, 168–174.

Plaut, V. C., Thomas, K. M., & Goren, M. J. (2009). Is multiculturalism or colorblindness better for minorities? *Psychological Science, 20(4)*, 444–446.

Ragins, B. R., Townsend, B., & Mattis, M. (1998). Gender gap in the executive suite: CEOs and female executives report on breaking the glass ceiling. *Academy of Management Executive, 12*, 28–42.

Riordan, C. M., & Shore, L. M. (1997). Demographic diversity and employee attitudes: An empirical examination of relational demography within work units. *Journal of Applied Psychology, 82,* 342–358.

Settles, I. H., Cortina, L. M., Malley, J., & Stewart, A. J. (2006). The climate for women in academic science: The good, the bad, and the changeable. *Psychology of Women Quarterly, 30,* 47–58.

Settles, I. H., Cortina, L. M., Stewart, A. J., & Malley, J. (2007). Voice matters: Buffering the impact of a negative climate for women in science. *Psychology of Women Quarterly, 31,* 270–281.

Settles, I. H., Jellison, W. A., & Pratt-Hyatt, J. S. (2009). Identification with multiple social groups: The moderating role of identity change over time among women-scientists. *Journal of Research in Personality, 43*(5), 856–867.

Seymour, E., & Hewitt, N. M. (1997). *Talking about leaving: Why undergraduates leave the sciences.* Boulder, CO: Westview Press.

Silverstein, L. B. (2006). Integrating feminism and multiculturalism: Scientific fact or science fiction. *Professional Psychology, 37*(1), 21–28.

Smith, J. W., Smith, W. J., & Markham, S. E. (2000). Diversity issues in mentoring academic faculty. *Journal of Career Development, 26,* 251–262.

Steele, C. M. (2010). *Whistling Vivaldi: And other clues to how stereotypes affect us.* New York, NY: Norton.

Sue, D. W. (2003). *Overcoming our racism: The journey to liberation.* San Francisco, CA: Jossey-Bass.

Sue, D. W., Capodilupo, C. M., Torino, G. C., Bucceri, J. M., Holder, A. M., Nadal, K. L. & Esquilin, M. (2007). Racial microaggressions in everyday life: Implications for clinical practice. *American Psychologist, 62*(4), 271–286.

Thomas, D. A. (1989). Mentoring and irrationality: The role of racial taboos. *Human Resource Management, 28,* 279–290.

Thomas, D. A., & Kram, K. E. (1988). Promoting career enhancing relationships: The role of the human resource professional. In M. London & E. More (Eds.), *Employee career development and the human resource professional* (pp. 49–66). Westport, CT: Greenwood.

Thomas, K. M. (2008). *Diversity resistance in organizations.* Applied psychology series. Mahwah, NJ: LEA.

Thomas, K. M., Johnson-Bailey, J., Phelps, R. E., Tran, N. M., & Johnson, L. (2013). Moving from pet to threat: Narratives of professional Black women. In L. Comas-Diaz & B. Green (Eds.), *The psychological health of women of color: Intersections, challenges, and opportunities.* Westport, CT: Praeger.

Thomas, K. M., Plaut, V. C., & Tran, N. M. (2014). *Diversity ideologies in organizations.* Applied psychology series. New York, NY: Routledge.

Towns, M. H. (2010). Where are the women of color? Data on African American, Hispanic, and Native American faculty in STEM. *Journal of College Science Teaching, 39*(4), 6–7.

Tsui, A. S., & O'Reilly, C. A., III. (1989). Beyond simple demographic effects: The importance of relational demography in superior–subordinate dyads. *Academy of Management Journal, 32,* 402–423.

Turban, D. B., Dougherty, T. W., & Lee, F. K. (2002). Gender, race, and perceived similarity effects in developmental relationships: The moderating role of relationship duration. *Journal of Vocational Behavior, 61,* 240–262.

Wilton, L. S., Good, J. J., Moss-Racusin, C. A., & Sanchez, D. T. (2015). Communicating more than diversity: The effect of institutional diversity statements on expectations and performance as a function of race and gender. *Cultural Diversity and Ethnic Minority Psychology, 21*(3), 315.

CHAPTER 3

BREAKING BARRIERS

Inspiring Stories About NASA Women of Color

Lisa Brown, Andrea Foster, and Barbara Polnick

In June 1963, the first woman in space was Valentina Tereshkova. Valentina was a Russian cosmonaut who spent more than 70 hours aboard Vostok 6 making 48 orbits around Earth. It was not until 20 years later that the United States launched the first American woman: Astronaut Mission Specialist Sally Ride, an astrophysicist. In September 1992, Mae Jemison became the first woman of color in space. While all of these women were astronauts—the traditional face of the National Aeronautics and Space Administration (NASA)—other women (including women of color) have made tremendous contributions behind the scenes in fields such as engineering, astronomy, physics, and aviation. In this chapter, we highlight the significant contributions made by some of these women of color, the barriers to success they overcame, and the important factors that influenced them to pursue careers in the fields of science, technology, engineering, and mathematics (STEM).

Women of Color in STEM, pages 57–77
Copyright © 2017 by Information Age Publishing
57

EARLY WOMEN PIONEERS OF NASA

In October 1957, an artificial, basketball-sized, Russian satellite named Sputnik I became the catalyst for a science renaissance (Powers, 1997). The United States public opinion of this launch created an illusion of a scientific and technological gap. Shortly after this launch, bountiful resources were directed to increase efforts in scientific education, aerospace, and technical endeavors, including the development of a new federal agency: the National Aeronautics and Space Administration (Powers, 1997). However, NASA was not the first organization in the United States designed to explore aviation.

An earlier national aeronautical laboratory, the National Advisory Committee for Aeronautics (NACA,) was founded on March 3, 1915 (Powers, 1997). Congress enacted legislation to form this independent government agency to coordinate efforts for aircraft technology. In 1920, NACA created the Langley Aeronautical Laboratory as a research and testing facility. During the next 30 years, NACA evolved into an amalgamation of new laboratories: Ames Aeronautical Laboratory, the Aircraft Engine Research Laboratory (renamed Lewis Research Center), and NACA Muroc Unit (renamed Edwards Air Force Base). Women worked in all of them.

During these early years, research in aerodynamics, airfoil shapes, aircraft designs, missile technology, and supersonic flight occurred at these different facilities. While this was mostly a "boys club," a few women worked at these facilities in traditional female roles as office workers, including secretaries, stenographers, and payroll clerks (Powers, 1997). Eventually, some women were hired to do the computing or calculations by hand and with slide rulers. As was standard practice by the federal government at that time, these *women computers* were unmarried or married without children and possessed degrees in mathematics. Powers (1997) recounted that in the federal government's scientific community, almost without exception, the early computers were women. Women were perceived to possess a natural ability to pay attention to details. The intensive gathering of data and analyzing this data was laborious. This data analysis process was lengthy before the age of the digital computers and calculators.

The first NACA professional woman was Pearl Young. As a 1919 graduate in physics, chemistry, and mathematics from the University of North Dakota, Young began her work at NACA Langley Memorial Aeronautical Laboratory in 1922. Her job duties at NACA included writing research reports to communicate and disseminate the extraordinary efforts and accomplishments of Langley. Young led the effort to ensure the technical reports would accurately and efficiently communicate the trailblazing efforts of the researchers (NASA, 2013). During World War II, Young moved to the NACA's Aircraft Engine Research Center in Cleveland, Ohio. Later, she taught physics at Pennsylvania State University and eventually worked at NASA, from which she retired in 1961.

Another pioneer at NACA was Katherine Coleman Goble Johnson, who was contracted at Langley Research Center as a research mathematician. Johnson's sister told her of an opportunity for African American women to apply for a pool position at an aeronautical facility in Virginia to perform math calculations. She applied for the position. After a year of persistence, Johnson was offered a job in the pool of "computers who wore skirts" (Johnson, n.d.). Katherine did not let the barriers of race or gender stop her. Her determination and assertiveness finally allowed her to go where no woman had gone before—the editorial meetings—where she was able to answer some questions the men could not. Johnson's work became more complex as the Space Race was advancing. For example, NASA officials asked her to verify the calculations the digital computers generated for John Glenn's historical orbital flight. Later, she calculated the Apollo 11 trajectory to the moon. Moreover, later in her career she worked on the Space Shuttle program as well as missions to Mars. In 1986, Katherine retired from NASA after 33 years of service. She spends her retired days tutoring young people often sharing words of wisdom such as

> Luck is a combination of preparation and opportunity. If you're prepared and the opportunity comes up, it's your good fortune to have been in the right place at the right time and to have been prepared for the job. (Johnson, n.d.)

As the aeronautical industry was taking off, the Cold War was beginning. NACA increased its time spent on missile technology. This increase resulted in the need for more data computation. Thus, more women were hired for data computation. The growth of women in aerospace had begun. According to the Workforce Information Cubes for NASA (NASA, n.d.) website, at the beginning of the 2014 fiscal year, NASA employed 6,294 females out of 18,068 employees overall. Of the 6,294 females, 1,613 were under the age of 40 and 1,368 were under the age of 30 (NASA, 2014).

METHODS

The primary purpose of this chapter is to illuminate the contributions of women of color who worked at NASA and to identify any barriers they may have encountered in the workplace. The authors also set out to discover significant factors that influenced these women to pursue STEM careers. A holistic case study approach was employed to conduct this research. Case study research starts from the compelling feature: the desire to derive an in-depth understanding of a small number of "cases" that are set in their real world contexts. These case studies are aimed to produce an insightful appreciation and new understandings about real world behavior and meaning in the lives of these women (Bromley, 1986).

The principal investigator for this study was a former female NASA employee. Four women of color (three African American and one Latina) volunteered to participate in this study. An open-ended, semi-formal interview protocol was used to guide these female participants to share their stories about their experience as women of color working at NASA. The names are not pseudonyms; these women approved the use of their real names. The participants were emailed the interview protocol in advance of a telephone interview. All participants have advanced degrees in a scientific field, and all but one (Candy) were working at NASA at the time of the interviews. Following NASA protocol, prior review and approval of the contents in this chapter were granted before publication.

After the interviews had been completed, transcripts were analyzed using a constant comparative method (Lincoln & Guba, 1985) to generate emerging common themes and new understandings. The unique cases of each of these four women are described in four sections in this chapter: Paths to NASA, Significant Contributions, Overcoming Barriers, Advice for Pursuing STEM Fields, and Attitudes and Early Science Experiences.

PATHS TO NASA

Dynae (38-year-old African American)

At the time of the interview, Dynae worked as the lead education professional development activities manager in the Office of Education at NASA Johnson Space Center (JSC) in Houston, Texas. When asked about her educational background leading to employment at NASA, she shared that she had wanted to be a pediatrician and pursued premed in college. However, in her senior year, she realized that courses such as genetics and anatomy did not hold her interest and she began to look at other career options. Both of her parents were educators. Dynae stated,

> Both of my parents were ahead of their time. It was the first introduction to professional learning communities (PLC's) I had. My father was a physical education teacher and my mother taught physical education and science.

After Dynae had graduated from the University of Houston with a degree in biology, she completed an alternative certification program to become certified to teach science to high school students. She taught at an inner-city school in the Houston area and pursued a master's of education degree. She stayed in teaching because she "liked watching them (the students) grow and function at a higher level." After many years in the classroom, she realized she was stymied. While her students were growing, she was not. Dynae's career interests in STEM soon led her to NASA's Aerospace Education Services Project. She worked at the NASA Headquarters, NASA Goddard Space Flight Center, and NASA Langley, and then joined the Johnson Space Center to work as an education specialist with NASA's Teaching from Space Office. Dynae continued her education achieving an online teaching certificate in 2014. In 2015, she completed her doctorate in education with a concentration in aviation and space educational studies from Oklahoma State University.

Patrice (56-year-old African American)

Patrice grew up in Houston's third ward, which was located in a poor part of the city. However, Patrice's parents taught her to pursue her dreams. Patrice stated, "There were no scientists in my family." But her mother encouraged her curiosity. Also, Patrice's sister played a critical role in her success. Patrice reported, "Seeing a sibling work very hard and reaching her goals was a driving force in my success. I had a role model in clear view at the right time." Patrice noted that throughout elementary and junior high school she was good at math, but was more interested in using math as a tool.

Because Patrice was identified as an academically talented student in high school, she was selected to work in a laboratory at the University of Houston during the summer of her junior and senior years. Patrice worked on a project studying the salt concentration of halophytes. It was this experience that solidified her career choice. The following year, she enrolled at the University of Houston and declared a major in biochemistry and received her doctorate in this field. After completing postdoctoral research, Patrice worked for a small, private biotech company, Genlabs Technologies, in the biotech corridor of Northern California for more than a decade.

Patrice returned to Houston to another small biotech company and was later employed at the University of Texas Medical Branch. Patrice eventually landed at NASA as a contract employee working at Universities Space Research Association (USRA). At the time of the interview, Patrice was the deputy project scientist for the Flight Analogs Project at NASA Johnson Space Center. She had been married 33 years, had two scientifically minded children, held eight United States patents as a co-inventor, and published more than 40 papers on her research of hepatitis E virus infections as well as coauthoring an abstract describing the research at NASA on ocular outcomes in head-down-tilt bed rest studies.

Trena (46-year-old African American)

Trena grew up in a Pennsylvania middle-class home asking "Why?" a lot. Throughout elementary school, she knew she loved science and math, and this passion continued throughout her high school years. Trena's school was mostly White. In her words, "There were only five students in my elementary school who were minorities." She shared that she was always interested in space since her father was an avid watcher of *Star Trek* and became even more so after the Challenger accident. During the interview, Trena recounted with a chuckle, "I used to watch *Star Trek* with my dad: It was our bonding moment. He knows all the dialog of *Star Trek* since he's seen them so many times." Early on, she decided she wanted to become a medical doctor, and when she was in high school, she volunteered in a nursing home. During her junior year, Trena had the opportunity to study abroad in Tonneins, France, where she was the only minority at her school. Her host father was a medical doctor. Trena shadowed him in the field, which solidified her desire to become a physician. However, when she graduated from Albright Reading College with a bachelor of science in premedical science, her path led to teaching. As a STEM teacher, she became aware of students who did not understand nor recognize the real-world applications of science and math in their lives. "I realized there was such a need for STEM education and that students don't realize how it affects their lives daily. I wanted to show them real-world connections of the importance of STEM."

Trena was awarded the Maya Angelou Teacher of the Year Award her first year of teaching. She earned a master's of science degree in developmental biology from American University and later earned her doctorate in environmental science from Oklahoma State University. Her first job at NASA was as a contract employee with the Urban and Rural Community Enrichment Program (URCEP). In this position, she was able to spend a month in a school district where she and her team members would conduct professional development for teachers. At the time of the interview, she was a civil servant at NASA Goddard Space Flight Center in the Office of Communications, where she familiarized the public and education communities with NASA and inspired the next generation of explorers.

Candy (61-year-old Latina of Puerto Rican heritage)

As hundreds of children, Candy was inspired by science fiction television shows. She was captivated by the fantasy worlds that came alive on the screen. Candy described these fictional environments as a stark contrast to the Bronx in New York City where she grew up in a Harlem culture. Candy stated,

My interest in science and technology began around the age of 5. I saw science fiction television shows and movies as exciting and adventurous visions of the future. I was fascinated by flying cars, space ships, aliens, and beautiful cities. People seemed to have access to food and clean housing. It was in contrast to the neighborhoods with which I was familiar. My family and relatives grew up in poverty.

Throughout her youth, Candy exhibited a strong curiosity about the world around her. Her parents encouraged her, but they did not understand much about science and were at a loss as to how to help her explore this field. Her father gave her an informal education on history and would take her to museums. Her mother suggested Candy take steno and typing so she could work as a secretary, a fallback plan if she could not get a job in science. Candy described her mother's talk. "She said I should lower my expectations because when she had followed her dream of being a reporter, she went to college for a year but then she got married and had her first child." Her mother had followed the trend of many other women at the time. For example, after World War II, most women were moved out of their wartime jobs back to traditional family roles when the men came home. Candy reflected,

> She [her mother] didn't know how to pursue a job as a reporter, and her dream probably was not as strong as mine. As a mother, she just wanted to protect me but sometimes she realized that would hold back so I could follow my own path.

Candy indeed followed her own path. In her teen years, she joined the Civil Air Patrol (CAP). Her father drove her to the meetings each week. The CAP experience enabled Candy to learn about aerospace education. Candy learned how to fly a plane at the age of 15 before she could even drive a car. Candy attended a women's college close to home. Douglass College provided her with the support she needed while taking science classes from Rutgers University. (Douglass had an agreement with Rutgers University to provide STEM classes for their students). Candy shared that often she was the only woman in the engineering classes. Candy stated, "I felt isolated in a class full of men. They definitely were not happy about having women in the class. They basically ignored me." After taking most of the science and engineering courses offered (e.g., astrophysics, astronomy, theoretical geology, etc.), Candy graduated in 1976 with an interdisciplinary major in space science. A day after graduating, she was offered a job in the astrophysics department at Princeton University. A few weeks after astronaut Sally Ride's historic launch, Candy was offered a job at the NASA Johnson Space Center. She worked as a software engineer on the Space

Shuttle program and then as a systems engineer on the International Space Station. Candy exclaimed,

> I felt as if my jaw dropped and my eyes grew big with the feeling that I had earned a place among the elite. I knew I had worked hard to get there. I was the little Puerto Rican girl who had achieved the impossible, the unattainable dream.

SIGNIFICANT CONTRIBUTIONS AT NASA

Dynae and Reduced Gravity

While working in NASA's Teaching from Space Office (TFS), Dynae was instrumental in the enhancement of the Microgravity eXperience [sic] (μGX) with the Reduced Gravity Education Flight Program at JSC. Eligible participants, students, and educators began developing a proposal for a reduced gravity experiment. The selected educators on the team then engaged in online professional development, which provided resources for classroom activities on microgravity to be used with the students on the team. The teams were provided a NASA mentor to collaborate with as they designed and fabricated their experiments to be tested. The teams tested their experiments on the Reduced Gravity aircraft that flies approximately 30 parabolic maneuvers over the Gulf of Mexico. This flight provided roller-coaster-like climbs and dips to produce periods of micro and hypergravity that ranged from 0 g's to 2 g's.

Dynae was able to use training in instructional design and apply it to the μGX. She also employed her doctoral coursework with online learning. By increasing the rigor and online components of the μGX, Dynae and her colleagues were able to address and satisfy the evaluation of the program. The project was awarded NASA's Desire to Excel Award in 2012 based on collaboration among the participant teams via an online platform because of the efforts by Dynae and her team. According to Dynae, team members had a richer dialogue among each other before meeting face-to-face the day before their flight on the Reduced Gravity aircraft.

Patrice and Microgravity

Ocular changes have been reported in astronauts who had been involved in long-duration space flight in low Earth-orbit. Patrice, along with a team, used flight analogs to research the intracranial pressures in human subjects to determine if ocular changes occurred. Also, Patrice researched the effects of fluid shifts in a simulated lunar environment via a bed rest study. Understanding the effects of microgravity on the human body is vital to astronauts who require long duration missions. Patrice reported that humans will live and work on other celestial bodies. She added that the research conducted at NASA not only mitigates the dangers of space flight to the astronauts, but is important in the development of new materials, medical protocols, and product development to make people's lives safer and healthier on Earth.

Trena and Public Outreach

Trena's contributions to NASA have been within STEM education. She has directly and indirectly inspired thousands of school-aged children in the wonderments of Earth and space science. Her work in the NASA UR-CEP enabled Trena to live and work in school districts across the United States (including Puerto Rico and the Virgin Islands) for a month-long period to provide professional development on NASA education resources to teachers of underrepresented students. Trena described what she learned from the experiences, saying,

> The time I spent in each community gave me a different perspective and it allowed me to personalize the NASA resources for the districts, teachers, and students. Also, it allowed me to develop a personal relationship with them and provided them with sustainability, since I was now their NASA point of contact—a person they could contact [for help].

Additionally, Trena worked on a NASA satellite project—the Sumoi-NPP (National Polar-orbiting Partnership)—where she was the education lead. The Sumoi-NPP was the first generation of satellites that orbited the Earth collecting weather data to improve weather forecasts and prediction models and increase an understanding of long-term climate change. NASA required an education and public outreach (EPO) for all funded missions by partnering scientists with educators to provide authentic science-based content to engage learners of all ages that broadened public participation in NASA missions.

Candy Improving Space Communications

NASA Johnson Space Center has been the heart of human space exploration since the Gemini program. It is known for Mission Control, astronauts, moon rocks, and space suits. Candy's office was located in the same building as the flight controllers and astronauts. Candy's work involved computerizing space operations. This task consisted of prelaunch to post-launch operations, testing of the computer, and software systems. According to Candy, "No day is ordinary!" Space operations ensure the astronauts are safe when in orbit. Additionally, Candy was a part of the Shuttle Amateur Radio EXperiment [sic] (SAREX). In this role, she helped write an antenna tracking computer code. This computer code enabled, for the first time, a 2-way television communication to occur between NASA-JSC and the space shuttle. Candy stated, "It was a major historic change in space communications we now take for granted. I used the camera to record images and radio equipment to call up to the shuttle."

OVERCOMING BARRIERS

Dynae Overcoming Barriers in the Lab

Growing up, Dynae was not discouraged to pursue a STEM career by family members, however, she was not encouraged to do so. Dynae stated,

> I knew a Black woman could be a teacher or open a hair salon. People usually aspire to be what you have examples of but, because I didn't see a Black person in the STEM fields, I wanted to achieve the impossible. I didn't want to be a disappointment to my family.

When Dynae was in undergraduate school at her first university, she stated, "I had a terrible experience. The organic chemistry laboratory only had enough laboratory equipment to build one apparatus for the entire class." She also voiced her frustration with her fellow classmates and stated, "I didn't want to have to teach the class because I was the only person who read the lab beforehand." Dynae later transferred to another university where she developed a great appreciation for science. She was placed in a professional laboratory environment and was held accountable for her learning.

Dynae highlighted one incident in her professional career where she believed her gender was more of a hindrance than her skin color. It was during an engineering challenge where she was the only female in the group. She stated, "I felt that I had to exert myself harder into the brainstorming session."

Patrice Meeting Gender Challenges in Research

Early on in her career, Patrice worked in groups that were predominantly male. Even her graduate and post-doc advisers were male. She stated, "I can probably pick out on one hand the number of occasions in my entire career where I was aware of someone hinting that my gender or my ethnicity was a factor of my success." She continued by saying, "It has never been an issue for me. Most people are so focused on the work that they don't care where the ideas come from if they are good ideas." Patrice stressed there were not that many women in research until recently, and when there were women they were in different research groups. She stated, "We tried to cross-utilize resources, and we didn't compete with each other." At the time of the interview, she was working with two other female scientists who all worked collaboratively playing to each other's strengths, which allowed everyone to complete each project successfully.

While not claiming it as a barrier, Patrice noted during the interview that she did not see people of color in the sciences during her youth. However, she posited, "I can't really think of any over-blatant circumstances where someone discouraged me. I have surrounded myself with people who have encouraged and supported me."

Trena Overcoming Gender Barriers in Environmental Sciences

The barriers Trena experienced seemed to stem from the degree she had chosen to earn as a minority female, which was a doctorate in environmental science. With a doctorate in environmental science, Trena worked in an environment where the male employees seemed to be more respected. Trena claimed,

> There are people who don't think environmental science is a true science. They think of it as more of a social science, and I feel that is an unfair assessment. [She continued,] I have been asked to do something, for example, give a talk to a school, and someone from upper leadership said, "We need to get someone who's a role model—a true scientist." So that's kind of a slap in the face. [Trena added,] I feel that I am not necessarily always respected as a female. Where, if there is a male, that they are more respected and in many situations, people go to that male first, and to me that's really discouraging. [She affirmed,] I see that [discrimination] a lot in the work environment. Across the country [they] are male dominated, Baby Boomers/Traditionalist, and we have got to change that. We have to get more Gen-Xers, Millennials, and females into science.

Candy Overcoming Age and Gender Barriers

Candy did not think race was so much a barrier, rather gender, and later in her career, age. She was told at an early age that Latina women did not have careers in science. The Hispanic culture encourages family, community, and mutual support. Candy believed that STEM did not nurture and support a collaborative environment but rather one of competition. She clarified her challenge,

> People got jobs to make a living. I wanted a job which was fun, exciting, and made a difference. My mother told me to take steno and typing so I could work as a secretary if I couldn't get a job in science.

When reflecting on her early years in the Civil Air Patrol (CAP) where she learned to fly a Piper Cub before she learned how to drive, she was confronted with sexism early on. In an interview with CNN (2011), Candy described a gender barrier she faced when completing one of the CAP challenges, "We were supposed to go find a businessman who was lost in the woods, but the girls were not allowed" (Saba, 2011). When sharing this story, Candy noted this was during an era before the women's rights movement was moved to the political forefront.

Other incidents only strengthened Candy's determination to succeed and overcome exclusion. Near retirement she affirmed, "Since I have experienced a lifetime of barriers due to my gender (though also support from men) and now age, I can imagine that an 'obvious' woman of color has a bigger burden." Candy noted that she always perceived herself as a woman of color; that stereotypes and negative ideas about people who look different still persist. She added "It is very wearying to handle issues that are unnecessarily personal. After a while, a woman just wonders whether it is worth having one's energy and enthusiasm smashed. It is lonely and isolating." Candy decided not to marry nor have children, but she did choose to take care of her elderly parents while still working. She felt some of her co-workers were not sympathetic to this additional home commitment. Candy noted that in addition to family conflict perceptions, "Intelligence and experience are not always appreciated by insecure coworkers no matter what gender. Generational differences can cause problems unless there is training to learn how to blend skills." As the number of Americans 60 years old and older grows, the workforce has not embraced this aging population. Candy summed up her feelings noting,

> Women, in particular, are more likely to be given fewer opportunities as they age. I have met many women who lost their confidence and self-esteem from a variety of the above issues. If there are any family or personal crises, women can be vulnerable to circumstances that they would otherwise be able to handle without crises. It is wrong to think that "a thick skin" or "toughening up" are solutions. Life happens in so many unexpected ways that can throw any strong person off kilter.

ADVICE FOR PURSUING STEM FIELDS

Dynae

As a STEM educator, Dynae believed, "Those of us in power of influence have the power to change students and to better the profession." She continued, "Every stakeholder has some benefit to each other." Dynae continued to teach because she, like most teachers, enjoyed watching her students grow and think at a higher level in the sciences. She boasted, "I liked watching their progress, especially the students who were at-risk, emotionally disturbed, or identified as needing modifications." These student populations can be challenging for some teachers, but Dynae persevered. When asked about her perseverance in pursuing her career, she explained, "When you start a large challenge, don't look at it as a large challenge but as smaller challenges. You attack each part with all the energy you have. And, ask guidance from the Almighty."

Patrice

Pursuing a career in STEM came in two parts for Patrice. The first part being what she called a "circumstance of exclusion," meaning the lack of role models of her same gender and ethnicity. Patrice clarified,

> There weren't too many people, in my immediate circle, that had a job that I wanted when I grew up. I know that sounds a little bit sad but it does help understand. I grew up in the late '50s and the early '60s where the education system was not open as much as it is today with respect to people of color, so, I really didn't see anybody with a job and so I was thinking at a very young age "Well, what do I want when I grow up?"

Patrice described a second characteristic for pursuing success in STEM: perseverance. She felt this was, and still is, a vital trait to have for success, not just for her but for the human race. She explained,

> My mom and dad were just incredible people and I grew up in an environment with my sister, where we were taught to pursue your dream . . . be willing to work for it and then pursue it. So, I had that inspiration and almost as long as I can remember, that if I just figure out what I wanted to do, I was going to have the support in order to do it—the support and the encouragement.

Patrice reflected on her days in school where she excelled in 8th-grade math and science, and "went into high school and got more science classes. I really honed in quickly on the things I enjoyed." When asked to give advice to future women in STEM, Patrice advised, "Pursue your passion because if you're passionate about it, then you are going to be persistent. STEM does require persistence." Patrice shared her belief that we should all help our youth to truly understand that, even though science and math can be fun, students should not be discouraged by the amount of preparation and work that must be done. She described the need for a balance.

> If you're not passionate about it, you're not going to get out of bed every day and do this. What often happens is some people don't realize that it is all new, but the failure rate for any experiment is 80%. If you can't deal with failure, then you are going to be turned off by this. The answers are there, but we aren't just smart enough to understand it so I am going to keep working at it until I can understand and explain it. It's that persistence.

According to Patrice, going to college was her only option. Patrice and her older sister grew up with that concept. She exclaimed during the interview, "It is not IF you were going to college but it just comes down to what day you're going! You WILL be going. We just knew it. We absolutely knew it." Patrice's sister played a tremendous role in Patrice's pursuit of a career in STEM. She explained that her sister is 9 years older and was also considered a trailblazer in chemical engineering. They shared a bedroom for 14 years. Patrice watched her sister, who was in college when she was in elementary school, study and struggle with her coursework, which impacted Patrice at a pivotal time. Patrice fondly recalled,

> I think the impact of actually seeing an older sibling work very hard, struggle, and come out on top is absolutely priceless. It is THE best life lesson ever. So that was my life when I was young. It was all about progress, success, and I was breathing the same air she was breathing. It was right there in front of me, so I knew I'd be able to do well in whatever I chose. I could see an older sister who was doing just that. She was definitely trailblazing.

Trena

Like most children, Trena was a curious child, specifically with science and the natural world around her, based on her self-reflection. Her educational pursuit in science began with medicine, but changed during medical school when she became a teacher. Most teachers feel a "calling" to the profession, and when Trena began to volunteer at a charter school, she was offered a job right away. Trena recalled,

> I guess I did well, so they asked me to become the science coordinator and internship coordinator. While teaching science, I called NASA to come in and

give a talk and that is when I met Octavia (the URCEP Lead). Two years later she called me and said that she was leaving NASA and told me to apply for URCEP. I did and that is how I ended up with URCEP at NASA.

Later in the interview, Trena confessed that the space program had always intrigued her. The Space Shuttle Challenger accident was one of those moments in time everyone remembers: Trena was no exception. She recalled during her interview, "I was in high school physics class. It got me thinking about why and how it happened. Then, it hit me that we have people in space doing work." With all of the opportunities available in the STEM field, Trena continues to be intrigued. She stated,

> STEM is so amazing. There are so many opportunities you can go into. There are so many fields of science you can go into. There's earth science, space science, engineering. To me, there are unlimited opportunities as well as the different career choices that are available. I like the fact that it changes daily so you are continually curious and you have to keep up-to-date. There are formidable facets. For example, you can combine medicine with engineering. I think it's fascinating how you can intermix these fields.

When asked to give advice to future women who want to pursue STEM fields, Trena was quick to say,

> Go into the STEM careers. Don't let anybody tell you that you can't do a STEM career. I feel this is a problem we have now in education. Students say they want to go into a STEM field, then when they get to college they are told "look to the left of you and look to the right of you and somebody is going to be gone." We can't accept that. We need to realize there is help out there for you. If you don't do well on the first test, give it a chance and try to stick it out.

Trena's dream for the future is more women in STEM than men.

Candy

Candy grew up in the age of an infant space program and knew she wanted to be an astronaut, yet Candy did not know how to maneuver through the educational system to achieve this dream. Her support came from Douglass College's counselors who provided the educational support to be successful, even when Candy contemplated dropping out of college. Candy recalled,

> The images of the future were strong within me. I really believed that progress would only lead to positive outcomes. I saw the pictures of the promising and better future on TV, in the movie theaters, and in books. There were pictures of families living happily on Earth and other planets. I really believed

that, eventually, I would be living and working on the moon permanently. I still believe the positive future is tied to space exploration.

When asked about perseverance when pursuing a career in STEM, Candy states, "Somehow, inside of me, there was something pulling me in the right direction."

ATTITUDES AND EARLY SCIENCE EXPERIENCES

Dynae

Researchers have been intrigued how science attitudes and achievement are correlated (Brown, 2011). Dynae had always been curious, but her attitude toward science evolved in middle school. This was probably due to her science teacher. Dynae remembers the energy her science teacher put into being a professional teacher and says, "My teacher took the time to step away from the textbook and gave us things to do." Dynae also had a science teacher at home, and recognized the energy and effort her mother gave to her students. While taking high school biology, Dynae gained a respect for scientific ways of thinking due to her teacher, Ms. King. The research in science education has shown teachers have the second strongest indicator of student attitudes on science (George, 2006). Dynae became an exceptional teacher in Houston and admits, "Being a scientist was not for me, but being an educator in science was the fit. I get to have bunches of fun!"

Patrice

Patrice grew up in an earlier generation than Dynae; however, they have common traits. Patrice exclaims,

> It was awe! It was just sheer awe! My sister was in college and I was in elementary school. I grew up in the inner city and had good teachers. My math teacher was legendary. She had a reputation that if you could get past her, then you were pretty good at it so there were various people around me who were there to help me develop and to create excellence. But definitely sheer awe. I loved science, still do.

When Patrice was in high school, she longed to visit a working science laboratory, not just her science classroom lab. She recalls,

> When I looked around, at arm's length, there was no one that I could say, "Can I come visit your lab?" There wasn't anybody in my extended family

that I could do that. There were a few physicians in my extended family, but I didn't want to go to the hospital, I wanted to go to a lab! School was the only place I could do that. I spent a lot of time in the school labs, but they were inner city school labs and they were limited in resources. At the time, I had not gone much outside of my physical community. My parents were very protective of our safety.

Patrice continued her recollection by stating,

In high school, I was yearning for the opportunities and it came at the end of the 11th grade. Westinghouse Talent Search offered a summer opportunity to the top academic students and there was an opportunity at the University of Houston (U of H). The summer after the 11th grade is when I finally went to see what a university lab was like. I had never been to a university lab except briefly to see my sister's chemistry lab. I was fascinated by it; I was definitely hooked. I had what I refer to as the research bug. Some people might refer to it as a drive. After that it was all a matter of how do I get back into the lab? What started out as awe, then very rapidly shifted to a desire to be a part of that re-search life. I think this is where being a bit of a free spirit and being young and unseasoned helped. I remember my first semester at the University of Houston and I did really well. I had spent the semester in biology and chemistry labs. I learned that I didn't want to lay my hands on a fetal pig ever again! I wanted a microscope—a high-powered microscope at that. The chemistry was fascinat-ing but I was looking for the application. What am I going to do with the chem-istry? Now what? The biochemistry lab became my new quest.

Patrice argued that your first years in college are part of your "teen years." Thus Patrice included her college experiences in this section. Pa-trice stayed in Houston and lived at home for her undergraduate degree. This was a conscious decision because she realized this approach would al-low her to focus on her studies while at home, and not have the influence of an unfamiliar environment. Patrice volunteered,

Most people were surprised that I didn't go into culture shock when I went to U of H [University of Houston]. Up to my college experience, everything in my life was African American—my family, my community, my church, my school, everywhere I went was 99% African American, and then I go to U of H and it's about 5% and I can't even see the other 4% because, in my col-lege—College of Science and Mathematics—it was less than 0.3% so there's very few like me, but I was okay with that. It's hard to be the only one. Some of our students will give up because they don't want to be the one to blaze the trail. They want to be on it, but they don't want to blaze it. I just had all this love and confidence from my family and all of this prior success that it didn't dawn on me that I wouldn't fit in.

High self-confidence in science is the leading factor to a higher attitude toward science (George, 2006). Patrice told a story of how, when she was a freshman, she was proactive in her learning.

> Literally, I walked into the dean's office, halfway through the second semester of my freshman year, and asked what did I have to do to get into a laboratory for the upcoming summer? To make a very long story short, I was prepared to take any opportunity that I had. What he said to me was that he appreciated me coming in. He recognized my enthusiasm and he was excited and he said, "Let me talk to the faculty and see what we can do for you." I had five faculty, half of the faculty in the biochem department, were interested in me. I went "Wow! I'm going to get a choice. I'm liking this." Honestly, there was no return for me. Who says you can't have choices? It wasn't until I finished my doctorate that the same dean told me, "You know when you first came into my office, I looked at you and thought I had never had a freshman come to me and ask that question. Everyone assumed that you would need more academic lab experience. It was just your enthusiasm." Having the choices, I figured out this is where I belong. I have the choices based upon my own merit. I can make my market. I have always felt very positive about science. In all my teen years, it was very positive for me. There are hurdles and politics but the reason I like science so much, because you are evaluated on your own merits. You get into that lab and you work really hard, and that's what you get evaluated on. Not if you have a Y chromosome or how much melanin you have in your skin. This field is awesome!

Trena

Children are born naturally curious about the world around them. Trena was no exception. She recalls, "I was always intrigued, curious. I was the one who enjoyed doing the labs—the biology and chemistry labs I had. I was always trying to figure out things. Asking questions like "Why?"

She knew she wanted to be a doctor, was even accepted into medical school, and was intrigued by the human body. To get some medical experience, she volunteered in a nursing home during her teen years. Even though Trena did not complete medical school, she still retains an active interest in medicine. She has maintained her medical assistant license. Trena describes the impact of her study abroad opportunity on her decision to pursue medicine. She explains,

> I was able to see how their [France] whole medical system worked. I was able to go see patients with my host father and I thought "Wow, this is really cool. I think I want to go into medicine." My teacher in France also took the time to explain the chemistry terms to me in English. All of my classes were taught

in French. Some of the terms in chemistry are the same as in English, but not all of them.

Trena's English teacher was influential in helping her to decide where to go to college.

Candy

Motivation and interest is necessary for learning to take place. Candy had the interest and motivation to learn as much about science as possible; specifically, space science and exploration. She asserted,

> I loved science and technology! For fun, I read books about lasers and antimatter after hearing about them on *Star Trek*. That TV show, in particular, embodied my dream of a future with women, people of color, former Cold War enemies, and aliens who lived and worked together for a common goal of peace.

Candy was in junior high school when she met a young lady who informed her of the Civil Air Patrol and learned CAP offered aerospace education. Candy recalls,

> I studied everything that CAP offered: military protocol, search and rescue, survival techniques, and especially aerospace education. It was the latter opportunity that made me decide to switch from Girl Scouts to CAP. Flying was an extra benefit. I became an activist promoting air and space. I learned to educate the public during CAP and Air Force events.

Civil Air Patrol is still offering aerospace education to today's youth and inspires them to pursue a career in aerospace.

CONCLUSIONS AND IMPLICATIONS

These four exceptional women grew up in four distinct decades (the 1960s, 1970s, 1980s, and 1990s) when the roles of women began to shift. In the 1960s, deep cultural changes were altering the role of women in American society. More females than ever were entering the paid workforce, and this increased the dissatisfaction among women regarding huge gender disparities in pay and advancement, and sexual harassment at the workplace. (Walsh, 2010). Over time, the feminist trends of the 1960s took hold, and over the subsequent decades changed relationships between the genders. According to Isserman and Kazin (2004), "Most young women, at least in the middle class, expected to have access to the same careers and to receive the same compensation as men." Through the intriguing stories of the four female NASA scientists, we have learned that each story is unique and is impacted by the eras in which they grew up. Candy grew up Latina in the turbulent 60s, when the academic expectations were influenced by cultural expectations for Latina women. She persevered and found ways to overcome these expectations and accomplished much in her career at NASA. At 61 years old, Candy faced an unexpected barrier: ageism rather than gender or race was a barrier to her future at NASA and she retired.

All three of the African American participants, Patrice, Trena, and Dynae whose formative years occurred during the '70s, '80s and '90s respectively, identified few barriers to their work in the STEM fields. None mentioned race specifically as a barrier to their success. A few gave examples of some gender bias, which seemed to shift as more and more women were encouraged to pursue STEM careers. They were encouraged and had supportive role models, parents, siblings, and counselors who helped pave the way for many contributions to the space program and STEM education. Perseverance, an innate curiosity and interest in science and mathematics, and significant role models seemed to be the most important factors in promoting women of color in STEM. At the time of this publication, photographs and stories of some of the women who work in STEM fields at NASA were available on the NASA website. A majority of these participants are women of color under the age of 40. Barriers have been lifted and more opportunities exist for women of color in STEM careers because of women like Candy, Patrice, Trena, and Dynae.

To mark Eileen Collins' historic flight as the first female commander of a space shuttle mission, Judy Collins (1999) wrote a song to commemorate this flight. The fifth verse foreshadows a girl who eventually achieves her goals: "For she led the way beyond darkness/for other dreamers who would dare the sky/she has led us to believe in dreaming/given us the hope that we can try."

REFERENCES

Bromley, P. H. (1986). *The case-study method in psychology and related disciplines.* New York, NY: Wiley.

Brown, L. O. (2011, May). *South Dakota secondary school students' science attitudes and the implementation of NASA's digital learning network's "Can a shoebox fly? challenge,"* (Unpublished doctoral dissertation). Oklahoma State University, Tulsa, OK. Retrieved from https://shareok.org/bitstream/handle/11244/7326/School%20of%20Teaching%20and%20Curriculum%20Leadership_038.pdf?sequence=1

Collins, J. (1999). *Beyond the sky.* Retrieved from http://chandra.harvard.edu/chronicle/

George, R. (2006). A cross-domain analysis of change in students' attitudes toward science and attitudes about the utility of science. *International Journal of Science Education, 28*, 571–589. doi: 10.1080/09500690500338755

Isserman, M., & Kazin, M. (2004). *America divided: The civil war of the 1960s.* New York, NY: Oxford University Press.

Johnson, K. (n.d.). Katherine Johnson, national visionary. *National Visionary Leadership Project.* Retrieved from http://www.visionaryproject.org/johnsonkatherine/

Lincoln, Y. S., & Guba, EG. (1985). *Naturalistic inquiry.* Newbury Park, CA: Sage.

NASA. (n.d.). *Workforce information cubes for NASA.* Retrieved from https://wicn.nssc.nasa.gov/

NASA. (2013, March 15). *Women@NASA: Women's History Month Shout Out: Pearl I. Young.* [Blog post]. Retrieved from https://blogs.nasa.gov/womenatnasa/2013/03/15/post_1363363908971/

NASA. (2014, October 15). *Workforce information cubes for NASA.* Retrieved from https://wicn.nssc.nasa.gov/

Powers, S. G., & United States. (1997). *Women in flight research at NASA Dryden Flight Research Center from 1946 to 1995.* Washington, DC: NASA History Office, NASA Headquarters.

Saba, M. (2011, July 7). Despite the naysayers, woman goes from Trekkie to NASA engineer. *CNN.com.* Retrieved from http://edition.cnn.com/2011/IREPORT/07/06/torres.shuttle.irpt/index.html

Walsh, K. (2010, March 12). *The 1960's: A decade of change for women.* Retrieved from http://www.usnews.com/news/articles/2010/03/12/the-1960s-a-decade-of-change-for-women

CHAPTER 4

MATHEMATICS LITERACY, IDENTITY RESILIENCE, AND OPPORTUNITY SIXTY YEARS SINCE *BROWN V. BOARD*

Counternarratives of a Five-Generation Family

Jacqueline Leonard, Erica N. Walker, Victoria R. Cloud and Nicole M. Joseph

ABSTRACT

In this chapter, the authors use Black feminist thought (BFT) to examine the mathematics education and the educational attainment of African American females in a matrilineal line that spans five generations. A cross analysis of school experiences, from a maternal great-great-grandmother to her great-great-granddaughter, reveal a portrait of segregation, desegregation, and re-segregation. The impact of these educational contexts on the mathematics literacy and mathematics identity of four African American women, and the hope and promise of a young girl in the class of 2026 are also presented. From

Women of Color in STEM, pages 79–107
Copyright © 2017 by Information Age Publishing
All rights of reproduction in any form reserved.

sharecropper schools in Mississippi to prestigious universities in the eastern United States, the challenges and successes of one family's struggle to obtain mathematics literacy and the American dream are discussed through the historical lens of *Brown v. Board* (Warren, 1954). Using this historical context, the specific experiences of these five females encourage a dialogue about a larger narrative: the mathematics attainment of all Black children.

The purpose of this qualitative study, which uses case study design, is to present and examine the mathematical experiences and educational attainment of five African American females. They represent five generations in one African American family whose roots began in rural Mississippi in the 1860s— nearly one hundred years before *Brown v. Board*. While the experiences of the females in this family are not meant to be generalized to all Black families, their struggle to obtain mathematics literacy can be used as a theme to understand the Black struggle for quality education pre- and post-*Brown v. Board*.

This study begins with a great-great-grandmother (now deceased) born in Washington County, Mississippi, in the 1910s during the Black Nadir and ends with her 6-year-old great-great-granddaughter, who began first grade in Delaware County, Pennsylvania, in the fall of 2014—60 years post-*Brown*. Descriptive content analysis of their mathematical experiences provides a sociohistorical (i.e., changes in society over time) account of five African American females' mathematics literacy and mathematics identity. Additionally, we describe the impact their mathematics education had on their career trajectories and everyday lives. These narratives are told through the historical lens of *Brown v. Board* (Warren, 1954).

REVIEW OF THE LITERATURE

The bodies of literature that support this study are mathematics literacy, mathematics identity, and the intersection of race and gender in mathematics education. Terry (2011) described literacy broadly as not only the ability to read and write, but also its importance for understanding literacy as the means to liberation and freedom. This view is grounded in Frankenstein's (1990) notion of *critical mathematics literacy* and Gutstein's (2006) notion of *reading and writing the world* with mathematics.

Mathematics Literacy

Mathematics literacy is using mathematics as a cognitive enterprise to communicate mathematically with others (National Council of Teachers of Mathematics, 2000), engage in society as an informed citizen (Moses & Cobb, 2001), and position oneself as a doer of mathematics for empowerment (Leonard, 2009). Thus, mathematics literacy is racialized and situated "within the larger contexts of African American, political, socioeconomic, and educational struggle" (Martin, 2006, p. 197) and the struggle for civil rights (Moses & Cobb, 2001).

Mathematics Identity

We examine mathematics identity among these five multigenerational females. Martin (2006) defined mathematics identity as "the dispositions and deeply held beliefs that individuals develop, within their overall self-concept, about their ability to participate and perform effectively in mathematical contexts and to use mathematics to change the conditions of their lives" (p. 206). Martin (2000) suggested that students with a well-developed mathematics identity are successful doers of mathematics. Students with well-developed mathematical identities have the following characteristics: (a) believe in their ability to perform in mathematical contexts, (b) understand the instrumental importance of mathematics, (c) realize there are constraints and opportunities in mathematical contexts, and (d) exhibit motivation and engagement in strategies to obtain mathematics knowledge (Clark, Johnson, & Chazan, 2009). The authors believe that individual and collective experiences should be studied and examined within the contexts of mathematics literacy, mathematics identity, and cultural practices as Black women. This study adds to the literature on Black feminism (Collins, 2009), Black resilience in mathematics (McGee, 2013), and Black self-determination (Dixson, 2011) offering a multigenerational analysis seldom seen in mathematics education research (Gholson, 2013).

The Intersection of Race and Gender

In this study, we not only examine the individual beliefs and mathematical understandings of five related but distinct females in a matrilineal line, but also how their identities are interwoven and intersect with race and gender. Specifically, we show how their mathematics identities are shaped and influenced by their mathematics attainment and positioning in the family across different generations. Using the lens of *Brown v. Board*, we present the counternarratives of five African American females, their struggle for mathematics literacy, and how it shaped or limited their access to higher education, STEM, and STEM-related careers. This study stands in contrast to the literature base on African American mathematics education in general, which is often related to gap-gazing (Gutierrez, 2008; Lubienski, 2008) and cultural deficit theory (Martin, 2006; McGee & Pearman, 2014; Terry

& Howard, 2013), rather than mathematics literacy, identity, resilience, and agency (Martin, 2000, 2006; Walker, 2012, 2014). Yet, narratives about mathematics achievement and attainment among African American females are sparse in the literature (Lim, 2008; Lubienski & Bowen, 2000). In the small number of studies that compare mathematics achievement among males and females, Lim (2008) claimed:

> The majority of previous studies of gender issues in mathematics education have focused on the differences between boys' and girls' motivational constructs, performance levels, or learning styles while ignoring the dynamic sociocultural context of their mathematics learning in and out of schools. (p. 308)

Thus, focusing on the intersection of race, gender, and mathematics attainment, this study adds to the research on both gender studies and mathematics education.

THEORETICAL FRAMEWORK

The theoretical framework that undergirds this study is Black feminist thought (BFT), which Collins (2009) describes as an epistemology used to validate Black women's knowledge and experiences. The core themes of BFT are "work, family, sexual politics, motherhood, and political activism" within the U.S. context of racial and gender oppression (Collins, 2009, p. 269). The principles of this epistemology rely on two types of knowing that derive from Black women's experience: knowledge and wisdom (Collins, 2009). In this way, Black women from all walks of life participate in a type of knowledge that is based on collective experiences that emerge from similar forms of oppression. Domestics had to learn how to function in two worlds: one where they were responsible for rearing White children, while simultaneously being viewed as inferior; and the other where they raised their children to resist such definitions and to strive for something better. In the narratives to be described, a great-great-grandmother's school and work experiences in rural Mississippi and later in an urban city in Missouri shaped and informed the educational trajectory of her granddaughter in St. Louis during the 1960s and 1970s. Thus, mother wit is valued alongside institutional knowledge, providing voice and legitimacy to four generations of women.

Black feminist thought uses dialogue to assess knowledge claims, promoting an ethic of care that is characterized by "personal expressiveness, emotions, and empathy...central to the knowledge validation process" and the ethic of personal accountability (Collins, 2009, p. 281–282). Black women validate each other's experiences through dialogue and storytelling that has its roots in "African-based oral traditions and in African American culture" (Collins, 2009, p. 279). BFT is used as a framework to discuss how mathematics literacy can be used to empower Black women to challenge oppression and the status quo.

We acknowledge that Black feminist thought as a framework has limitations. As a social theory, it lies at the intersection of "race, class, gender, sexuality, ethnicity, nation, and religion" and can only partially tell the entire story (Collins, 2009, p. 12). The hope of *Brown v. Board* (Warren, 1954) 60 years ago was that the United States would turn the corner on race and racism to provide all students with equal access and educational opportunity. The *Brown* decision took a first step toward eradicating the separate but equal doctrine that perpetuated Jim Crow for a half century and reversed Black advancements in politics and education acquired during Reconstruction (Patterson, Niles, Carlson, & Kelley, 2008; Rucker & Jubilee, 2007). However, the voices of Black women and their educational experiences, particularly in mathematics, are often missing from the extant literature (Walker, 2014). Thus, BFT is a powerful analytical and theoretical tool to examine the ways in which seemingly neutral educational policies and practices reproduced gendered and racialized mathematics education in African American communities. These policies are evident in the counternarratives of a five-generation family. From a sharecropper school system in Mississippi with burgeoning class sizes and high dropout rates to a suburban school district, the females in this family experienced segregation, desegregation, or resegregation. Such educational contexts had and continue to have an impact on their mathematics education and educational attainment in general.

RESEARCH QUESTIONS

The research questions that guide this study on five African American females in a matrilineal line are as follows:

1. How do the counternarratives of a five-generation matrilineal line of African American females compare and contrast in terms of their mathematics literacy, mathematics identity, and resilience?
2. What role did mathematics literacy and social agency play in terms of educational opportunities and career paths?
3. How do their mathematics education and educational attainment illustrate a broader social and political context of race, class, and gender?

To answer these research questions, we engaged in descriptive content analysis of the counternarratives, document analysis of historical records and artifacts, and comparative analysis to find themes and patterns from multiple data sources.

METHODOLOGY

We used the counternarrative or counterstorytelling approach to examine the mathematics literacy, identity, and resilience of a five-generation matrilineal line. Solorzano and Yasso (2002) present three general forms of counterstorytelling: (a) personal stories or narratives told in first-person, (b) other people's stories or narratives told in third-person, and (c) composite stories or narratives constructed through various forms of data, historical records, or archives. In this paper, we employ all three of the aforementioned methods of counterstorytelling to examine historical data, school records, and test data that span 70 years of schooling from the rural South to the urban East Coast. These sources also include data obtained from interviews and questionnaires as well as oral history (i.e., recollections and oral traditions told by elders to members of successive generations). Two authors of this paper are members of the five-generational family reported in this study. To ensure validity and reliability, an unrelated third party analyzed the qualitative data to find emergent themes.

Data Analysis and Data Sources

While counternarratives are used to uncover the use of simple language and thick descriptions, we also examined anecdotal records and artifacts to understand the varied mathematical experiences of each family member by using descriptive content analysis (Neuendorf, 2002). The data sources consisted of artifacts and documents that spanned more than 70 years. Those data included census records, report cards, SAT and GRE scores, interviews, and questionnaires collected at different time periods. Additionally, oral stories were used to describe the mathematical experiences and educational attainment of four adult women and one child who represent five generations in one family. These stories revealed details about these Black females' mathematical literacy, identity, resilience, and educational opportunity that can be used to tell a larger narrative about the education of African American children.

Participants and Settings

The participants in the study are members of the Cross family (all names are pseudonyms (see Figure 4.1 for family tree). Results of recent DNA testing revealed the ancestry of this family is 76%–80% Yoruba (West African tribe near Nigeria) and 20%–24% European. Tracing the maternal side of the family tree through census records, seven generations of the Cross family have resided in Oktibbeha County, Mississippi, since 1860.

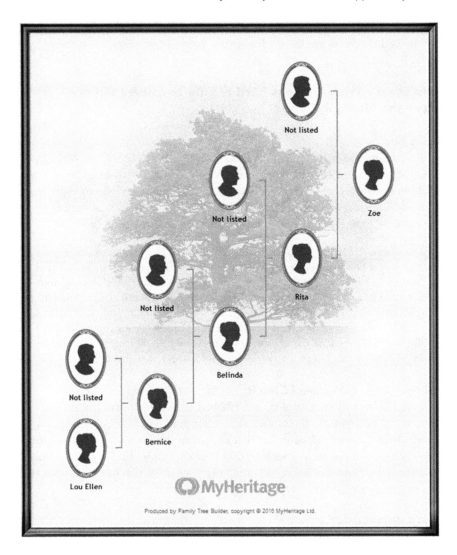

Figure 4.1   Cross maternal family tree.

THE COUNTERNARRATIVES

We present the individual counternarratives of five females in a matrilineal line to illuminate their early life, school experiences, mathematics literacy, mathematics identity, and resilience within historical and educational contexts. Each counternarrative is unique, exploring the individual and social agency that influenced each girl's life. The counternarratives begin with Lou Ellen, the great-great-grandmother. Living into her 90s, she had a strong influence on the family for nearly seventy-five years.

Lou Ellen's Story: "It was hard for me because I did not have the learning."

Early Life

Lou Ellen was born in Washington County, the heart of the Mississippi Delta, during the 1910s. The family moved during her early childhood years, and she was reared in Oktibbeha County. Lou Ellen's responses to a questionnaire administered by her great-granddaughter, Rita, in 1997 as part of a college course, reveal many nuances about her school and adult life.

> I was born in Leland, Mississippi. I grew up in Starkville, Mississippi, on my grandmother's farm. I loved that farm very much. I have a cousin still on that farm now, but it much different. [My grandparents] had nine children—four boys and five girls. My grandparents owned their own land... raise the children and take care of the land. [My father] worked on a dairy farm; he helped to milk the cows. He got paid for working. We raised all our food. [Mother] did not work; she took care of the house and children. My mother died when I was 10 years old. I lived with my oldest sister after she married.

Historical and Educational Contexts

Lou Ellen went to school in the 1920s. During this period, the agrarian South was dotted with farms and sharecroppers. However, teaching was a stable, high-status profession for Blacks during this period. Ladson-Billings (2005) noted there were about 66,000 Black teachers in the United States in 1910. Unable to teach in the North, many of these teachers taught in the South (Tillman, 2004).

School Experiences

Lou Ellen often told stories of how she and her sisters had to walk 10 miles to school. The stories revealed the nature of the one-room schoolhouse where reading, spelling, and figuring were the lessons of the day. Given the demands of farm life in rural Mississippi, it was common for Black students to work on the farm instead of attending high school, which was not compulsory. Although Blacks represented 29% of all high school students, only 5% of Black children were enrolled in high school in the South during the 1910s (Anderson, 1988; Rucker & Jubilee, 2007).

> I was not able to go to high school. My father could not send us to high school. It was three of us. He could not pay for us to go.... We did not have a lot of money but that was no problem. We had food and shelter, and we was [sic] happy then.

Lou Ellen's statement implied the family could not afford for her to attend high school. If she was old enough to work in the fields or perform day work, the family needed her to bring in additional income. Although she did not complete high school, she had aspirations to further her education. "I wanted to go to college and learn a traid [sic] to work with older peoples [sic] and to help peoples [sic] that can't help themselves."

Mathematics Literacy and Mathematics Identity

Although there were no copies of school records, Lou Ellen often told her family that she completed school as far as the eighth grade. While her literacy in mathematics was unknown, she read the Bible on a daily basis and was able to fix anything that was broken. She often said she was good at *figuring*, which was evident by her ability to manage and save money.

Life Choices and Career Trajectory

As a young adult in the 1940s, Lou Ellen made a life-changing decision. She left her family in Mississippi and relocated to St. Louis, Missouri, during the Great Migration. There were relatives in St. Louis that helped her to get settled. She joined the African Methodist Episcopal Church, where she was a member for 65 years before her death in 2010.

> I been without a job, without food, and [did not] know where I would get my next meal or get money for rent, but the Lord made a way for me to get a job. It was hard to get a job without training or education. It was hard for me because I did not have the learning. So I wint [sic] back to school. My first job was day work.

Lou Ellen lived and worked in St. Louis as a baker, cook, and dietician until she was 70 years old. Because of her self-determination to leave Mississippi and start a new life, Lou Ellen influenced her daughter, Bernice, to leave Mississippi as well. Thus, her decision to relocate led to opportunities that changed the career trajectories of both women. She shared her pride as a Black elder and offered advice to her progeny.

> It is nice to be Black at any age. It does not [matter] what color you are. Age does not change anything. I am proud to be Black. I am proud [to] be what God intended for me to be. Glad I am Black.

> Stay in school and get [some] learning. Do not smoke or drink. Don't let men take advanted [sic] of you. Don't let your relationships into fear [sic] with your education or with religion.

Bernice's Story: "I wanted to finish high school, but I needed a job."

Early Life

Bernice was born in Oktibbeha County, Mississippi, in the late 1930s. She was the only child living in the household. She appeared to live an uncomplicated life with her mother and stepfather prior to matriculating in school. When she was 7 years old, her life became complicated after her mother, Lou Ellen, left for St. Louis. Because Lou Ellen was uncertain that she could find a job right away, she left Bernice with an aunt in Mississippi who could provide a home and a nurturing environment.

Historical and Educational Contexts

There were two educational philosophies that were prevalent during the 1940s: classical (liberal arts) and industrial (technical) education influenced by DuBois and Carver, respectively (Russell, 2014). During this period, many Black students learned applied mathematics, which allowed them to learn a vocational trade. However, other Black students, influenced by DuBois's philosophy, studied algebra and plane geometry in high school (Russell, 2014). Interestingly, the high school mathematics curriculum in Oktibbeha County, Mississippi, was predominantly influenced by DuBois since 10th- through 12th-grade students took algebra, geometry, and trigonometry in high school.

School Experiences

School records revealed that her mother, Lou Ellen, registered Bernice for school at the age of 5. Education in the South often took place in segregated schoolhouses like the one shown in Figure 4.2. The photograph

Figure 4.2 Schoolhouse in Oktibbeha County, Mississippi.

shows Bernice smiling as she stood among 50 members of the 3rd-grade class at the Oktibbeha County Training School (OCTS).

Mathematics Literacy and Mathematics Identity

Examination of report cards revealed that Bernice earned B grades in 1st-grade arithmetic and As and Bs in second grade. Her grades dropped to Cs in grades third through fifth. By sixth grade, her arithmetic grade slipped to a D. However, attendance records also showed 17 absences during her 6th-grade year. These absences no doubt had an impact on her performance. When asked about these absences, Bernice replied:

> When I was old enough, I had to stay home to watch Auntie's younger children while she went to work. I also stayed with another Aunt sometimes who lived farther away from the school. If the weather was bad, I couldn't go. My other aunt lived more than 10 miles from the school. I had to leave at 6 a.m. to walk to school to get there before 8:30 a.m.

Because of D grades in arithmetic and history, Bernice had to attend summer school to be promoted to the seventh grade. However, her grades in mathematics showed little improvement. When asked about her grades, Bernice stated, "Math gets harder as you go along, and you need someone to help you. Auntie had an 8th-grade education and a family of her own, and I didn't have anyone to help me with my homework."

In high school, Bernice was enrolled in a course that used a book called *Math at Work*. George Washington Carver and the current thinking of the day may have influenced such a text. While her behavior was good, and her grades in English and reading were passing, she reluctantly claimed, "I was not good in math." She earned a D grade in general math in ninth grade. In 10th grade, she was enrolled in algebra but later withdrew from the course (see Table 4.1). When queried about this, Bernice said:

> In grade 10 you had algebra, geometry in grade 11, and trigonometry in grade 12. There was [sic] four years of math in high school. It was difficult for me because I did not understand the concepts. There were 40 or 50 students in my elementary classes. In high school, students came from the surrounding areas and there could be 90 in one class. Mom and Auntie dropped out of school to work on the farm. I was the first one to go to high school, but I dropped out in the 10th grade.

Life Choices and Career Trajectory

As an adult, Bernice did not lose sight of her desire to finish her high school education. She enrolled at a community college in St. Louis during the 1970s and completed studies to earn a GED and later an associate's

TABLE 4.1	Generational Mathematics Achievement: High School Courses and SAT Scores						
Family Member	High School Type	8th grade course	9th grade course	10th grade course	11th grade course	12th grade course	SAT math score[a]
Bernice	Oktibbeha County Training School, Starkville, MS Enrollment: NA Minority: 100%	General Math D	Mathematics for Work D	Algebra W	Withdrawn	Withdrawn	NA
Belinda	Public High St. Louis, Missouri Enrollment: 2,500 Graduation Rate: 50% Minority: 99%	General Math A	Algebra I A	NA	Geometry W	Algebra II/ Trig A	510 81st percentile[b]
Rita	Public High School Howard County, Maryland Enrollment: 1,155[c] Graduation Rate: 90% Minority: 66%	Pre-Algebra B	Algebra I A	Geometry/ Trig A	Algebra II Honors A	Calculus, AP A, Score 3	560 72nd percentile[d]

[a] SAT scores scaled 200–800
[b] Percentile Rank is for all students only
[c] Enrollment, graduation, and minority data from 2012
[d] SAT recentered in 1995

degree. This self-determination opened the door of opportunity. Bernice was able to get a better job where she became a union worker at a local bakery chain. Her wages doubled, enabling her to become a homeowner and to move from working-class to lower-middle-class status. This decision impacted her life and the lives of her mother and children, who were able to enjoy the comforts of homeownership.

Belinda's Story: "I Decided to Go Back to College"

Early Years

Belinda was born in Missouri in the late 1950s. She was Bernice's older daughter and one of three siblings born in St. Louis. She responded to the same questionnaire, which was administered by her daughter Rita in 1997. Belinda's responses revealed details about her life and upbringing during the 1960s and 1970s.

> I remember looking out the window of my neighborhood when I was 4 years old and liking what I saw. Streets were lined with brick apartments and bunga-low houses dotted with trees, flowers, and green grass. My neighborhood con-sisted of corner stores and confectionaries owned by Blacks and Jews. There was a grocery store, library, and several clothing and shoe stores a few blocks away.

Historical and Educational Contexts

Two major events defined the 1950s: the U.S. Supreme Court deci-sion on May 17, 1954, known as *Brown v. Topeka Board of Education* and the launch of Sputnik by the Russians on October 4, 1957. As a result of Sput-nik, children in the 1950s and 1960s were introduced to "new math" (Berry, Pinter, & McClain, 2013). A chapter on sets was common in every textbook as new math became synonymous with set theory (Berry et al., 2013; Raimi, 1995). Despite the millions of dollars spent to design the curriculum, the new math program was a failure (Raimi, 1995). Mathematics achievement scores dropped during this period revealing students, in general, were worse off than they were before new math was introduced.

School Experiences

De facto segregation existed in the St. Louis Public Schools when Be-linda began matriculating in 1963, despite the passage of *Brown v. Board* almost 10 years earlier. Belinda attended a K-8 neighborhood school for 9 years. The majority of her teachers were Black, and some lived in the community. Discipline was strict, and parents unequivocally supported the teachers. "My neighborhood [school] was all Black.... [My mother] was a hard worker. Her unhappiness inspired me to do better. I valued education as the key to success and worked hard in school. I valued family."

Mathematics Literacy and Mathematics Identity

Belinda disliked mathematics in elementary school because teachers tended to focus on rote memorization and computation if they taught mathematics at all. While she did not remember what mathematics curriculum was used, she recalled studying set theory (i.e., new math) in seventh and eighth grade using old books that were passed down from White schools. Belinda's 8th-grade teacher was an African American woman who liked teaching math. She spent a great deal of time teaching the class how to solve word problems, fractions, decimals, and percent. Working with rational numbers (i.e., fractions) was Belinda's earliest recollection of enjoying mathematics, and she realized that she was good at it.

The 8th-grade teacher recommended that Belinda take algebra in ninth grade at the local high school. To her surprise, she enjoyed solving quadratic equations and using the foil method to distribute binomials. Her grade in algebra I was an A, reflecting the time and effort she put into the course. Unlike the schools in Mississippi in the 1950s, 4 years of mathematics were not mandatory in the St. Louis Public Schools in the 1970s. Therefore, Belinda appealed to the high school counselor to skip geometry and take algebra II/ trig instead. Permission was granted, and she earned an A in algebra II/trig as well. In her senior year, Belinda's score on the SAT was higher than most students who attended her predominantly Black high school (see Table 4.1). Encouraged by her counselor, teachers, and college-bound peers, Belinda decided to attend college in New England.

> My biggest challenge was staying focused on completing my education. I dropped out of college to get married. Family and belonging were important to me. Because I could type, I took jobs as an office clerk. It was hard to emerge from the domesticated role of being a clerical worker and mother. I decided to go back to college.

Life Choices and Career Trajectory

Belinda's decision to return to college was one of self-determination. She enrolled in the teacher education program at a private urban university in the Midwest during the early 1980s. She graduated with a B+ average and a teaching credential in general science, and she began teaching science at a middle school in a nearby suburb. After relocating to Texas with her family, Belinda obtained a master's degree in mathematical sciences and taught middle grades mathematics for 8 years. Ten years later, she obtained a PhD in mathematics education in the late 1990s from a research university in the eastern United States; Belinda eventually became a tenured professor.

Her life choices and career trajectory firmly planted the Cross women in the middle class.

> The Civil Rights Movement gave me a militant attitude, but I believe I am tolerant of others. The women's movement gave me strength to break out of stereotypical jobs for women and to pursue mathematics education and ordained ministry.

Rita's Story: "I was accepted to an Ivy League university."

Early Years

Rita, Belinda's older daughter, was born in the late 1970s on a military base in the South. Three years later, the family relocated back to Missouri after her father was honorably discharged. Rita started kindergarten at the age of 4 because she had a fall birthday. She was most often the youngest student in her class. Rita initially attended elementary school at a private Christian school in Missouri and later two public elementary schools in Texas when the family relocated. The racial makeup of the private school in Missouri was predominantly White, whereas the public schools in Texas consisted mainly of African American and Latino/a students. During her adolescent years in Texas, Rita attended a small, private, predominantly White Episcopalian school for seventh and eighth grade.

Historical and Educational Contexts

On the educational front, the National Commission on Excellence in Education presented a report titled *A Nation at Risk* (Gardner, 1983). During this time, U.S. students were compared with their international counterparts and found to be lagging, particularly in mathematics and science. In response to public criticism of the report, many states began requiring algebra I as a graduation requirement. From 1982 to 1992, student enrollment in algebra I and advanced mathematics courses increased dramatically: algebra I from 65% to 89%, algebra II from 35% to 62%, and calculus from 5% to 11% (Raizen, McLead, & Rowe, 1997).

Mathematics Literacy and Mathematics Identity

In elementary school, Rita was part of the talented and gifted program where she enjoyed solving logic problems. She learned early on that she was good in mathematics and enjoyed word problems. Throughout high school, Rita was placed in honors or advanced placement mathematics courses. Responding to a protocol in 2013 provided by her mother Belinda, she shared her mathematics experiences.

> In my math classes in high school, I was usually the only Black person in class. There was a 99 club where the students' average grades were 99 or higher for

each report card, and there were at least 20 to 30 students in that club, if not more. I was a member of the 99 club as well.

In the middle of 11th grade, Rita moved to the East Coast to finish high school, as her mother was pursuing a PhD. The high school demographics were primarily mixed. African American and White students attended high school together as a result of a planned community that prided itself on developing neighborhoods to house both middle-class and affluent families. Rita remembered her algebra II and calculus teacher was a mentor and role model. "He was very encouraging and advised me while applying to college. He was very excited when he found out I was accepted to an Ivy League university, and encouraged me to attend that school over others."

After graduating from the Ivy League university, Rita was admitted to a master's degree program in allied health. Note the growth in quantitative reasoning on her GRE scores as shown in Table 4.2 compared to her SAT scores in Table 4.1. After obtaining the advanced degree, Rita began a career in allied health that has spanned 14 years. She credits her positive experience in mathematics as a factor in acquiring higher education, obtaining a stable job in healthcare, and maintaining the middle-class lifestyle she enjoyed as a child.

Zoe's Story: "Every number plus zero is the same number."

Early Years

Zoe was born in a research hospital in Pennsylvania prior to 2010. She is Rita's only daughter. Zoe has one brother who is 18 months older than she. Prior to enrolling in a neighborhood public school, Zoe and her brother attended daycare less than a mile from their home. At the daycare, Zoe learned to recognize the alphabet, counting numbers, calendar, shapes, and colors. She also enjoyed playing with dolls and playing house.

Historical and Educational Contexts

Notwithstanding, one of the most important legal cases in recent history was *Parents Involved in Community Schools v. Seattle Public School District* (2007; Dixson, 2011). The crux of this case was deciding whether a school district could remedy racial segregation voluntarily. Race was considered, among several factors, to determine admission to highly demanding Seattle high schools. Parents filed a lawsuit, contending that admission based on race was unconstitutional (Dixson, 2011). The Supreme Court ruled in favor of the parents, stating that the way race was used to admit students was unconstitutional and violated the 14th Amendment. Some legal scholars saw this case as overturning *Brown v. Board* (Warren, 1954) offering no remedy for school resegregation (Dixson, 2011) and leaving Black parents with few

TABLE 4.2 Generational Mathematics Achievement: College Mathematics Courses and GRE Scores				
Family Member	College Information	College Statistics	College Mathematics Courses	GRE Scores[c]
Bernice	St. Louis Community College St. Louis, Missouri Public Two-Year College	Gender: 66.8% F; 33.2% M Black: 45.7% Asian: 0.04% Hispanic: 0.02% White: 37.0% Other: 0.05% Total Enrollment: 7,232[a]	General Math—C	NA
Belinda	Boston University, Boston, Massachusetts Private St. Louis University, St. Louis, Missouri Private Jesuit	Gender: 57.6% F; 42.2%M Black: 8.3% Asian: 8.2% Hispanic: 0.04% White: 72.3% Two or more races: 0.04% FT Undergraduate: 7,716[b]	College/Algebra Trig—B Calculus—A Calculus II/Analytic Geometry—B+ Trigonometry—A	570 53rd percentile
Rita	University of Pennsylvania Philadelphia, Pennsylvania Private Ivy League	Gender: 51.3% F; 48.7% M Black: 7.1% Native American: 0.3% Asian: 18.6% Hispanic: 8.1% White: 46.2% Two or more races: 2.2% International: 10.9% FT Undergraduate: 10,324[b]	Calculus I—C– Calculus II—B Intro to Stats I—B+ Intro to Stats II—C+	660 81st percentile

[a] STLCC data from 2007
[b] SLU & Penn data from 2011
[c] GRE scores scaled 200–800

choices other than charter and neighborhood schools (Leonard, McKee, & Williams, 2013; Morris, 2004).

School Experiences

Zoe currently attends a public school in Pennsylvania where she began kindergarten in the fall of 2013 with a great deal of exposure to technology. Her kindergarten teacher reported that Zoe knew how to count up to 40 and was an active listener in class. According to Child Trends, a research center based in Maryland, 4 million children (52% White; 23% Hispanic/ Latino; 16% Black/African American; 5% Asian/Pacific Islander; 2% multiple races; and 1% American Indian/Alaska Native) started kindergarten in the U.S. as the class of 2026 in fall 2013 (Samuels, 2013). This class has been described by Samuels as happy, resilient, and eager to learn.

Mathematics Literacy and Mathematics Identity

During kindergarten, Zoe enjoyed counting various objects, such as light displays during the Christmas season as her mother drove the car. She often shouted out math problems such as "2 + 2 is 4 and 3 + 3 is 6." When her mother asked her how she knew, Zoe said, "I already know that." She

Figure 4.3 Zoe and friend using iPad mini.

frequently played games on her mother's iPhone and iPad (see Figure 4.3). Zoe also had a LeapPad that she used to play math games. Her grandmother, who is a mathematics educator, heard her count backwards from 12 during the Christmas holidays: "12, 11, 10, 9, 8, 7, 6, 5, 4, 3, 2, 1, 0." Surprised to hear Zoe state the number zero, her grandmother wondered how deep Zoe's mathematical understanding was at the age of 5.

A few days later while riding in the car, Zoe asked, "What's zero plus 3?" Her older brother responded the answer was three. The next week Zoe asked the same question again. Her grandmother explained that any number plus zero was that number and drilled both children by asking: "What's 4 + 0? 10 + 0? 25 + 0? 200 + 0?" They responded in unison: 4, 10, 25, and 200. Several days later, her grandmother asked, "What's 0 + 300?" Zoe responded 300. Then her grandmother asked, "Why?" Zoe responded, "Zero plus 300 is 300 because 300 plus zero is that number." A few minutes later, she told her brother, "Every number plus zero is the same number." Thus, not only was Zoe able to recognize zero as a number, but she was also able to generalize the *zero property of addition*, regardless of the order of the addends. As a kindergartener, Zoe's brilliance in mathematics suggests that Black children are capable of learning much more mathematics, and their mathematics identity can be developed as young children (Leonard et al., 2013).

Zoe also modeled her teacher at home by posting grids on the wall and counting down to a reward: "When we get to the number 17, we will have a dance party!" Her mother encouraged math concepts by dividing hot dogs and pancakes into parts or cutting a pizza into slices. She often asked Zoe, "Would you like your pizza cut into quarters or halves?" After Zoe responded, her mother told her, "You know math!" In kindergarten, Zoe aspired to become either a teacher or a boss.

DATA ANALYSIS

The counternarratives describing the mathematics experiences of five generations of Cross females (Lou Ellen, Bernice, Belinda, Rita, and Zoe) in many ways reflect the 20th-century history of school mathematics in the United States. As described earlier in this paper, many contemporary narratives of the history of mathematics education emphasize key historical landmarks, such as the Sputnik launch in 1957, the "new math" of the 1960s, and *A Nation at Risk* in 1983 as well as their impact on school curriculum, instruction, and assessment. However, these counternarratives also reveal a simultaneously occurring story: that of how one particular set of American citizens—Black Americans—were finally gaining legal access to rights as citizens. The *Brown v. Board of Education* decision in 1954, the Civil Rights Movement of the 1960s, along with increased attention to standards and equity as described in *A Nation at Risk* had profound implications for education generally and mathematics specifically. Thus, to consider the mathematical lives of these five African American females, and African Americans in general, without attending to the broader historical, educational, and social contexts would be ahistorical and incomplete. When comparing and contrasting the counternarratives, two themes emerge: Mother Wit and Like a Boss. We draw upon Black feminist thought as a theoretical framework to analyze these themes within a sociohistorical context (i.e., changes in society over time).

"MOTHER WIT": THE DRIVE FOR EDUCATION WITHIN CONSTRAINED OPPORTUNITY

We see this broader historical context writ large in Lou Ellen and Bernice's stories. The South, as others have described (Anderson, 1988; Morris & Monroe, 2009), holds an important place in education for African Americans. Here is where most African Americans were enslaved and thus barred from educational opportunity. Thus, a sharecropping system was developed that kept Blacks in poverty. Indeed, the education provided for Blacks in Mississippi and other southern states during this period was minimal, inadequate, and relegated African Americans to second-class citizenship designed to maintain the status quo (Rucker & Jubilee, 2007). Despite significant obstacles to Black education in the South, Black parents valued education (Mizell, 2010). Moreover, Blacks supported community schools, which were largely built, maintained, and supported by all-Black communities (Anderson, 1988).

The quest for education was also at times hampered by the financial realities of living in the agrarian South. Children were needed for labor—on the farm or at home—and schooling was often interrupted. In the case of Lou Ellen, families simply could not forego the financial benefit of additional laborers working the farm. Thus, for this generation of young people, going to school would have decreased family income significantly.

Further, Lou Ellen and Bernice's description of family life resonates with the broad and extended family networks of many African Americans in the South. For a variety of reasons, children lived not only with their parents, but also with grandparents, aunts, uncles, or older siblings. At times, schooling was interrupted due to family obligations: Bernice was entreated to stay home and look after younger cousins because her aunt had to go to work. Demands of family and work also prevented Bernice from getting help with her math homework. The limited education of her elders adversely affected Bernice's educational trajectory. As was discovered in a study of African American mathematicians who described cases of older generations of family members being born "too early" to benefit from advances in civil rights (Walker, 2014), Lou Ellen's desire to go to high school and college was thwarted by her circumstances. There is evidence that Lou Ellen exhibited talent ("able to fix anything that was broken") that was unrealized within a traditional educational context, in part because she was Black and arguably because she was a woman.

In Black mathematicians' descriptions of family members who exhibited mathematical talent but were undereducated, the men often worked at skilled and technical but menial labor. Women, however, were in most cases limited to the domestic sphere whether they worked in their homes or were domestics in the homes of others. Lou Ellen's "cautionary tales" to her own descendants—about getting an education and not allowing relationships with men to interfere with education or progress in life—are deeply centered in a Black feminist ideology of self-determination. The emphasis on acquiring education to support oneself, helping extended family members, and not "fall" while prominent among African American women, did not have the same urgency among White women of a similar era (Giddings, 1984; Jones, 1985).

The tension between vocational and classical education in terms of what was "most appropriate" for African Americans was evident in Bernice's experience: Although classes like algebra, geometry, and trigonometry were offered to 10th through 12th graders, a high school course that Bernice took in the ninth grade used a book called *Math at Work*. Bernice felt her lack of progress in mathematics limited her opportunities for employment. Therefore, she exhorted her progeny to do better and learn more than she had. Although she had not benefitted from direct intervention on the part of her mother or aunt, she was determined to help her children go even further in school and to be successful. In the urbanized Midwest, there were varied opportunities for employment—better paying than the farm and domestic jobs of the South—and more opportunities for young people to be exposed to educational and social experiences. Bernice's quest for education continued when she earned her GED and was able to secure better employment benefitting not just herself, but her elders and descendants.

LIKE "A BOSS": HONORING AND REDEFINING "WOMEN'S WORK" IN MATHEMATICS AND BEYOND

The self-determination ethic inspired the mathematical lives of Bernice's descendants, Belinda and Rita. Belinda, who was born just after the *Brown v. Board of Education* decision, experienced mathematics at a time when educational opportunity was increasing for Blacks, and the traditional curriculum in mathematics was changing. Unlike her mother, who took standard courses in arithmetic and algebra, Belinda recalled studying set theory in addition to traditional mathematics topics in her neighborhood school. For many schools in the South, the *Brown* decision did not ensure speedy desegregation. Likewise, Belinda's school had a predominantly Black teaching force, with teachers and their families living and working in the same community. She attended a progressive high school where she was able to take advanced mathematics courses up to precalculus, if she chose to do so. Belinda's daughter Rita, like many Black children of the 1970s and 1980s attending integrated schools, still found herself one of only a few Black students in advanced mathematics classes. The narrative about advanced mathematics classes "being the most segregated places in American society" (Stiff & Harvey, 1988) is a familiar one to high-achieving mathematics students, educators, and researchers (Walker, 2006). Disturbingly, there is significant evidence that even when Black students are qualified for these courses, they are shunted into lower-level courses (Oakes, 1995) or they may self-select lower-level courses themselves to avoid the isolation they experience in advanced courses (Walker, 2006).

Like high-achieving students describing family members whose own experience in school was not indicative of their mathematics potential (Walker, 2006), Belinda saw her mother's life as a cautionary tale: working hard at unsatisfying labor because of limited education and lack of success in school. Knowing the narrative of her mother's interrupted education, she knew that she had to do well in school to avoid having similar experiences. Belinda advocated to take advanced mathematics courses and defined her path through the high school mathematics curriculum. She graduated from high school and attended college, but interrupted her college education to get married. As Belinda described it, the pull of family life was strong. Nevertheless, she continued her education in mathematics and mathematics education, becoming a teacher and later a professor. Her daughter, Rita, attended an Ivy League university, and although she is not in a mathematics career, she described mathematics as being an important means to securing her university education and well-paying career. Rita's daughter, Zoe, is a beneficiary of her grandmother's mathematical expertise and her mother's encouragement of mathematics discussion and learning. In addition, she undoubtedly benefits from the ease of access to technology, which supports mathematics learning through games and apps. What Zoe sees in her mother and grandmother are women who are invested in and committed to her education, and who have time to talk to her about math. Despite Zoe's elders, Bernice and Lou Ellen, not having this luxury of time to devote to their descendants' education, the lessons they imparted—directly and indirectly—about determining one's future are evident. That Zoe wants to "be a boss" is a testament to the sacrifices of her elders and her freedom to declare herself as such without censure.

DISCUSSION

The multiple and interlocking layers of race, gender, and mathematics among these five generations of females are of interest from a historical perspective, to be sure, but also have significant implications for how we consider these constructs in current educational settings. Much of the literature on race and mathematics focuses on racialized hierarchies of performance, with little attention to the role of gender and cultural contexts. Much of the literature on gender and mathematics omits discussion of race, and focuses on (White) women's attitudes toward and performance in mathematics. However, more recent literature (e.g., Walker, 2001; Riegle-Crumb, 2006) and cross-sectional analyses of national datasets show that the picture is considerably more complex. For example, African American girls have very positive attitudes toward mathematics, higher than those of their White and Latina counterparts, and are as likely as White boys to persist in advanced mathematics classes in high school. The societal meme that women are not good in mathematics or are not confident in mathematics largely does not apply to Black women.

Yet, given the counternarratives of these five females, mathematics has multiple meanings. Despite their interest in school, educational opportunities for Lou Ellen and Bernice were limited, and their mathematical trajectories were cut short. We hear about math enjoyment from Belinda and Zoe, while Rita sees it as more of a driver to facilitate access to college and career. For Belinda, who saw the struggles of her mother and undoubtedly heard the stories from her grandmother, school was a way to ensure social mobility and success, as it was for many African Americans in the United States. However, without the TRIO programs instituted by the Johnson administration, educational attainment and economic success may have been limited during the 1970s.

Further, in a time of significant economic stress, it is important to consider that some of the same choices that Lou Ellen and Bernice had to make are those that resonate with young women of color today. Given that girls are still more likely than their brothers to be called upon to provide domestic care for elderly relatives and younger siblings, the impact of these experiences on their schooling might be considerable. How do we ensure that close familial ties and a desire to support their families do not conflict with girls' mathematics success?

Finally, and rather disturbingly, there is substantial evidence that opportunities to learn mathematics are more limited in rural educational settings. Various reform movements in mathematics and school organization may not necessarily be aligned: as one example, course offerings in small high schools (a popular school organization reform) in mathematics are often limited. Despite their best efforts to stay in school and commit to their education, a ceiling effect in terms of coursework can affect Black girls' college and career chances.

While the last century has brought great progress, in many ways these cautionary tales abound. The mathematical experiences of five generations of Black women and girls show the strides Blacks have made in education and professional settings. However, there is still much to be done to ensure that children of color have opportunities to determine their paths.

CONCLUSIONS

This study examined the mathematical experiences and educational attainment of five African American females in a matrilineal line that spanned five generations. Their mathematics literacy and mathematics identity developed differently due to various educational opportunities based on sociohistorical contexts. The elder women, who grew up prior to *Brown v. Board*, had family responsibilities that hindered their educational attainment. Nevertheless, the elders seized opportunities to advance their education by enrolling in training programs or returning to college. They also encouraged the women in younger generations to stay in school and avoid the distractions that might derail their education. While effort, resilience, and perseverance were important factors in actualizing successful careers, school segregation and integration had an impact on Belinda and Rita's academic preparation, respectively. Segregation is hegemonic and disadvantages students of color. Yet, caring teachers pushed African American students and influenced students like Belinda to succeed. In contrast, attending integrated schools provided Rita with broader opportunities to learn than her mother, grandmother, and great-grandmother. Nevertheless, being the only African American in advanced mathematics courses was intimidating and isolating for Rita. Yet, these experiences prepared her to succeed at an Ivy League institution, while her mother dropped out but later returned to college.

The counternarrative of this family is not complete because the educational journey continues for young Zoe. At the present time, Zoe attends a predominantly African American school in a suburban school district near a large urban city. Her future is dependent upon the strength of family support and learning opportunities provided by the school district, or her mother's ability to relocate to a better district in the future. While the success of previous generations of women is no guarantee, the family legacy of educational attainment is a strong predictor of Zoe's future success. What remains to be seen is whether the nation turns the corner in the 21st century to deeply invest in the mathematics education of African American females.

RECOMMENDATIONS

This study reveals the challenges that African American females face in mathematics classrooms in public school systems in the United States. The literature reveals they are underserved when it comes to opportunities to learn advanced mathematics (Leonard, 2009; Walker, 2012, 2014). Low enrollment in advanced courses, lack of rigorous coursework, poor perceptions of ability, and feelings of isolation hinder the success of African American women in mathematics. Given that most careers require more mathematical knowledge than in the past, three recommendations emerge from this study. The recommendations are to: (a) continue to advance efforts to remedy segregation in public schools (Dixson, 2011), (b) broaden opportunities for African American girls to take advanced mathematics and science courses, and (c) support longitudinal studies on the STEM education of African American girls.

While we acknowledge educational progress for African American children since the passage of *Brown v. Board*, evidence suggests that public schools remain highly segregated along racial and economic lines (Berry et al., 2013; Dixson, 2011; Leonard et al., 2013). As evident in this study, middle-class African American families often live in large urban cities or first-tier suburbs where schools serve predominantly Black and brown children. African Americans continue to be underserved by receiving a different kind of mathematics education than their White counterparts (Berry et al., 2013; Martin, 2006). Until academic success cannot be correlated with one's zip code, the intent of *Brown v. Board* remains unrealized.

Broadening opportunities for African American children in general and African American girls in particular requires broader access and creative innovation. To promote student success in science, technology, engineering, and mathematics (STEM), some schools and districts are implementing cutting-edge programs like robotics and game design as early as third grade in afterschool clubs (Leonard et al., 2016; Repenning, Webb, & Ioannidou, 2010). However, encouraging girls to participate in these activities during afterschool clubs has been challenging (Leonard et al., 2016). What has been successful in some school districts is offering robotics and game design classes during the regular school day. In these settings, female and minority students have reported high self-efficacy on video gaming and use of computers when a combination of robotics and game design is offered (Leonard et al., 2016).

Connecting robotics and game design to problem solving and mathematics may help to increase the need for learning advanced mathematics, particular among young African American females who are growing up in a gaming culture. For students like Zoe, who are intrigued with iPads and tablets, opportunities to learn mathematics and computational thinking through robotics and game design hold promise. Computational thinking is a problem-solving process that promotes algorithmic thinking (Wing, 2006). In fall 2015, Zoe's grandmother, Belinda, facilitated a study on computational thinking in Zoe's school district. This study will unpack teacher learning and facilitation of robotics and game design as well as student learning in STEM and development of 21st-century skills. The impact on African American students and girls in these schools has yet to be realized.

Finally, we recommend conducting longitudinal studies to examine the relationship between African American girls' exposure to innovative STEM curriculums and role models, and their persistence in advanced mathematics courses and academic success. Such studies are needed to understand issues related to recruiting and retaining African American women as STEM majors and professionals. From Euphemia Lofton Haynes (first African American woman to receive a PhD in mathematics in 1943) to Tasha Inniss, Sherry Scott, and Kimberly Weems (first three African American women to earn PhDs in mathematics from the same institution in 2000), the counter-narratives of African American women continue to challenge the notion that mathematics is a White male endeavor. It is our hope that young girls like Zoe will benefit from their history and pursue careers in mathematics.

REFERENCES

Anderson, J. (1988). *The education of Blacks in the South, 1860-1935*. Chapel Hill, NC: University of North Carolina Press.

Berry, R. Q., III, Pinter, H. H., & McClain, O. L. (2013). A critical review of American K-12 mathematics education, 1900-present: Implications for the experiences and achievement of Black children. In J. Leonard & D. B. Martin (Eds.), *The brilliance of Black children in mathematics: Beyond the numbers and toward new discourse* (pp. 23–53). Charlotte, NC: Information Age.

Clark, L., Johnson, W. & Chazan, D. (2009) Researching African American mathematics teachers of African American students: Conceptual and methodological considerations. In D. B. Martin, (Ed.). *Mathematics teaching, learning, and liberation in the lives of Black children* (pp. 39–62). New York, NY: Routledge.

Collins, P. H. (2009). *Black feminist thought* (2nd ed.). New York, NY: Routledge.

Dixson, A. D. (2011). Democracy now? Race, education, and Black self-determination. *Teachers College Press, 113*(4), 811–830.

Frankenstein, M. (1990). Incorporating race, gender, and class issues into a critical mathematical literacy curriculum. *Journal of Negro Education, 59*, 336–347.

Gardner, D. P. (1983). *A nation at risk*. Washington, DC: The National Commission on Excellence in Education, U.S. Department of Education.

Gholson, M. L. (2013). The mathematical lives of Black children: A sociocultural-historical rendering of Black brilliance. In J. Leonard & D. B. Martin (Eds.), *The brilliance of Black children in mathematics: Beyond the numbers and toward new discourse* (pp. 55–76). Charlotte, NC: Information Age.

Giddings, P. (1984). *When and where I enter: The impact of Black women on race and sex in America.* New York, NY: Quill.

Gutiérrez, R. (2008). A gap-gazing fetish in mathematics education? Problematizing research on the achievement gap. *Journal for Research in Mathematics Education, 39,* 357–364.

Gutstein, E. (2006). *Reading and writing the world with mathematics: Toward a pedagogy of teaching for social justice.* New York, NY: Routledge.

Jones, J. (1985). *Labor of love, labor of sorrow: Black women, work, and the family from slavery to the present.* New York, NY: Basic Books.

Ladson-Billings, G. (2005). *Beyond the big house: African American educators on teacher education. Multicultural education series.* New York, NY: Teachers College Press.

Leonard, J. (2009). "Still not saved": The power of mathematics to liberate the oppressed. In D. B. Martin (Ed.), *Mathematics teaching, learning, and liberation in the lives of Black children* (pp. 304–330). New York, NY: Routledge.

Leonard, J., Gamboa, R., Buss, A., Mitchell, M., Fashola, O. S., Hubert, T., & Almughyirah, S. (2016, June). Using robotics and game design to enhance children's spatial reasoning and computational thinking skills. *Journal of Science Education and Technology,* 1–17

Leonard, J., McKee, M., & Williams, Y. M. (2013). Not "waiting for superman": Policy implications for Black children attending public schools. In J. Leonard & D. B. Martin (Eds.), *Beyond the numbers and toward new discourse: The brilliance of Black children in mathematics* (pp. 95–120). Charlotte, NC: Information Age.

Lim, J. H. (2008). The road not taken: Two African American girls' experiences with school mathematics. *Race Ethnicity and Education, 11*(3), 303–317. doi: 10.1080/13613320802291181

Lubienski, S. T. (2008). On gap gazing in mathematics education: The need for gaps analyses. *Journal for Research in Mathematics Education, 39,* 350–356.

Lubienski, S. T., & Bowen, A. 2000. Who's counting? A survey of mathematics education research 1982–1998. *Journal for Research in Mathematics Education 31,* 626–633.

Martin, D. B. (2000). *Mathematics success and failure among African American youth: The roles of sociohistorical context, community forces, school influence, and individual agency.* Mahwah, NJ: Erlbaum.

Martin, D. B. (2006) Mathematics learning and participation as racialized forms of experience: African American parents speak on the struggle for mathematics literacy. *Mathematical Thinking and Learning, 8*(3), 197–229. doi :10.1207/s15327833mtl0803_2

McGee, E. O. (2013). Growing up Black and brilliant: Narratives of two mathematically high-achieving college students. In J. Leonard & D. B. Martin (Eds.), *The brilliance of Black children in mathematics: Beyond the numbers and toward new discourse* (pp. 247–272). Charlotte, NC: Information Age.

McGee, E. O., & Pearman, F. A. (2014). Factors in mathematically talented Black male students: Snapshots from kindergarten through eighth grade. *Urban Education, 49*(4) 363–393.

Mizell, L. (2010). "The holy cause of education": Lessons learned from the history of a freedom-loving people. In T. Perry, R. P. Moses, J. T. Wynne, E. Cortes,

& L. Delpit (Eds.). *Creating a grassroots movement to transform public schools* (p. xvi). Boston, MA: Beacon Press.

Morris, J. E. (2004). Can anything good come from Nazareth? *American Educational Research Journal, 41*(1), 69–112.

Morris, J. E., & Monroe, C. R. (2009). Why study the U.S. South? The nexus of race and place in investigating Black student achievement. *Educational Researcher, 38*, 21–35.

Moses, R. P., & Cobb, C. E. (2001). *Radical equations: Math literacy and civil rights.* Boston, MA: Beacon.

National Council of Teachers of Mathematics. (2000). *Principles and standards for school mathematics.* Reston, VA: Author.

Neuendorf, K. A. (2002). *The content analysis guidebook.* Thousand Oaks, CA: Sage.

Oakes, J. (1995). Two cities' tracking and within-school segregation. *Teachers College Record, 96*(4), 681–690.

Patterson, J. A., Niles, R., Carlson, C. & Kelley, W. L. (2008). The consequences of school desegregation in a Kansas town 50 years after *Brown. The Urban Review, 40*, 76–95.

Raimi, R. A. (1995). *Whatever happened to the new math?* Retrieved on September 19, 2013 from http://web.math.rochester.edu/people/faculty/rarm/smsg.html

Raizen, S. A., McLeod, D. B., & Rowe, M. B. (1997). The changing conceptions of reform. In S. A Raizen & E. D. Britton (Eds.). *Bold ventures: Patterns among U.S. interventions in science and mathematics* (Vol. 1; pp. 97–130). Boston, MA: Kluwer Academic.

Repenning, A., Webb, D., & Ioannidou, A. (2010). *Scalable game design and the development of a checklist for getting computational thinking into public schools.* Proceedings of the 41st ACM technical symposium on computer science education (pp. 265–269). Milwaukee, WI: Special Interest Group on Computer Science Education.

Riegle-Crumb, C. (2006). The path through math: Course sequences and academic performance at the intersection of race-ethnicity and gender. *American Journal of Education, 113*, 101–122.

Rucker, W. C., & Jubilee, S. K. (2007). From Black Nadir to *Brown v. Board*: Education and empowerment in Black Georgian communities—1865 to 1954. *The Negro Educational Review, 58*(3/4), 151–168.

Russell, N. (2014, April). *The mathematics education of African Americans, 1866–1954.* Paper presented at the 2014 Annual Meeting of the American Educational Research Association. Philadelphia, PA.

Samuels, C. (2013). A look at this year's kindergarten class. *Education Week.* Retrieved on August 27, 2013, from http://blogs.edweek.org/edweek/early_years/2013/08/child_trends_a_bethesda_md-based.html

Solorzano, D. G., & Yasso, T. J. (2002). Critical race methodology: Counter-storytelling as an analytical framework for education research. *Qualitative Inquiry, 8*(1), 23–44.

Stevens J. (2007). Stevens, J. dissenting. Parents Involved in Community Schools, Petitioner v. Seattle School District No. 1 et al. Retrieved on October 19, 2016 from http://www.law.cornell.edu/supct/pdf/05-908P.ZD

Stiff, L. & Harvey, W. B. (1988). On the education of Black children in mathematics. *Journal of Black Studies, 19*(2), 190–203.

Terry, C. L, Sr. (2011). Mathematical counter-story and African American male students: Urban mathematics education from a critical race theory perspective. *Journal of Urban Mathematics Education, 4*(1), 23–49.

Terry, C. L., Sr., & Howard, T. C. (2013). The power of counterstories: The complexity of Black male experiences with racism in pursuit of academic success. In J. K. Donner & A. Dixson (Eds.), *The resegregation of schools: Education and race in the twenty-first century* (pp. 71–98). New York, NY: Routledge.

Tillman, L. C. (2004). (Un)intended consequences? The impact of *Brown v. Board of Education* decision on the employment status of Black educators. *Education and Urban Society, 36*(3), 280–303.

Walker, E. N. (2001). *On time and off track? Advanced mathematics course-taking among high school students.* (Unpublished doctoral dissertation.) Harvard University, Cambridge, MA.

Walker, E. N. (2006). Urban high school students' academic communities and their effects on mathematics success. *American Educational Research Journal, 43*(1), 41–71.

Walker, E. N. (2012). *Building mathematics learning communities: Improving outcomes in urban high schools.* New York, NY: Teachers College Press.

Walker, E. N. (2014). *Beyond Banneker: Black mathematicians and the paths to excellence.* Albany: State University of New York Press.

Warren, C. J. E. (1954). Brown v. Board of Education. *United States Reports, 347,* 483.

Wing, J. M. (2006). Computational thinking. *Communications of the ACM, 49*(3), 33–35.

PART II

WOMEN OF COLOR IN STEM:
STORIES OF STRUGGLES AND SUCCESS

CHAPTER 5

THE FULFILLMENT OF A MOTHER'S DREAM

An African Woman's Story of Struggle and Success in Science

Cailisha L. Petty and Catherine Dinitra White

In general, the outlook of African American students aspiring to become scientists is disappointing and bleak. In 2011, African Americans received just 7% of STEM-related undergraduate degrees and were also awarded approximately 4% and 2% of master's and doctoral degrees, respectively (Calabrese Barton, Tan, & O'Neil, 2014). African Americans continue to be underrepresented in science classrooms, as science majors, and in science professions. Of the 2% of practicing African American PhD scientists, a much smaller fraction is African American women. African American women face the unfortunate dichotomy of being both highly visible yet invisible in American society (Collins, 2000). Similarly, they are virtually invisible in scientific society. When African American women are allowed access to science, they often must contend with isolation, marginalization, and racialization as well (Brickhouse & Potter, 2001; Carlone & Johnson, 2007; Hurtado, Cabrera, Lin, Arellano, & Espinosa, 2009; Lewis, 2003; Malone & Barabino, 2009; Scantlebury, Tal, & Rahm, 2007).

Women of Color in STEM, pages 111–133
Copyright © 2017 by Information Age Publishing
111

With the gravely disproportionate number of African American women in science, there is a lack of diversity in scientific research areas. The problem is tremendously significant because minority scientists are more likely to study issues specific to the minority community (Hurtado et al., 2009). Scientists very often conduct research on topics that are of importance to them and their lives. Additionally, the approach of scientific inquiry is not diversified if the persons gaining access to research opportunities continue to be overwhelmingly male, and more often than not, White males.

Though literature that focuses on the experiences of African American women in science is sparse (Ong, Wright, Espinosa, & Orfield, 2011), there are successful African American women who have endured despite the almost impossible odds. The stories of successful African American women in science who have persisted despite living in a racist and sexist society should be privileged. The position, plight, and history of African American women are unique because of their struggle to survive and thrive in postslavery America. For this very fact, the perspective of African American women is different and unique; therefore, there is a need for research that captures the perspective of the African American woman.

In this chapter, the authors present the narratives of an African American female scientist, Dr. Cynthia Niema Anderson (pseudonym), who was one of five participants in a larger study. The purpose of the study was to explore the experiences of successful African American women in science and understand how they had crafted narratives of success, and persisted despite the odds. By understanding how successful African American female scientists have persevered through the stories they tell about themselves and their experiences, we can provide aspiring Black female scientists with the wisdom of experience from those who have traveled the path before them. In addition, with a light shone on the barriers that impede the path into science, the scientific community can be held accountable for the role it plays in perpetuating practices that inhibit access and participation for African American women.

As we seek to understand the narratives of an African American female scientist, the research was driven by the following questions:

1. What are the life stories of a successful African American woman in science?
2. What have been the facilitators and barriers encountered by an African American female scientist?

THEORETICAL POSITIONING

In this chapter, we employ Black feminist thought and critical race theory as theoretical positions to privilege the lived experiences of an African

American woman who has completed her PhD in science. Black feminist thought (BFT) is a useful framework to examine the unique experiences of African American women who face multiple forms of oppression (Collins, 2000). There are six characteristics of BFT, and the two most significant to this study are (a) commitment to social justice, and (b) heterogeneous collectivity. The first is a commitment to social justice—not only for Black women, but justice for all (Collins, 2000). The significance of combating oppression in its multiple forms is defined as intersectionality. By not identifying the multiple, overlapping, intersecting forms of oppression, Black women will never be fully empowered (Collins, 2000; Parsons & Mensah, 2010). The second significant characteristic is diverse responses to common challenges (Collins, 2000; Parsons & Mensah, 2010), also known as heterogeneous collectivity. Although a collective with shared group knowledge and common lived experiences, African American women navigate barriers caused by oppression with various strategies.

The other lens utilized in this study was critical race theory (CRT). CRT is a movement by those who are committed to "studying and transforming the relationship between race, racism, and power" (Delgado & Stefancic, 2001, p. 2). There are six basic tenets of CRT, three of which are salient in this study. First, racism is ordinary, normal, and endemic in American society (Ladson-Billings, 2009; Taylor, 2009). Racism is deeply rooted in American culture and institutions. The next relevant tenet is the concept of intersectionality (Delgado & Stefancic, 2001). No person is one single lineage, affiliation, or identity. Intersectionality speaks to the idea that everyone has multiple, overlapping, often conflicting identities. Intersectionality can be defined as "an intersection of recognized sites of oppression" (Delgado & Stefancic, 2001, p. 51). The third significant tenet of CRT is voice of color or narrative (Bell, 2009; Ladson-Billings, 2009; Solórzano & Yosso, 2009). "Stories can name a type of discrimination; once named, it can be combated" (Delgado & Stefancic, 2001, p. 43).

The use of narrative is embraced by CRT because it gives credence to the experiences as people of color as illustrations of oppression and racism. It demands that the racism be viewed through the eyes of the oppressed, rather than from a White perspective (Bell, 2009). "Critical writers use counterstories to challenge, displace, or mock these pernicious narratives and beliefs" (Delgado & Stefancic, 2001, p. 43). Slave narratives, Indian storytelling, and Latino novels are ways that various ethnic groups have recorded their histories. By hearing, seeing, and feeling the perspective of someone else's experience, we make room for understanding. Narratives that are powerfully written can help to adjust people's thinking and mindsets.

By using BFT and CRT as a lenses, we attend to and look for evidence of not only blatant forms of racism, but microaggressions that affect the path of the participant into science. Microaggressions are the verbal, nonverbal, and environmental slights, snubs, or insults whether intentional or unintentional that communicate hostile, derogatory, or negative messages to target persons solely based upon their marginalized group membership (Sue, 2010). Most specifically, CRT requires that we use a methodology that captures the counternarratives that disrupt the dominant narrative of experiences in science. By using narrative analysis as a methodology of inquiry, we captured Niema's experiences and privileged her voice and the meanings she gave to her experiences.

METHODOLOGY

Collecting and analyzing the stories told by African American female scientists about their experiences is an ideal method to deeply and intimately understand how these women successfully persevered in a professional society that is traditionally both racist and sexist. We privilege their voices as we gathered authentic stories and the meanings given to their experiences. The methodology we chose to collect and examine these experiences was narrative inquiry (Clandinin, 2013; Clandinin & Connelly, 2000). There is no story until it is told. The story comes to life as it is being told. Before that moment, it did not exist. The research provides a safe space for the participant to create and share their stories. The researcher then interprets the experiences and events of these actions and activities.

> People shape their daily lives by stories of who they are and others are, and as they interpret their past in terms of these stories. Story . . . is a portal through which a person enters the world and by which their experience of the world is interpreted and made personally meaningful. (Clandinin, 2013, p. 13)

Narrative inquiry goes beyond observation because the teller is, in turn, allowing space for the researcher to come to an understanding of how they construct their stories and ultimately how they construct themselves (Clandinin & Connelly, 2000). The power and potential of narrative inquiry is to reveal the individual in all of their complexity and uniqueness (Clandinin, 2013).

In this chapter, we highlight the narrative of one African American woman, Niema, a participant in a larger research study. Niema was chosen by purposeful selection (Maxwell, 2005). She was recruited for the study because she had successfully obtained a PhD in an area of science. There were three criteria for participants: African American, female, and academic status. Additionally, the women were recruited across the spectrum of academic status (doctoral candidate, postdoctoral scholar, assistant professor, associate professor, and full professor). By doing so, the sample was diversified with the intention of encountering variety in their experiences that span several decades. Niema was the associate professor in the study.

In narrative inquiry, in-depth interviews are most often the tool used to elicit stories. (Clandinin, 2013; Elliott, 2005). The interview is not just a means for collection of data, but it is also the place where meaning is made of the data. The interview process consisted of two semi-structured interviews. The first focused on the path that led the women into science. The second set of interview questions focused on where they were currently and their perceivable futures in the science.

The data analysis was built upon Clandinin and Connelly's (2000) and Clandinin's (2006) model of narrative inquiry, which explores narratives as a means to understand experience. The transcripts from the interviews were professionally transcribed and the narratives were organized chronologically to create order. Each narrative was then reviewed to identify the theme of each story and titles were created to categorize the stories. From Niema's narratives, three major narrative themes were created: stories about curiosity ("being nosy"); stories about undergraduate research experiences; and stories about being a serious scientist. A single, powerful, individual narrative, A Story About Fulfilling a Mother's Dream, is the final story presented in the findings of this chapter.

As the stories were reviewed and analyzed, storylines were identified. The storylines provided context and the meanings Niema made of her experiences. All of the storylines were then pooled together into one of two major categories: storylines of tension and storylines of cooperation, which are presented in the discussion of this chapter.

In the following section, we introduce Dr. Cynthia Niema Anderson and share her narratives. All the names of persons and places have been replaced with pseudonyms to protect the anonymity of the participant.

FINDINGS: THE NARRATIVES OF AN AFRICAN AMERICAN WOMAN IN SCIENCE

Cynthia Niema Anderson received her bachelor's degree in biology in 1996 from Ida B. Wells University, a southern historically Black college and university (HBCU). Niema then attended Washington Carver University, a midwestern predominately White institution (PWI) where she received her doctorate in immunology and microbiology in 2002. In 2006, Niema joined the faculty of Frederick Douglass University, a southern HBCU, and became a tenured associate professor of biology in 2012. In the following section, Niema's voice is privileged as raw and powerful narratives are presented. We begin with stories about being a little Black girl interested in science and her experiences at school. Next, we present stories from Niema's years at Wells University and her doctoral program at Carver. The third set of narratives are stories from her experiences at Douglass University, where she began her professional career. We end this section with a powerful story about a special bond shared between Niema and her mother.

Stories About Curiosity: "Being Nosy"

> *When I talk to my mom we always joke around because we say other people say its curiosity. We know it's just being nosy. That's the bottom line.*
>
> —Niema

As we ventured back to the earliest moments in life when Niema recalled first feeling connected to science, she described herself as curious little girl who wanted to learn more, wanted to know why, and asked "What if" questions. Niema explained that her relationship with science began by feeling connected to the natural world. When asked about when she first felt connected to science, Niema took us outside and told stories about being with her sister, father, and mother. She described her parents as "outdoorsy" and credited them for sparking and fostering her interest in science. Her mother was a science teacher and on warm summer days when the skies were a crisp blue and fluffy clouds danced across the landscape, she would teach her daughters the names of clouds. Niema remembered being impressed by how much her mother knew about nature. Her father, a truck driver, also possessed knowledge about the natural world and taught his daughters many informal science lessons. For example, there was the time the girls learned about "click beetles." Niema's father caught one and tied thread around its legs and said, "Ok, you have to look real close so you can see how the wings work and how the legs move." Niema was in awe as they watched the beetle and observed how the click sound was made by the beetle rubbing its legs together.

Niema recalled numerous memories similar to these. On summer nights, they chased and collected lightening bugs in jars to make a nightlight to illuminate the girls' bedroom. And there was the time her mother woke her up from a deep slumber in the middle of the night to look at the stars through a huge telescope she had brought home. Niema's mother was her first official and "unofficial" science teacher. This unique relationship served as the fuel to ignite her spark ablaze. Niema's description of her early experiences highlights the various ways in which she was exposed to science at home. She described her relationship with science as being very natural. "It was like drinking water," she said. Niema's narrative introduces the storyline of being connected to nature. This connection was fostered by Niema's parents and access to science outside of school.

Her mother, Mrs. Anderson, was her first science teacher, but Niema also credited other science teachers for nurturing her interest. Mr. Anderson, her 2nd-grade teacher, started a science club to foster his students' interests in science. Niema remembered Mr. Howard as an impressive and passionate teacher. He took a significant interest in the lives of his students. He created the science club for his elementary school students and it was evidence of his commitment to developing future scientists and exposing students to science beyond the classroom. Mr. Howard had his young science club members write letters to NASA and they received a package back with posters and picture of Mars. Niema reminisced about several other impressive science teachers who taught with hands-on learning activities that made science fun and interesting. For example, one teacher did a diffusion demonstration, and another taught her class about waves by having them to play with Slinkys. Niema's memories of science in the classroom introduces the storyline of influential science teachers who helped to deepen her passion for science and influenced her decision to major in science in college.

Stories About Undergraduate Research Experiences

After graduating from high school, Niema attended Ida B. Wells University, a small southern HBCU, and majored in biology. She recalled receiving a tremendous amount of mentoring, support, and encouragement in college. She distinctly remembered being given one-on-one attention. "My support system was wonderful and broad. In my department, my adviser, she was just wonderful. She is one of the people that I really give credit for keeping me in science. I also had a research adviser who was outstanding." Just as with her science teachers during Niema's K–12 years, at Wells University Niema had professors and advisers who took the time to mentor her. This attention nurtured her passion for science:

> My research adviser was named Dr. Josh Phillips and I love him to death. He was a microbiologist. He gave me my first real research experience and it was so much fun because it was outside. We went to the fauna forest in West Virginia and collected water samples and stayed in a cabin. It was really cool because I learned how to do field work with him and I'd never done that before. He also had a project where he studied the effects of hurricanes on erosion. I thought it was amazing, I didn't know that you could do that. They were very impactful and from my advisers to every teacher that I had, everybody…It wasn't just that they wanted you to do well, they expected you to do well.

As a Maximizing Access to Research Careers (MARC) scholar, Niema participated in research experiences at Wells University during the semester and then over the summer she traveled to research programs at other university. She also had the opportunity go to Australia for six months and conduct research. When she was asked if there was ever a time that she felt invisible or alone as an undergraduate student, she talked about traveling to New York one summer. Niema did a research program at Henrietta Lacks University (PWI), and out of 25 students she was the only African American, the only ethnic minority. She said, "A lot of times, I felt extremely lonely." While there, Niema recalled having to contend with racism for the first time. She also spoke about an experience that had a very lasting impact on her.

> I went to a summer program in undergrad at Lacks University in New York and I was working with a post-doc and he was awesome...And he never meant any harm, but he and his wife were having a baby and we were talking about what he was going to name his baby. And it was a group of us. There were other students. There were graduate students and other post-docs. And I remember he turned to me and he said "Well Niema, your parents were so smart." And I said, "Why?" He said, "Because they gave you a name that you can use in business and one that you can use at home." And it took me a minute, and I was like "What was he talking about?" And my first is Cynthia, and my middle name is Niema.
>
> And I remember, I didn't get mad at him because I knew that he didn't mean any harm. He just didn't know any better. That day when I got back to the apartment, I called my dad. Because my dad gave me the name Cynthia. And I told him, I said, "Daddy, I hope you never think I'm ashamed of my name or I hope you never take offense." But I told him, "Every chance I get, I will be called Niema. I don't care if I'm at home. If I'm at the office. Wherever it is." And, now it's so funny because now when people call me Cynthia, I know its people that don't know me. But that was very, very telling. And it could have...if I were a different person, that could have ended very badly, but I was raised that you should use every opportunity as an educational experience. Not use it to show out. So ... you know.

This experience introduces the storyline of contending with racism and altered how Niema chose to operate in the world by changing how she wanted others to identify her. She chose to defy the status quo and define herself by her own terms and by a name that embraced her ethnicity. Unfortunately, Niema also had another extremely uncomfortable experience that she said stayed with her all of her life. It occurred when she spent a semester in Australia. It was a study abroad program supported by the National Institutes of Health. That summer, Niema conducted research in physiology and learned about science in a different context because she was outside of the United States. Outside of the realm of science, Niema also learned people's perception of Americans was positive in general, but differed for African Americans in particular. She recalled being asked what gang she was in and how many children she had because the perception was that the majority of African American women were in gangs and had lots of children very early in life. Niema described one very unsettling experience in Australia:

> The gentleman that I worked with, he as a post-doc in the physiology lab. Very nice…just a very sweet person, and he was German. No…he was Dutch. And I remember he asked me and one my friends if we wouldn't mind baby-sitting for him and his wife one night. And we were very happy to. You know I love playing with little kids. And so we were at their house and they had shown us a little bookshelf with all of the reading material that we could read to the little boy. And I remember there was book in there and it's called the *Little Pickaninny*. I will never forget it. And on the front of the book it had picture of little Black child. It was a cartoon drawing. And if you remember how Buckwheat looked.…I forgot the name of that show with Alfalfa (*The Little Rascals*).

> The picture looked like that and so the little child on the book had the pig-tails that were sticking everywhere. They had little bows on them. It was a very dark skinned child and it really made me think, how was this scientist seeing me? It made me really question that. And so I have carried that with me all my life. I'm always wondering how I'm being perceived.

Niema's experiences forced her to question how other people saw her. Her research experiences with her mentors at Wells University and abroad struck a chord with her and she became excited about a future in research. Niema's experiences as a HBCU undergraduate reinforced and solidified her passion for science. These experiences were in cooperation with who she was and who she was becoming as an emerging scientist. Within her narratives, the storyline of early research experiences was introduced. Within research, Niema "first felt like scientists and saw science as a possible future." Also, the storyline of support and mentoring by HBCU professors and advisers was quite evident. The one-on-one support Niema received made her feel important and valued because of the time and energy her mentors were willing to spend on her.

Unfortunately, however, she also had to contend with antagonistic forces that made her feel insecure. Niema's narrative in this section reveals the storyline of feeling insecure, invisible, and alone. Niema experienced feeling uncomfortable during her summer program at Lacks University in New York because she was the only student of color in the group. She also became very insecure regarding how she was being perceived because of her experiences in Australia. The experiences created a heightened sense of insecurity as she contended with racist interactions that affected the way she saw herself, and ultimately how she wanted to be addressed by others. She chose Niema instead of Cynthia to embrace, preserve, and defend her African American culture.

Stories About Becoming "A Serious Scientist"

Niema graduated from Ida B. Wells University in May 1996, and began a PhD program at Washington Carver University (WCU), a midwestern PWI, in microbiology and immunology the in the fall. The PhD program was difficult, especially the first year. When she talked about her years in graduate school, she remembered having a very strong support system in her family, church, and friends. Without them, "I wouldn't have survived the first year." For Niema, a huge factor that made the environment difficult was the fact that out of ten graduate programs in the School of Medicine, she was only one of six African Americans. Specifically, in her program, the only other African American to complete the program had graduated in the 1970s. Niema found a support system in her involvement in the MBRS (Minority Biomedical Research Support) program. "So one of the things that really helped me was that all of the graduate students had to mentor the undergraduate students. So I felt like I had to get through ... I had to figure out how to make this work so I could help the undergraduates keep their motivation. And figure out that they could make it work too. So that really helped."

If she had not had a strong support system, Niema does not believe that she would have survived the first year. Niema's support system was undoubtedly her reason for staying. She credited the MBRS program with keeping her on the path, as well as her roommate, Vanessa. Vanessa was an African American young woman also enrolled in a doctoral program at WCU, who Niema said would "threaten her life" when she would ever talk about quitting. She also had her sister and a friend from back home who jumped on the road and came to see about her whenever she sounded down or stressed out. The storyline of support is reinforced by the actions of Niema's sister and friends.

There were several times when she considered quitting, and Niema recalled two in particular during the first year that caused her to contemplate not going back a second year. The first experience was during a rotation when her graduate adviser walked over to her and said: "You know, I really don't know if you should be a scientist. You really think like a technician, so I don't think you know how to think like a scientist. You should probably think about being a technician." Her comment crushed Niema because she thought that she was doing a good job. This incident caused her to begin to feel very insecure and incompetent, a feeling that she first remembered having during her research experience in New York. The second incident occurred in the research lab.

> My PI came to me one day and he wanted me to make up a certain solution, like a three millimolar solution of something. And I remembered doing it in class. I remembered seeing other people doing it, but I just didn't have that

much experience making that particular type of solution. And I just remember I just froze. I couldn't think, I started sweating, I had to leave the lab. I was just so . . . it just blew my mind, and then I was upset with myself because I was thinking, "This is so irrational. Why am I having this issue?" And it took me a very long time to get over that, because I was afraid to go ask him for help even though he was my superior. I didn't want him to think that he had let this person in the lab that couldn't even make a solution. I was afraid to ask my other colleagues in the lab for help, because, to me, they were like superstars. They came from these schools where they were really, overly prepared, even before coming. They just seemed to never have any issues, but for me, I felt like I was the problem child in the laboratory. That made it very difficult and those two instances really caused me to think twice about whether I should even be in science, and it's sad because they're such *minor* things. It was just really, *really* scary. . . . [T]he whole first year of graduate school was when I questioned whether or not this was what I was supposed to be doing. What kept me there was my support group. If I didn't have the students and faculty in the MBRS program, I probably wouldn't have made it.

These experiences highlight the external barriers that threatened Niema's continuation in the program, but Niema also had internal conflicts.

One barrier was my self-perception. The way I saw myself . . . I was very unsure of my own capabilities at that time. And I remember asking myself several times, "Why did they let me into this program?" I just couldn't figure it out.

Niema knew she was smart, but she just could not figure out how to navigate the program and she found this to be very difficult. Additionally, Niema felt the overwhelming burden of needing to succeed because no other African American had completed the program in more than 20 years. She was the only African American in her program. Niema said, "Because no African American had graduated from that program in many many years, I knew that people were counting on me to be successful. It was just too much pressure."

Niema also struggled with her courses for the first time in her life. Everything moved very fast and even though she knew how to study, she found herself really struggling in the first year. Niema soon realized that part of her problem was a difference in the culture. Other students were doing well because they were studying together and had access to old tests. Niema had not been extended the invitation to join a study group and therefore did not have the same access to material like her colleagues. After meeting and getting to know Linda, Niema started doing better in class. Linda invited Niema over to her house and she taught her how to study for biochemistry and also gave her access to the old tests. Linda was a former teacher and one of her classmates in biochemistry. With Linda's help, "my grades skyrocketed." Niema credited Linda with being a key member of her support system and one of the reasons why she did not quit after the first year.

Despite the obstacles during her first year, in 2002 Niema received her PhD in microbiology and immunology at Washington Carver University. After returning home, she began the TEAM (Teacher Education And Mastery) postdoctoral fellowship at South East University, a large southern PWI. Niema knew that she wanted to continue teaching because of her experiences teaching in the MBRS program. The TEAM program was a great training program, and she thoroughly enjoyed her experience. Niema began the postdoctoral program in 2002 and met her husband while in the program. Her future husband was also a TEAM fellow, and they married in May 2006.

In August 2006, Niema completed her postdoctoral fellowship and was hired as an assistant professor in the Department of Biology at Frederick Douglass University (HBCU). After interviewing at Douglass, she was confident that she had found the right fit because of how she felt during the interview and how she feels about work right now.

> In my workplace, it actually feels great because I think this is probably the first time that I feel that my opinion is highly valued. People were really interested in hearing my opinion ... and that made me feel so good because I hadn't had that feeling probably since undergrad.

Niema's decision to join the Douglass biology faculty was because of the way she felt during the interview process. She was interviewed by three African American female scientists, the chairperson of the department as well as the cochairperson and another faculty member. The women all responded very positively when she answered questions and shared her ideas about research and teaching: "And when I gave my answers, their response was so positive ... it was just a positive environment. And that's what made me want to come here."

Niema was pleased with her decision to come to Douglass. She became an active member of the faculty and received accolades for both teaching and mentoring in her research lab. However, even though Niema had an overwhelmingly positive experience at Douglass, she explained there were still a few barriers.

> I think one of the biggest barriers is the way that I perceive myself. Sometimes I am extremely hard on myself because I know that I'm female and because I know that I'm an African American woman. A lot of times I feel like I have to be so far above the mark.

Niema's insecurity persisted and she believed that just being an African American female scientist was a barrier because she put pressure on herself to be as perfect as possible and worried about how others perceived her.

She described it as "feeling like we're representing every African American *ever!*" Niema recalled this feeling started in graduate school and continued. Within this vignette, the storyline of overwhelming burden is introduced and reinforced. It was a familiar feeling that Niema remembered experiencing before in graduate school.

Niema felt that her biggest challenge was getting over some of the interactions she faced in the past that now shaped how she interacted with people. She looked at her husband, an African American male scientist, and envied his confidence and the way he interacted with other scientists at conferences:

> I just look at him and he has this demeanor. He's just strolling around, talking to people, shaking hands, and I'm sitting back there thinking, "Man, it must be great to be a guy." I wish I had that, and it's not just confidence, it's almost like . . . I don't even know how to describe it, it's like being in the same pack. I think, as a female scientist, I'm much more comfortable with other female scientists than I am with other male scientists, unless I know the male scientist really well. He can talk to anybody, male or female, he doesn't care.

All these years later, Niema still carried the burden of feeling as if she needed to be over-prepared and that she was representing the entire race. The insecurity was still there, but she believed that she was getting to the point where she was becoming happy with herself. At the time of our first interview in the summer of 2014, Niema had become a mother. Her first daughter, April, was born in 2012. In the fall of 2012, she completed her tenure and promotion package and was promoted to associate professor. That was an extremely tough period in her life because she was physically, mentally, and emotionally exhausted. Niema had a very difficult pregnancy and was sick pretty much the entire time, but she still had teaching duties, academic advisees, and students in the lab.

By our final interview in the fall of 2015, her second daughter, Maria, was just about six months old. Becoming a mother changed her life and changed how Niema saw her future in science. The demands of being a research scientist created friction with the demands of motherhood. "In order to be really productive in the laboratory, you have to be there. And so when I was in my post-doc and before I had a baby, you know I would be in the lab [at] 8:00 or 9:00 at night." Being a mother now required her to leave each day by 5 p.m. Niema's teaching load had not been reduced, and her service to the department and university had actually increased. Yet, she had less to time to complete everything because of the demands of motherhood. "I haven't been able to add any extra hours in my day. My hours have been cut because of daycare. At 5:00, I have to be on the road. And that's just how it is." Niema's narrative in this section introduces the storyline of family and children.

Furthermore, Niema explained that the politics of science were not conducive to mothers, especially in terms of the tenure clock.

> As a faculty member, one of the scariest things is trying to get tenure. Depending on the university, that tenure clock may stop. It may stop for a certain amount of time, it all depends on the institution. Here (at Douglass), we actually have the ability to halt the clock, but it won't halt for like a year. We can take maternity leave, they'll give us paid maternity leave for I think it's 12 weeks. If you need to go beyond that, then you have some issues. The way science is set up as a whole it really is not setup for women with children or people with children period. Because if you have to take time off for a sick child, let's say you get a call from daycare today. If you are a bench research scientist, your experiments don't care. You're still expected to get the same number of publications, you're expected to have the same level of productivity. There are no differences there.

Within this vignette, the sexist environment of science was evident as Niema discussed policies that place a burden on expectant women and new mothers. The storyline of sexism is revealed. The rules were designed for men, so unfortunately facing issues like the tenure clock, maternity leave, and the demands of family created a new set of challenges for Niema to negotiate.

Ultimately, Niema came to realize that although she still loved science and research, her experience with mentoring students had led to a new passion. "My passion now is really with students." She developed a university-wide professional development program to support students who wanted to go professional. Niema became committed to helping them follow their dreams by "helping them figure out what they needed to do in order to be productive while they were in undergrad." Niema explained,

> And all it took was working closely with one student who graduated and then getting into professional school. And that did it for me!! I was like, "Oh, I gotta keep doing this!" But yeah, that's my passion, but I still love research. I love science. But there are so many aspects of it that just turned me off at this point in my life.

As Niema embarked in perhaps a new direction in her career, she poignantly described what being an African American woman in science meant to her.

> I think that it means that you have to be a very strong person. You have to be thick-skinned. I am not thick-skinned naturally. This is something that I really had to develop over time. But I think because of how we may be seen by others or how we may be perceived before people really know us. I think that is means that you have to be on your Ps and Qs. And still science is a very male dominated. And nonminority dominated field, if you really think about the

research area. And so I just think that it's really important because I've spoken to other scientists before, mainly Caucasian American scientists, and I tend to get these looks like "Oh, she actually *knows* this."

When I think back to the time in Australia and the *Little Pickaninny* book that I told you about. And wondering if he saw me that way. I think I have carried that with me all my life. So when I go out of the country or when I just go out of NC. I'm always... or when I go off campus, I'm always wondering how I'm being perceived. That's why I'm so careful about being very professional and making sure that I really, really know what I'm talking about. Because I want people to look past my exterior. I don't want them to see a woman. I don't want them to see my ethnicity. I don't want them to even see my nationality. I want them to see that I am a serious scientist who knows what I'm talking about.

A Story About Fulfilling a Mother's Dream

It was spring of 2002 and Niema was making preparations to wrap up everything at WCU and go home. She did not want to stay a minute longer than she had to. It had been a long and rough 6 years, but she had made it. Niema was about to defend her thesis in March, and she was tired and debated whether or not she would move back home right away or wait until after graduation. She soon discovered that she did not have a choice in the matter. Niema's mother insisted that she stay and graduate. It was an important moment for her mother and she was not going to let Niema miss the graduation ceremony.

Mrs. Anderson had actually started a doctoral program right after she graduated from Ida B. Wells University, Niema's alma mater, in 1968. She started a program at a large PWI in the north, but left early because she had no support. Niema never even knew that her mother began a PhD program until she was in graduate school herself. "Now I can understand why if I had an issue I would just go directly to her and she would be able to give me advice that I just thought was miraculous, but now I know it's because she went through it too."

Mrs. Anderson was a tremendous source of advice for Niema because she came up against the same issues and had similar experiences. She was one of very few minorities in the microbiology PhD program at Prosperity University, but at that time there were no programs in place to support students of color. Mrs. Anderson felt alone. She also shared with Niema that there was still a lot of racism around so she did personally experience some racism while she was there. Another issue was that she was from the South. She was in the Midwest, which is a completely different culture. And the course load, she found to be extremely difficult. She shared with me that a lot of times people wouldn't study with her.

Mrs. Anderson was left to figure things out on her own.

So when Niema would come to her mother about the struggles that she was experiencing, her mother could relate and would give her advice on how to handle a situation and how to conduct herself.

> One of the best pieces of advice that she gave me was that once you are accepted to a PhD program, she said, "People already know that you are intelligent enough to complete the program. That's not the question.... Sometimes you have to treat it like an endurance test. If you can endure it, you will get through it." She also said, "Don't start off talking. Start off listening. When you go to your program, make sure you listen. Listen to how people speak to each other. Listen to how they communicate with one another and the things that they do. And you kinda follow that model because that's how they're successful at that time in that program." She would always tell us to "start off listening. Look at how people are doing things and then work your way in." And that was good advice.

Mrs. Anderson motivated and pushed Niema when times were tough. On more than one occasion, Niema would call home and cry about something she was going through at the moment. Her mother would only listen and then very simply ask, "Now what are you going to do about it?" Mrs. Anderson wasn't the type of mother to coddle her daughters.

> She would pat you on the back and tell you to pull your pants up and keep going. That's the type of person my mom is. She's very strong and I love that. I love that about her now. She's always helped keep me going that way.

Niema reminisced about speaking to her mother about how she felt about Niema's success.

> It was a point in her life where she was extremely proud because she always told me she feels like I lived her dream. And so, for her to be able to come to my graduation... I didn't realize at the time how important it was for her. I remember calling her. It was right before my thesis defense, and I was exhausted. I was just ready to go home. And I said, "Well Mama, I don't think I'm going to stay for graduation. I think I'm going to go ahead and move back home." And she said, "I don't understand why you think that's your degree. This was a *joint* effort." She said, "That's my degree, too! So, yes ma'am, you're gonna walk across that stage." And so, I actually ended up moving out the day after graduation. If nothing else happened, she was going to see me march across that stage. And for me, to this day, it makes me teary-eyed because I know how important it was to her. And so, I feel like our paths have been so common, and I feel like I am really doing what she wanted me to do, but she would have never told me that she wanted me to do it. So I'm glad that I could do that for her.

DISCUSSION

After we completed crafting the presentation of Niema's narratives, we revisited our research questions to remind us of our original motivation for narratively inquiring into the life of an African American woman in science. Unfortunately, during the journey into science, very few African American women have been able to defeat the antagonistic forces that rise up against them and triumph. Therefore, we wanted to collect and examine life stories of success. As we looked back at our research questions and aligned them against Niema's narratives, we began to better understand not just the stories and experiences that she shared, but more importantly the meanings Niema made of the experiences and the effect they had on her life.

Our main research question was: "What are the life stories of a successful African American woman in science?" From Niema's narratives, we discovered various storylines of cooperation and tension. Storylines of cooperation were experiences that aligned with who she was and who she was becoming as a scientist. For example, "influential teacher" and "mentoring and support" were storylines of cooperation. On the other hand, storylines of tension were the experiences that created friction and butted up against who Niema was and challenged her goal of becoming a scientist. Examples would include storylines of "contending with racism" and "feeling invisible, insecure, and alone." The storylines of cooperation and tension helped us to address the following research question: "What have been the facilitators and barriers encountered by an African American female scientist?" By attending to the storylines and the meanings the Niema made of her experiences, we began to articulate the influences that contributed to her success, as well as describe potentially damaging distractions. In the following section, we reflect upon the storylines of tension followed by the storylines of cooperation.

Unexpected Barriers: Storylines of Tension

Niema's narratives revealed several important storylines that illustrated the unexpected barriers she faced that were potentially damaging. Storylines of tension included feeling insecure, invisible, and alone; contending with racism and sexism; family and children; and, overwhelming burdens.

Within her narratives the storyline of feeling insecure, invisible, and alone was reinforced. She experienced this feeling while in college when away during the summer, but as Niema entered graduate school she felt this way again. There was insecurity because she felt unsure about her preparedness. Niema was entering a doctoral program directly from completing her bachelor's degree. There were other students with more education and life experiences in her program. In addition, there was an added level of insecurity because she was the only one or one of a few African Americans in the room. Ong and colleagues (2011) found that women of color encountered problems because very often they were coming from environments filled with encouragement and support (HBCUs) into environments where they experienced social isolation and academic difficulties. Furthermore, feelings of loneliness and not being accepted affects a woman's sense of self and can lead to social stratification and low expectations (Ong et al., 2011).

Additionally, the storyline of contending with racism and sexism was revealed. Although at times manifested as subtle microaggressions, Niema contended with racism on several different occasions such as the comment about her parents being smart when naming her, not being invited to study sessions, the *Little Pickaninny* book, and Niema's research mentor stating that she thought more like a technician. Studies have found that the prevalent cultural belief in White male superiority played out as microaggressions in everyday practices that affected the experiences of women of color (Ong, 2005). As a coping strategy to downplay their differences, women of color in these environments often altered their mode of thinking, dress, speech, and behavior.

Niema also discussed the storyline of family and children. Niema had the unique experience of having her first daughter while her tenure clock was ticking. At Douglass, she was able to "stop" the clock briefly after her daughter was born, but she emphatically believed that science was not conducive to women with families. As she shouldered the burden of workloads, pregnancy, and children, Niema began to feel as if it is almost impossible to continue at the laboratory bench and have a family as well. Previous literature reports that when women are present in higher education, they are largely concentrated in lower level positions, such as assistant professor, and at a lower pay rate (Easterly & Ricard, 2011; Eisenhart & Finkel, 1998). One of the reasons noted for lower pay and the concentration of women in lower level positions is that very often for men there is less pressure to negotiate both home and work responsibilities (Easterly & Ricard, 2011; Eisenhart & Finkel, 1998; Heilbronner, 2012).

Another dominant storyline from Niema's narratives are the storylines of overwhelming burdens. Niema felt the very heavy burden of representing her race. Racialization is described by Malone and Barabino (2009) as "related to stereotype and never being able to escape being seen as a Black (or minority) person" (p. 495). Niema recalled, "Feeling like we're representing every African American *ever!*" Because of this burden, Niema felt like she always had to be extremely good at whatever she did. She knew that others would watch and judge her performances not as individual actions, but as representations of her race and gender. With so few African American women in science, she felt the burden of desperately needing to succeed.

If she did not make it, her failure would reinforce the stereotype that Black people do not belong and cannot make it in science. She was burdened with a massive responsibility. Niema discussed still feeling that way even as a seasoned professional. She felt the need to be over-prepared. She wanted to leave no room for criticism.

Confidence and Competence: Storylines of Cooperation

We define storylines of cooperation as the narratives that aligned with Niema's interest and desire to learn more about science and to become a scientist. These storylines were in cooperation with her identity as an African American woman in science. The storylines of connected to nature, influential science teachers, early research experiences, and support and mentoring all contributed to her passion for science and her desire to become a scientist. When she considered leaving, Niema had enough support externally and enough motivation internally to persist. The positive experiences reinforced Niema's confidence in her scientific ability and contributed to what made her feel good about being a scientist.

To begin, Niema fondly remembered several teachers that she credited for developing her emerging interests in science. She knew the teachers by name and described the activities she did in class and after school in science club. Niema's stories remind us of the research study in which several students described "doing science" as "doing school" (Varelas, Kane, & Wylie, 2011). What made the experiences so important was that the teachers she deemed as significant had encouraged her to "do science" and not just "do school." Varelas et al. (2011) explained that some students in their study described "doing science" as staying in their seats, working hard, and not talking too much. These descriptions align with a "pedagogy of control" and compliance rather than engaging students in "doing science" (Varelas et al., 2011). Authentically engaging in science can be messy, loud, and disorganized, and requires a teacher dedicated and talented enough to recognize the needs of his or her students.

Next, Niema's experiences with undergraduate research reinforced her desire to pursue science. The importance of research experiences was supported by multiple studies that identified postsecondary experiences in science that positively impacted engagement and achievement. These experiences included developing competence through participation in authentic science practices (Hurtado et al., 2009) and the support and recognition of "scientific" others (Carlone & Johnson, 2007; Hurtado et al., 2009; Malone & Barabino, 2009; Rao & Flores, 2007). Participation in research experiences allowed the women to develop competence by obtaining scientific research skills as well as developing relationships with research mentors from whom they received support and recognition.

Additionally, the storyline of support and mentoring, specifically at HB-CUs, was reinforced throughout Niema's narratives. Niema was very comfortable during her undergraduate years and later when she was hired at a HBCU. In this environment, there was not the pressure that she described when she entered other environments where she was the only African American female. She did not have to carry that weight. Niema's experiences echoed findings reported in Ong and colleagues' (2011) literature review about African American women's experiences in science. Several studies described in their review illustrated that supportive environments in STEM are found in minority serving institutions, specially historically Black colleges and universities (HBCUs). The key characteristics found in these institutions were openness, lack of stigma when remediation is required, high expectations, and supportive faculty student relationships (Ong et al., 2011).

Furthermore, HBCUs and women's colleges produced far greater numbers of African American female PhDs in biological and physical sciences "because of their deliberate efforts to establish an infrastructure to recruit and retain students in these fields. That infrastructure included supportive faculty, strong sense of community, curricula that encouraged collaboration and real-world applications, and programs designed to promote success" (Ong et al., 2011, p. 191).

Lastly, the support from Niema's mother was critically important in her journey. Studies show that family and community support may be the most influential factor that encourages women of color in STEM (Russell & Atwater, 2005). Russell and Atwater's (2005) research of senior African American biology students identified three factors of parental influence: encouragement, acceptance, and high expectations. Studies have also shown the influence of mothers as a strong, consistent, supportive force (Ong et al., 2011).

IMPLICATION: SUSTAIN AND ENHANCE SUPPORTIVE STRUCTURES

Niema's narratives provide direction for an evolved postsecondary experience for African American women science majors. Research enrichment program like MARC and MBRS provided Niema with the opportunity to experience science and also receive mentoring and support. We believe one way to enhance the effectiveness of these programs might be to ensure that students are connected to a larger network of scientists of color. Ong (2005) recommended that departments "should provide opportunities for multiplicity by structurally and financially supporting these members' (female and minority) participation in local associations, such as formal groups for women and minorities" (p. 612). She recommended conference events sponsored by national associations for underrepresented members, such as the American Physical Society's Committee on the Status of Women in Physics, the National Association of Black Engineers, and the National Conference of Black Physics Students.

Similarly, Espinosa (2011) noted that academic relationships formed through organizations like these are important because when women of color attend PWIs, they struggle to connect with their White and/or male peers. Memberships in academic organizations may help women of color feel more connected to the STEM community at large. One of the most important displays of support for Niema was when individuals showed up physically and supported her. Niema's sister and friend would jump in the car and drive 12 hours to come and check on her. Because of this kind of support, when Niema became the MARC director at Douglass for a few years, she visited her students when they were in summer research programs at various schools across the country. When asked why visiting and physically checking on the students was important to her, Niema replied:

> That's really important, because number one I know the culture of science. I know the culture of research laboratories. Every place is different and it's very important for students to be placed in a situation where they can feel that they're going to be successful and where they are *actually* going to be successful. It's also important so that the people who are over the programs can see us. They need to know that we are that student's support, and that if something goes wrong we're going to pull those students out. So it's really important for that to happen. I recommend that for everybody who's working with students.

We believe that this kind of support should be provided more often. Programs could possibly fund visits to institutions where their students are placed so that we know the type of environments where students are being trained and to ensure they are being adequately supported.

CONCLUSION

Niema's narratives illustrate the necessity for continuous, open, and honest conversations regarding the experiences of African American women who aspire to succeed in science. Dr. Cynthia Niema Anderson's success is a cause for celebration among women of color, but also a time to pause and realize that sexism and racism still present barriers that create stress and pressure that African American women must contend with and struggle to overcome. Without strong systems of support in place and a strong definition of self, success is nearly impossible. Niema was able to rise above isolation and oppression to live her mother's dream. Her mother had no support; therefore, despite tremendous potential, she left. Collins (2000) emphasizes the importance of the relationships among African American women as support for each other in the struggles of everyday life in America. These supportive relationships were key. Niema's mother, sister, friends, and other African American female scientists all played a major role as sources of encourgement and support. As we look toward the future and work diligently to increase the number of women of color in science, we must listen closely to the counterstories of dreams deferred and dreams realized, so that more little girls who love science are able to dream big and rise high.

REFERENCES

Bell, D. A. (2009). Who's afraid of critical race theory? In E. Taylor, D. Gillborn, & G. Ladson-Billings (Eds.), *Foundations of critical race theory in education* (pp. 37–50). New York, NY: Routledge.

Brickhouse, N. W., & Potter, J. T. (2001). Young women's science identity in an urban context. *Journal of Research in Science Teaching, 38*(8), 965–980.

Calabrese Barton, A., Tan, E., & O'Neil, T. (2014). Science education in urban contexts: New conceptual tool and stories of possibilities. In N. G. Lederman & S. K. Abell (Eds.), *Handbook of research on science education* (pp. 246–265). New York, NY: Routledge.

Carlone, H. B., & Johnson, A. (2007). Understanding the science experiences of successful women of color: Science identity as an analytic lens. *Journal of Research in Science Teaching, 44*(8), 1187–1218.

Clandinin, D. J. (2006). Narrative inquiry: A methodology for studying lived experience. *Research Studies in Music Education, 27*(44), 44–54.

Clandinin, D. J. (2013). *Engaging in narrative inquiry.* Walnut Creek, CA: Left Coast Press.

Clandinin, D. J., & Connelly, F. M. (2000). *Narrative inquiry: Experience and story in qualitative research.* San Francisco, CA: Wiley.

Collins, P. H. (2000). *Black feminist thought.* New York, NY: Routledge.

Delgado, R., & Stefancic, J. (2001). *Critical race theory: An introduction.* New York, NY: New York University.

Easterly, D. M., & Ricard, C. S. (2011). Conscious efforts to end unconscious bias: Why women leave academic research. *Journal of Research Administration, 42*(1), 61–73.

Eisenhart, M. A., & Finkel, E. (1998). *Women's science: Learning and succeeding from the margins.* Chicago, IL: University of Chicago Press.

Elliott, J. (2005). *Using narrative in social science research: Qualitative and quantitative approaches.* London, England: Sage.

Espinosa, L. L. (2011). Pipelines and pathways: Women of color in undergraduate STEM major. *Harvard Educational Review, 81*(2), 209–241.

Heilbronner, N. N. (2012). The STEM pathway for women: What has changed? *Gifted Child Quarterly,* 0016986212460085.

Hurtado, S., Cabrera, N. L., Lin, M. H., Arellano, L., & Espinosa, L. L. (2009). Diversifying science: Underrepresented student experiences in structured research programs. *Research in Higher Education, 50,* 189–224.

Ladson-Billings, G. (2009). Just what is critical race theory and what's it doing in a nice field like education? In E. Taylor, D. Gillborn, & G. Ladson-Billings (Eds.), *Foundations of critical race theory in education* (pp. 17–36). New York, NY: Routledge.

Lewis, B. F. (2003). A critique of literature on the underrepresentation of African Americans in science: Directions for future research. *Journal of Women and Minorities in Science and Engineering, 9,* 361–373.

Malone, K. R., & Barabino, G. (2009). Narrations of race in STEM research settings: Identity formation and its discontents. *Science Education, 93*(3), 485–510.

Maxwell, J. A. (2005). *Qualitative research design: An interactive approach.* Thousand Oaks, CA: Sage.

Ong, M. (2005). Body projects of young women of color in physics: Intersections of gender, race, and science. *Social Problems, 52*(4), 593–617.

Ong, M., Wright, C., Espinosa, L. L., & Orfield, G. (2011). Inside the double bind: A synthesis of empirical research on undergraduate and graduate women of color in science, technology, engineering, and math. *Harvard Educational Review, 81*(2), 172–208.

Parsons, E. C., & Mensah, F. M. (2010). Black feminist thought: The lived experiences of two Black female science educators. In K. Scantlebury, J. Butler Kahle, & S. N. Martin (Eds.), *Re-visioning science education from feminist perspective* (pp. 13–24). Rotterdam, the Netherlands: Sense.

Rao, V., & Flores, G. (2007). Why aren't there more African-American physicians? A qualitative study and exploratory inquiry of African-American students' perspectives on careers in medicine. *Journal of National Medical Association, 99*(9), 986–933.

Russell, M. L., & Atwater, M. M. (2005). Traveling the road to success: A discourse on persistence throughout the science pipeline with African American students at a predominantly White institution. *Journal of Research in Science Teaching, 42*(6), 691–715.

Scantlebury, K., Tal, T., & Rahm, J. (2007). "That don't look like me." Stereotypic images of science: Where do they come from and what can we do with them? *Cultural Studies in Science Education, 1*(3), 545–558.

Solórzano, D. G., & Yosso, T. J. (2009). Critical race methodology: Counter-storytelling as an analytical framework for educational research. In E. Taylor, D. Gillborn, & G. Ladson-Billings (Eds.), *Foundations of critical race theory in education* (pp. 131–147). New York, NY: Routledge.

Sue, D. W. (2010). *Microaggressions in everyday life: Race, gender, and sexual orientation.* Hoboken, NJ: Wiley & Sons.

Taylor, E. (2009). The foundation of critical race theory. In E. Taylor, D. Gillborn, & G. Ladson-Billing (Eds.), *Foundations of critical race theory in education* (pp. 1–13). New York, NY: Routledge.

Varelas, M., Kane, J. M., & Wylie, C. D. (2011). Young African American children's representations of self, science, and school: Making sense of difference. *Science Education, 95*(5), 824–851.

CHAPTER 6

NAVIGATING THE STEM LANDSCAPE

Examining the Role of Spatial Reasoning for Women of Color

Samina Hadi-Tabassum

On January 16, 2005, Harvard University's former president, Lawrence Summers, made public comments on sex differences between men and women and how they may relate to the careers of women in science. In particular, Summers spoke of the underrepresentation of women among tenure-track faculty at elite universities in physical science, math, and engineering. Summers' words sparked a lengthy debate that continues today regarding gender disparities in the sciences, studies of bias and discrimination, and innate and acquired differences between the sexes. According to the United States Department of Commerce report (Beede, Julian, Langdon, McKittrick, Khan, & Doms, 2011), women account for half of the nation's college-educated workforce but still occupy less than 25% of STEM jobs. Moreover, women of color hold just 8% of the STEM jobs. Before we examine this debate about women of color, however, the literature on sex

Women of Color in STEM, pages 135–155
Copyright © 2017 by Information Age Publishing
All rights of reproduction in any form reserved.

differences in math and science is filled with inconsistent findings, contradictory theories, and emotional claims that are often unsupported by solid and substantial evidence. Despite all the fury over the data, clear and consistent messages can be found in which there are real and, in some cases, sizable sex differences with respect to the gender gap in math and science, especially in the area of spatial reasoning (Rahman & Wilson, 2003).

Studies have made strong corollaries between academic achievement in the sciences and some significant factors, such as background knowledge in the sciences, attitude toward the sciences, biological differences, curricular emphasis, and even differences in spatial reasoning. When it comes to the basic categories of cognition—how we negotiate the world and live our lives, and our concept of objects, of numbers, of people, of living things, and so on—there are no differences between the sexes. However, there are cognitive differences in some instances when it comes to spatial reasoning in science and math: male students are better at mentally rotating three-dimensional shapes, while female students are better at visual memory; and male students are better at mathematical problem solving, while female students are better at mathematical calculation (Pinker, 2005). Since research has shown that the largest and most consistent gender difference in cognition is spatial reasoning with effect sizes ranging from medium to large (Halpern, Beninger, & Straight, 2011; Voyer, Voyer, & Bryden, 1995), emphasis on spatial reasoning is statistically significant in closing the gender gap in math and science.

In this chapter, I specifically focus on spatial reasoning and how sex differences in spatial reasoning across all ages and demographics can give male students leverage in science achievement. When one examines the lives of famous scientists and famous scientific discoveries, the mental manipulation of objects in three dimensions gains prominence in the memoirs and journals of many physicists and mathematicians. Descartes and Tesla, for example, claimed to have hit upon their discoveries through dynamic visual imagery and only later set these visualizations down in equations. Well-developed spatial skills have been shown to lead to success in engineering, computer science, and chemistry (Wilhelm, 2009). Spatial reasoning is thus crucial to how we navigate the scientific landscape; in particular, spatial reasoning skills can give students leverage in understanding complex science and math concepts, such as learning proportional reasoning in mathematics and visualizing three-dimensional molecules in chemistry, which are difficult topics to teach using traditional language-analytical methods on paper alone. The spatial orientation of orbitals, molecular geometries, crystal structures, and the R and S configurations of organic molecules all require heightened visualization and mental manipulation in two or three dimensions, often through the use of computer technology (Coleman & Gotch, 1998).

A significant body of research exists that examines gender differences between males and females in general when it comes to spatial reasoning, and often the studies cite males performing better (Kerns & Berenbaum, 1991; Silverman, Choi, & Peters, 2007). However, a lack of research is evident that focuses on specific racial and cultural groups; in particular, the spatial reasoning ability of women of color (Jackson, Wilhelm, Lamar, & Cole, 2015). Much of the research creates a heightened binary between male and female spatial reasoning without examining the complexities of identity development along race and ethnicity.

Gender supersedes race and ethnicity so that there is hardly any demographic information regarding the research subjects themselves. Spatial reasoning studies focus on the singular identity of gender rather than the intersection of both race and gender to examine the subject from a holistic perspective. The intersection of race and gender would not distract from the analysis of spatial reasoning, instead perhaps the experiences of women of color in the sciences are very different kinds of experiences than White women in the sciences, just as they are on college campuses in which women of color experience greater stress due to a sense of alienation and a lack of support in predominantly White institutions (Berger & Lyon, 2005). Examining the concept of the double bind, therefore, is a form of intersectional research that must simultaneously examine the identity of race and the identity of gender. Even though one identity may disappear in certain contexts, such as women of color and White women working together in an all-female school setting with gender disappearing as a variable, most research contexts nevertheless should require the examination of both identities through social observation and their separate outcomes.

For example, Livingston, Rosette, and Washington (2012) found that Black women and White men did not receive backlash when they displayed dominant behaviors in the workplace in relation to their White female and Black male colleagues, who did face a backlash. The work-related experiences of Black women are therefore qualitatively different from the work-related experiences of White women and Black men. If race had been collapsed together, researchers would never have analyzed the differing levels of significance and the type of social significance that Black women carry in the workplace, which might have been overlooked otherwise. Therefore, we must stop ourselves from conducting research in which race and ethnicity are collapsed together (Latina/o and Black subjects collapsed together), sexualities are collapsed together (homosexual, heterosexual and transsexual identities collapsed together), social class collapsed together, and ability backgrounds collapsed together (disabled Black men versus abled Black men).

Researchers should not hesitate to analyze complex individual identities. Differences in individual experiences in the sciences, for example, will perhaps lead to differences in outcomes. The reliability of research conducted with only one type of social group and then generalization of those results for other social groups should be questioned. A specific educational program that works with Black females may not work the same way for Black males. Intersection research has been popular in certain disciplines such as business, communication, and political science; however, in education there is a lack of research that examines the subidentities of their research subjects. There is a need for more intersection research as well as the need to reexamine the reliability and validity of research that has collapsed race and gender together. The concept of *reconceptualization* argues that researchers must extend the analysis of gender as a unitary category to a dynamic relational analysis of gender, race, and social class (Azzarito & Solomon, 2005). Retesting existing theory in spatial reasoning is a much needed next step. The more inclusive we are about demographics, then perhaps the more nuisances we can find with our research results. Due to this lack of intersection research in spatial reasoning studies, this chapter will first define spatial reasoning, then examine gender differences in spatial reasoning, and end with the concept of the double bind in spatial reasoning.

DEFINING SPATIAL REASONING

Spatial reasoning can be defined as (a) the transforming and relating of mental images in space and time; (b) symmetries of inherent cortical activity patterns in the visual cortex, medial parietal, and left frontal regions of the brain to compare physical and mental images; and (c) natural temporal sequences of those inherent cortical activity patterns (Grandin, Peterson, & Shaw, 1998). According to cognitive psychologists, even newborns possess a structured cortex, often very pliable at that age, in which performing spatial-temporal tasks can enhance the synchrony of neural firing activity in the cortex. Pattern recognition processes in which students have the ability to create, maintain, transform and relate complex mental images, even in the absence of external sensory input or feedback, lead to heightened cortical activity in the brain (Leng & Shaw, 1991). Students who harness spatial reasoning skills enter a virtual reality of sorts in which they can visualize underlying problems, anticipate and correct for problematic patterns that might develop, and even rotate objects and spatial planes through mental mapping.

Furthermore, spatial reasoning can be categorized as two main functions: spatial visualization and spatial orientation (Coleman & Gotch, 1998). Spatial visualization entails recognizing the relationships of a visual representation with respect to its parts and external frame of reference, such as recognizing, retaining, and recalling configurations in which movement of the figure or parts of the figure occurs. Examples of spatial visualization tasks include acknowledging the difference between various types of orbitals in chemistry as well as reading two-dimensional architectural drawings. However, spatial orientation is the ability to remain clear about changing orientations where visual stimuli are present, such as imagining simple and rigid transformations of whole objects. Spatial orientation, which focuses on the rotation of objects, is considered to be more fundamental to enhancing spatial ability because it goes beyond visualization and examines mathematical movements of objects across time and space. The object assembly task, for example, improves spatial reasoning skills greatly because it requires students to form a mental image of an object and then orient tangible objects to reproduce ideally that very same mental image.

Also, spatial reasoning showed much stronger relationships with quantitative reasoning than with verbal reasoning; in fact, spatial reasoning and verbal reasoning are only weakly correlated (Robinson, Abbott, Berninger, & Busse, 1996). Verbal reasoning is defined as drawing on a form of reasoning using declarative knowledge composed of facts and concepts. On the other hand, quantitative reasoning is defined as drawing on a form of reasoning using the manipulation of numerical quantities, while spatial reasoning can be defined as drawing on a form of reasoning using visual or spatial relations, motions, distances, or a combination of these (Ayala, Shavelson, Yin, & Schiltz, 2002).

If students are given a globe of the Earth within a cardboard box and a flashlight, and are asked to explain how the amount of sunlight changes throughout the day as well as throughout the year, they need to understand the sun's position in relation to the Earth, the Earth's rotation, and the relationship between the position of the sun and shadows cast on Earth. These forms of content knowledge rely heavily on spatial reasoning, in particular spatial orientation. Spatial reasoning skills are enacted by even preschool children through such classroom activities as playing musical instruments, arranging pieces of a puzzle, assembling objects, and navigation through physical space. However, they need to be enacted upon early in the child's life to have long-lasting effects later in her academic career, thus enhancing the hardware for spatial reasoning in the brain and the development of spatiotemporal maps of cerebral activity (Bower, 1994).

THE GENDER GAP IN SPATIAL REASONING

The existence of sex differences in spatial abilities is a well-established fact in the field of psychology, even though it remains fairly controversial elsewhere (Voyer, 1997). Several factors have been proposed as possible causes for differences in spatial performance: differential experiences and socialization, sex-role identification, sex hormones and rate of maturation, choice of strategy, cerebral lateralization, genetic complement, and the recessive trait on the Y-chromosome. Other factors proposed are the inferior parietal lobe, which is generally larger in male brains and that is involved in spatial and mathematical reasoning; and the corpus callosum, which carries communications between the two brain hemispheres, is generally larger in women's brains and is involved in verbal reasoning, etc. New positron emission tomography (PET) and MRI technologies have created images showing a structural difference between the male and female brain and these differences can affect how we learn, especially the argument that women are wired for language and men are wired for spatial reasoning.

Due to the fact that many cortical areas in the female brain are used for verbal-emotive functioning, "the female brain does not activate as many cortical areas as the male's does for abstract and physical-spatial functions, such as watching and manipulating objects that move through physical space and understanding abstract mechanical concepts" (Gurian & Stevens, 2004, p. 57).

Wallentin (2009) performed an extensive review of gender differences in language among children and concluded that

> a small but consistent female advantage is found in early language development. But this seems to disappear during childhood. In adults, sex differences in verbal abilities and in brain structure and function related to language processing are not readily identified. If they exist, they are not easily picked up with the research methods used today. (p. 181)

Gender disparities in spatial reasoning, however, remain consistent throughout the lives of men and women, especially in such spatial tasks as navigations strategies and geographical orientation (Iachini, Sergi, Ruggiero & Gnisci, 2005). Often, the dichotomy between nature and nurture, and biology and psychology comes back to the forefront regarding sex differences in spatial performance.

Furthermore, the gender gap is closing much faster in mathematics than in science, especially in specific subject areas such as chemistry and physics—both of which require high degrees of spatial reasoning (Coleman & Gotch, 1998). The MRT (mental rotation test) has been used for several decades to assess sex differences in spatial ability: a three-dimensional mental rotation test containing 20 paper-and-pencil items in which subjects are required to indict which of the rotated figures below match the original target object. In the MRT test, students are presented with a picture of an object; the correct choices are identical to the chosen object, but in rotated positions. Thus, to complete the task, the student must hold a picture of a complex shape in his or her mind and mentally rotate it in three-dimensional space (Casey, Nuttall, & Pezaris, 2001). According to Voyer (1997), females tend to perform tasks slowly and carefully in relation to the males, and tend to complete fewer items on the timed MRT assessment. However, it has been argued that the sex differences in the MRT are due to differences in the levels of spatial ability as opposed to the speed of processing. Even when females are given unlimited time, they never reach the level of accuracy on the MRT as the males. The difficulties female students have mentally rotating complex three-dimensional objects derives largely from their failure to keep track of the details of the object being rotated and not from fundamental difficulties with the rotation itself. One task that most female students had difficulty with involved rotating a thin box around an axis formed by a dowel that skewered the box. When the box was not at right angles to the dowel, the female students struggled in their attempt to rotate mentally the box around the dowel (Voyer, 1997).

From the earliest age it can be measured, boys show better ability at spatial tasks (i.e., imagining a 3-D object laid out flat), though girls have a better memory for placement of objects. For example, boys 3 to 5 years old were faster at copying 3-D models of Lego pieces than girls (McGuinness, 1993). Moreover, even in gifted classrooms male students were more advanced in spatial reasoning tasks than female students of comparable age and IQ. Even though male students performed better on spatial-reasoning tasks, they did not necessarily have an overall superiority; in other words, the female students were not that far behind regarding measured performance of such spatial assessments.

The age at which males begin to exhibit higher spatial reasoning has been contested as well. Some studies found spatial ability differences in normally developing males and females 9 to 13 years of age, whereas other studies have found the differences emerging after puberty (Robinson, Abbott, Berninger, & Busse, 1996). In terms of socialization, by 3 to 6 years of age, children begin to play more exclusively with same-sex peers, and research shows that boys begin to play very differently from girls; for example, boys tend to focus on forms of play that challenge spatial boundaries and explore thresholds (Honig, 2006). Often, the toys that boys play with, such as fast-moving cars and magnetic trains, help them understand how to maneuver and navigate through bounded space; unlike girl toys such as dolls and tea sets that help them to develop interpersonal and intrapersonal social skills, as well as richer language interchanges through pretend play. Studies have also shown that girls tend to have fewer out-of-school spatial experiences than boys, such as roaming neighborhood streets on their bikes, climbing trees and playing organized tag (Frick, Daum, Wilson, & Wilkening, 2009).

Researchers have also proposed that male students excel on tasks that require manipulation of information using working memory, such as when mentally rotating objects; while female students excel in tasks that require rapid access to and retrieval of information in long-term memory, such as during verbal reasoning (Casey, Nuttall, & Pezaris, 2001). Young girls generally articulate words earlier and have better vocabularies than boys at an early age. Girls are seemingly better at controlling dynamics and language. Also, the quality and length of their utterances is better, fewer pauses in their speech, and improved word articulation. Females tend to have higher reading scores and are more able to associate English letters and language sounds, which may have to do with the connection between the left and right hemispheres. Today, boys are at greater risk for poor verbal skills, whereas girls are at a greater risk for poor spatial skills, leading to the literacy gap between boys and girls with boys lagging behind their female peers in writing and reading assessments (Moir & Jessel, 1989; Rich, 2000). However, a verbal-skills curriculum is emphasized at greater length in the elementary school curriculum in comparison to a spatial-skills curriculum, thus putting girls at a greater disadvantage from the beginning in math and science.

Furthermore, in the first grade, girls were found to use concrete manipulatives to calculate solutions to basic math and science problems, whereas boys used the mental representation of numbers and retrieval strategies for solving math and science problems (Casey, Nuttall, & Pezaris, 2001). In turn, girls were found to use concrete solution strategies like modeling and counting, while boys tended to use more abstract solution strategies that not only reflected conceptual understanding, but also helped them extend their understandings. Next, when students are presented with a complex task that can be solved through multiple different strategies, males and females sometimes differed in the strategy that they preferred. For example, if a task can only be solved by representing the geometry of the layout, we do not see a difference between males and females.

However, if the task can be accomplished either by representing geometry or by representing individual landmarks, girls tend to rely on the landmarks, and boys on the geometry. When you compare the shapes of two objects of different orientations, there are two strategies. Students can attempt a holistic rotation of one of the objects into registration with the other, or they can do point-by-point feature comparisons of the two objects. Male students are more likely to do the first; female students are more likely to do the second. Furthermore, many math and science problems require a solution by drawing a diagram using spatial reasoning or by laying out a step-by-step algorithmic solution that is linear, logical, and deductive. Boys as a group depend often on spatial strategies when solving mental rotation tasks, while girls as a group tend to use verbal, analytical strategies for solving such tasks (Casey, Nuttall, & Pezaris, 2001).

Finally, the mathematical word problems on the SAT-M very often allow multiple solutions. Both item analysis and studies of high school students engaged in the act of solving such problems suggest that when students have the choice of solving a problem by plugging in a formula or by doing

Venn diagram-like spatial reasoning, girls tend to do the first and boys tend to do the second. Thus, girls are at a disadvantage when test items cannot be solved by previously memorized algorithms (Spelke, 2005).

Overall, boys more frequently than girls show early signs of interest and ability with numbers and quantitative relationships. Moreover, parents become sensitive to these differences in cues from boys versus girls and react differently toward boys and girls, with the common occurrence of boys being pushed toward math and science by their parents early on (Robinson, Abbott, Berninger, & Busse, 1996).

Children's expectancies about their success in math and science, which can be measured through self-confidence and anxiety measures that are often based on parental beliefs, start diverging along gender lines beginning in the first grade as well. One study found that female students had lowered self-confidence about their capabilities in math and science when compared with male students who carried their higher degrees of self-confidence throughout their schooling, regardless if the female students had higher grades in math and science. In another study using the Trends in International Mathematics and Science Study (TIMSS) data from multiple countries, researchers found that spatial skill measures, in comparison to self-confidence measures, accounted for about twice the indirect mediational effect between gender differences in mathematics performance among high school students. Thus, for female students, strengthening spatial reasoning is going to give them an advantage, regardless of self-confidence in mathematics (Casey, Nuttall, & Pezaris, 2001).

Another form of sex differences is spatial anxiety. In studies examining navigation skills between men and women, a greater degree of spatial anxiety was reported by women (Hund & Minarik, 2006). Lawton and Kallai (2002) examined individual differences in way-finding strategies and spatial anxiety. They asked participants to report which strategy they preferred when navigating through the environment: orientation strategies maintaining a sense of one's own position in relation to a given a point (e.g., "I know which direction I am going because I keep moving north.") or route strategies using a particular route to get from place to place (e.g., "I ask for directions telling me whether to turn right or left at particular landmarks."). Men reported using orientation strategies more than did women, whereas women reported using route strategies more than did men. Participants also completed measures of spatial anxiety and general anxiety through a self-reported questionnaire, which was then correlated with their performance on the navigation task itself. The spatial anxiety scale measured the extent to which participants felt anxious when following directions and navigating in unfamiliar environments. Women reported more spatial anxiety than did men on the questionnaires.

Furthermore, women who followed directions containing Euclidean descriptors navigated more slowly than did women and men who followed directions containing landmark descriptors. These findings suggest that there is a correlation between women's spatial anxiety and their performance on spatial navigation tasks; however, it is not a causal relationship per se (Hund & Minarik, 2006). In an afterschool program using underwater robotics, for example, being able to master spatial navigation tasks is essential and the degree to which a young woman's spatial anxiety affects her interest and pursuit of engineering programs needs to be examined.

Wraga, Helt, Jacobs and Sullivan (2007) conducted an important study right after Larry Summers' proclaimed that women do not have the intrinsic aptitude for math and science. Their team of researchers used functional magnetic imaging to examine the neural structure underlying shifts in women's performance of a spatial reasoning task induced by positive and negative stereotypes. Three groups of participants performed a task involving imagined rotations of the self. Prior to scanning, the positive stereotype group was exposed to a false but plausible stereotype of women's superior perspective-taking abilities; the negative stereotype group was exposed to the pervasive stereotype that men outperform women on spatial tasks; and the control group received neutral information. The significantly poorer performance they found in the negative stereotype group corresponded to increased activation in brain regions associated with increased emotional load. In contrast, the significantly improved performance they found in the positive stereotype group was associated with increased activation in visual processing areas, and to a lesser degree, complex working memory processes. These findings suggest that stereotype messages affect the brain selectively, with positive messages producing relatively more efficient neural strategies than negative messages.

SPATIAL REASONING, WOMEN OF COLOR AND THE DOUBLE BIND

Since gender alone explains only a portion of individual variation in spatial ability (Caplan & Caplan, 1994), identifying other developmental factors that promote spatial ability is an important research goal (Halpern et al., 2007; Hyde & Lindberg, 2007). Hyde (2005) noted that within-gender variation across race and ethnicity is larger than between-gender differences in the sciences. Neisser et al. (1996) argued that understanding the source of such within-gender differences is critical, and that such questions are socially, as well as scientifically, important. For many women of color, the interest and motivation for math and science gets cut off much earlier than their White male and White female peers who maintain interest and motivation up through junior high (Berryman, 1983). For Latina American students, their self-efficacy of math and science drops the lowest as they move into secondary education, which is not the case for African American female students who have the highest degrees of self-efficacy (Leslie, McClure & Oaxaca, 1998; MacCorquodale, 1988). Asian American females tend to have higher degrees of self-efficacy within mathematics in comparison to their White female peers due to their mother's emphasis on effort as opposed to their perception of mathematical ability (Tsang & Yip, 2007).

Regarding overall achievement in math and science, Asian American females perform at a higher level than their Native American, African American and Latina American peers. Muller, Stage, and Kinzie (2001) found that socioeconomic status, prior grades, parental beliefs about math and science, and internal locus of control were significant positive predictors of Asian American girls' 8th-grade science achievement. Kim, Rendon, and Valadez (1998) found differences in 10th-grade math performance and educational aspirations among six Asian American ethnic groups: South Asians (Indian and Pakistani) were more likely to have the highest scores and Southeast Asians (Vietnamese, Laotian, Cambodian, and Thai) were more likely to have the lowest scores of the two outcomes. An interaction effect between gender and race and large subgroup variance indicated a need for separate analyses by subgroup to assess within-group differences. Although race and ethnicity differences are greater among the female students than male students, women of color are nonetheless caught in that double bind of both race and gender differences—a multithreat phenomenon.

Social-psychological research suggests that cultural stereotypes can affect the educational attainment, learning, and retention of women of color in math and science and racial minorities more generally. Individuals that belong to these groups may become weary of being seen through the lens of negative stereotypes and suffer from what researchers call stereotype threat. Social-psychological research suggests that cultural stereotypes can affect the educational attainment, learning, and retention of women in math and science, and of racial minorities more generally. Individuals that belong to these groups may become weary of being seen through the lens of negative stereotypes and suffer from what researchers call *stereotype threat* (Inzlicht & Mangels, 2007). Within this duality of race and gender, there is also the variable of socioeconomic status and the trifecta of race, gender, and class and its effects on women of color in STEM careers. Native American, African American, and Latina American female students are overrepresented in terms of lower levels of parental education and incomes in comparison to their Asian American counterparts (MacCorquodale, 1988).

Beth Casey and colleagues at Boston College (2001) found that the roles of family socioeconomics and home learning experiences had a greater impact on 1st-grade girls' spatial and mathematical skills than the category of race and ethnicity. For both arithmetic and spatial skills, the mothers' spatial skills and spatial reasoning were correlated with race. Casey's findings demonstrate that socioeconomic context impacts not only students' levels of performance, but also their capacity to apply basic cognitive skills, like spatial reasoning, to their academic performance (2001). Furthermore, in households with low educational levels, men are exposed to significantly richer spatially-enriched environments than women who often remain rooted at home where they care for their children and do the cooking and cleaning. Ostrosky, Ardila and Rosselli (1999) found that Latino men participated in diverse activities throughout the day that required moving around the city spatially, handling money, interacting with a variety of people, and receiving a constant flow of information on many social and political events, unlike the Latina women who were at home. The intersecting analysis of race, gender and class seems paramount in developing a better understanding of which social environments lead to heightened spatial intelligence in young women of color.

At the same time, there has not been much research examining the spatial reasoning of women of color in relation to their same-race male peers (Espinosa, 2011). Although they generally outperform men of the same racial backgrounds, underrepresented women of color still lag behind their same-race male peers in achieving bachelor's degrees in physics, computer science, and engineering—disciplines requiring a great amount of spatial reasoning (National Science Foundation, 2007). Asian American women, despite being categorized as a model minority, earned less than 10% of all physical science degrees and only 6% of engineering degrees granted to women (National Science Foundation, 2007; Wu & Jing, 2011). The double bind for women of color was highlighted in a seminal study in which Asian American women's math performance decreased when their gender identity was salient, but improved when their Asian identity was salient (Shih, Pittinsky, & Ambady, 1999). In contrast, Asian American women performed better on a verbal test when their gender identity, not Asian identity, was made salient (Shih, Pittinsky, & Trahan, 2006). Similarly, female participants primed with the achievement-oriented identity of being a private college student performed better on a mental rotation task as compared to the performance of participants who were primed to think about their gender or a task-irrelevant identity (McGlone & Aronson, 2006). Thus, Asian American women assimilated to self-relevant stereotypes, both positive and negative, when taking spatial reasoning assessments.

Research studies also point out the structural and systemic challenges that women of color face, which includes: (a) the lack of opportunities to acquire the spatial reasoning skills needed for STEM due to higher levels of poverty found in their elementary schools; (b) the overrepresentation of women of color in high schools and colleges without strong math and science programs; (c) the lack of strong mentors and coaches who can provide the scaffolding needed for the STEM pipeline; and (d) the need for colleges and universities to focus on retention rates of women of color in STEM pathways (Oakes, 1990). Hoffman, Gneezy and List (2011) found that the cultural world of the female student plays a key role in spatial reasoning. They used a large-scale incentivized experiment with nearly 1,300 participants to show that the gender gap in spatial abilities, measured by time to solve a puzzle, disappears when we move from a patrilineal society to an adjoining matrilineal society. The role of culture and its effects on women of color in the sciences is an anthropological and sociological question: what kinds of cultural worlds help promote women of color in the sciences as well as hone in on their much needed spatial skills.

Sex differences in spatial reasoning have also been documented by researchers in previous decades who examined populations outside of the United States. One can conclude that there is a universality when it comes to the edge that men have in spatial reasoning skills—whether it is in Japan (Mann, Sasanuma, Sakuma, &Masaki, 1990; Silverman, Phillips, & Silverman, 1996), in Scotland (Berry, 1966; Jahoda, 1980), in Ghana (Jahoda, 1980), in Sierra Leone (Berry, 1966), or in India, South Africa, and Australia (Porteus, 1965).

A more recent study conducted by Silverman, Choi, and Peters (2007) assessed the universality of both male and female spatial specializations across multiple countries and ethnic groups, using an interactive Internet study hosted by the BBC, comprising more than 250,000 participants in 226 countries across the world. The data from 40 countries were culled from 128,360 males and 116,533 females. Participants were also divided into self-identified ethnic groups based on categories listed in the demographic questionnaire for the BBC survey: Black/British, Black/other, Chinese, other Asian (including East Indian), Middle Eastern, mixed and White.

Silverman, Choi, and Peters' (2007) prediction that men would score significantly higher than women on a test of three-dimensional mental rotations in all seven ethnic groups and 40 countries proved true. Close to their prediction, women scored significantly higher than men on a test of object location memory in all seven ethnic groups, and 35 of the 40 countries in which they had to recall objects from a screen viewed for 60 seconds through a point and click task—therefore measuring memory and perception more so than spatial reasoning. Significant main effects favoring females in the object recall task were found for each of the seven ethnic groups and 35 of the 40 countries. This study unequivocally supported the universality of the male advantage in three dimensional mental rotation tasks across different cultures. The test of correlation between effect sizes for male and female biased tests provided no support for the notion that society-based, sex-role stereotyping practices are relevant to sex-related spatial differences as measured by these assessments. Nor did the correlations for both tests' effect sizes replicate prior findings of a socioeconomic factor

factor. None of this, however, implies the absence of an environmental role in the ontogeny of spatial sex differences across different cultures.

Gaulin and Hoffman (1988) pointed out a definitive environmental variable in the orientation-type spatial performance between males and females. They stated that larger home ranges for males (the area within which the individual becomes familiar and regularly visits), which begin in the toddler age, can create an advantage for males when it comes to spatial reasoning. The argument they pose is that when boys first become mobile, regardless of race and ethnicity, they are innately programmed to explore a wider area of space outside their immediate environments. This argument is grounded in the evolutionary theory that males are innately wired to hunt across a large spatial terrain often in silence, while our ancient female ancestors were wired to gather nuts, tubers, and berries in concentrated spatial areas with a need to vocalize across the terrain. Therefore, males may be innately programmed to explore larger areas than females from an early point in ontogeny, which may represent a critical period in which sex differences in spatial strategies develop in response to the differential requirements for navigating larger versus smaller spaces. The prevailing adaptation hypothesis states that the superior performance of human males over females on spatial navigation tasks is an evolutionary adaptation related to the specific cognitive demands associated with hunting or navigating a larger home range (Jones, Braithewaite, & Healy, 2003).

Several cross-cultural comparisons of sexual dimorphism in spatial ability have been conducted in which the morphological, physiological, and behavioral differences between male and females have been highlighted. Mann et al. (1990) compared sexual dimorphism in mental rotation performance tests using high school students in the United States and Japan. Both nations showed a similar male performance advantage. Silverman et al. (1996) produced a similar result comparing Japanese and Canadian subjects. Owen and Lynn (1993) reported male advantage in spatial performance among White, Black, and Indian subjects in South Africa, congruent with studies based in industrial nations.

Silverman et al. (2007) found the familiar male spatial ability advantages in mental rotation performance across seven ethnic groups and 40 countries, which is perhaps the most expansive such cross-cultural comparison to date (Murphy, Wynne, O'Rourke, Commins, & Roche, 2009). The uniformity of results across cultures, together with the data showing that testosterone enhances spatial ability, argues against the idea that culture plays a major role in the observed sexual dimorphism in spatial ability; instead, it argues for innate differences.

One can, therefore, argue that women of color have a disadvantage in the sense that they might be raised in an environment with limited spatial mobility due to the confines of their physical and social community. Women of color in the United States are more likely to be raised in communities with higher degrees of violence and crime that then leads to a limited home range size and therefore a male bias for spatial abilities with minority males more likely to venture outside of the house than minority females (Gorman-Smith & Tolan, 1998). Three-quarters of African American children have been exposed to neighborhood violence in their lifetimes (Aizer, 2008). Spatial anxiety might increase for young minority girls who are afraid of leaving their homes, even remaining confined to a safe place in the back of the home and not near front windows (Bowean, Gorner, & Sege, 2014).

Most existing research has concluded that exposure to violence leads to restricted emotional development, aggressive behavior, and poor school outcomes. However, this literature fails to account for the fact that children exposed to neighborhood violence are highly disadvantaged in other ways: they are more likely to have limited home range size and perhaps lower degrees of spatial reasoning. The long-term effects of living in a violent community with a smaller house range size have not been explored and need further research.

ADDRESSING THE GENDER GAP
THROUGH CURRICULAR INTERVENTIONS

Can curricular interventions improve spatial reasoning in female students and give them leverage in science achievement? Several educational programs have been designed specifically to teach visual-spatial skills to girls so their performance would be equivalent to boys, such as all-girl high school science classes, training in imagery and mental rotation skills, computer learning opportunities, or self-discovery training in visual-spatial reasoning for co-ed classes. Outcome evaluations of such programs often show improvement in girls' performance on visual-spatial tasks so that gender differences are reduced or eliminated on some tasks. One can argue that women's visual-spatial skill levels are malleable with changes in educational methods. Training studies that involve short-term interventions on specific spatial tasks have been found to improve spatial skills with equal benefits for boys and girls (Casey, Nuttall, & Pezaris, 2001).

The Michigan Tech Project received funding from NSF (National Science Foundation) in 1993 to develop a course and materials for improving spatial skills. Female students were around 17% of the group tested on a spatial-visualization test, and 43% failed the pretest during the orientation to their engineering program. Course topics included 2-D to 3-D object transformations, 3-D coordinate systems, object translations, object scaling, object rotations, object reflections, cross-sections of solids, and surfaces and solids of revolution. Handheld models were used wherever possible, but the computer lab also utilized modeling software. By developing and implementing a course to improve spatial skills, the university positively impacted the performance and retention of engineering students, particularly women of color, and gains were statistically significant (Sorby, 2007). Furthermore, even at the high school level, the integration of concrete and computer models might positively affect cognitive performance in spatial reasoning (Coleman & Gotch, 1998). When teaching molecular geometry and hybridization, for example, measuring bond lengths and bond angles using hands-on, ball-and-stick models, as well as computer simulation models, can be the kind of curricular exposure female students in secondary settings need to enhance their science background when entering rigorous science college programs.

In elementary education settings, Piagetian-type tasks that focus on spatial visualization and that developed mental imaging abilities can become successful forms of curricular intervention. According to Piaget, spatial competence is attained when children gain the ability to use a Euclidean system of reference to organize spatial experience. For example, teachers can ask students to predict the location of water surfaces in tilted bottles that are half-filled. The students draw a line representing the water level in the bottle of water tilted at various angles such as 0, 45, 90, 135, and 225 degrees—thus generating an image of a half-filled bottle of water and mentally rotating it to different orientations (Casey, Nuttall, & Pezaris, 2001). A student's assessment on this task would be the proportion of water lines within 5 degrees of the exact horizontal line. Another lesson activity includes giving students mechanical devices such as gears, levers, wheels, and pulleys, and asking them to visualize on paper the effect of rotating or manipulating one part of the device and its relation to another part of the device.

Furthermore, in terms of pedagogy, both male and female students need to be encouraged to apply spatial strategies when solving problems in math and science, especially before the high school level when it might be too late. Teachers need to provide in-class modeling of spatial as well as analytical solutions to the same problems and to require both types of problem-solutions for homework assignments ranging from word problems to calculus (Casey, Nuttall, & Pezaris, 2001). If students are using manipulatives to solve a problem, such as base-ten blocks, then they should also be required to represent their solution on paper, as well to not bypass this pictorial level, which allows them to visualize solutions using imagery as well as helping them internalize their thinking. Measurement problems in mathematics may require spatial solutions; however, problems with known algorithms may not.

An arts curriculum focusing on music and fine arts can also enhance spatial reasoning. The reading of music by sight, for example, involves the audiation of tonal and rhythmic patterns, comprehension of a graphic notation system with both spatial and textual qualities, and highly coordinated kinesthetic action in performance. Neuroscientists have investigated brain activity during music sight-reading using PET and MRI (magnetic resonance imaging) technology. They found areas of the brain for processing spatial information were activated—parallel but distinct from verbal reasoning areas of the brain—due to the need for identifying the spatial location of notes (Gromko, 2004). Neural networks associated with spatial reasoning can also be activated by the reading of languages; however, recent research has found that learning to read 2,500 pictorial symbols in Chinese has yielded a 5-point advantage on IQ tests, compared with scores of Westerners whose languages are based on alphabets (Bower, 2005). Visual and spatial tasks are required to read and write Chinese, for example, and thus Chinese students in this particular study were ranked as highly efficient visualizers; however, further research is still required.

REFERENCES

Ayala, C., Shavelson, R., Yin, Y., & Schultz, S. (2002). Reasoning dimensions underlying science achievement: The case of performance assessment. *Educational Assessment, 8*(2), 101–121.

Azzarito, L. & Solomon, M. (2005). A reconceptualization of physical education: The intersection of gender/race/social class. *Sports, Education and Society, 10*(1), 25–47.

Beede, D., Julian, T., Langdon, D., McKittrick, G., Khan, B., & Doms, M., (2011). Women in STEM: A gender gap in innovation. *U.S. Department of Commerce, Economics and Statistics Administration.* Retrieved from http://www.esa.doc.gov/sites/default/files/womeninstemagaptoinnovation8311.pdf

Berger, J.B., & Lyon, S.C. (2005). Past to present: A historical look at retention. In A. Seidman (Ed.), *College student retention. formula for student success* (pp. 1–29). Stanford, CN: Praeger.

Berry, J. W. (1966). Temme and Eskimo perceptual skills. *International Journal of Psychology, 1*, 207–229.

Berryman, S. (1983). *Who will do science?* Washington, DC: The Rockefeller Foundation.

Bowean, L., Gorner, J., & Sege, A. (2014, April 21). Shootings of 5 kids rattle neighborhood: 'I don't want to get shot'. *Chicago Tribune*, A1.

Bower, B. (1994). Tuning up young brains. *Science News, 146*(9), 146.

Bower, B. (2005). Reading system may boost Chinese scores. *Science News, 16*(7), 99.

Caplan, P. J., & Caplan, J. B. (1994). *Thinking critically about research on sex and gender.* New York, NY: Harper Collins.

Casey, B., Nuttall, R., & Pezaris, E. (2001). Spatial-mechanical reasoning skills versus mathematics self-confidence as mediators of gender differences on mathematics subtests using cross-national gender-based items. *Journal for Research in Mathematics Education, 32*(1), 28–57.

Coleman, S., & Gotch, A. (1998). Spatial perception skills of chemistry students. *Journal of Chemical Education, 75*(1), 206–209.

Espinosa, L. L. (2011). Pipelines and pathways: Women of color in undergraduate STEM majors and the college experiences that contribute to persistence. *Harvard Educational Review, 81*(2), 209–240.

Frick, A., Daum, M. M., Wilson, M., & Wilkening, F. (2009). Effects of action on children's and adults' mental imagery. *Journal of Experimental Child Psychology, 104*, 34–51.

Gaulin, S. J., & Hoffman, H. A. (1988). Evolution and development of sex differences in spatial ability. In L. Betzig, M. B. Mulder, & P. Turke (Eds.), *Human reproductive behavior: A Darwinian perspective* (pp. 129–152). Cambridge, MA: Cambridge University Press.

Grandin, T., Peterson, M., & Shaw, G. (1998). Spatial-temporal versus language-analytic reasoning: The role of music training. *Arts Education Policy Review, 99*(1), 11–14.

Gorman-Smith, D., & Tolan, P. (1998). The role of exposure to community violence and developmental problems among inner-city youth. *Development and Psychopathology, 10*, 101.

Gromko, J. (2004). Predictors of music sight-reading ability in high school wind players. *Journal of Research in Music Education, 52*(1), 6–15.

Gurian, M., & Stevens, K. (2004). With boys and girls in mind. *Educational Leadership, 62*(3), 21–26.

Halpern, D. F., Beninger, A. S., & Straight, C. A. (2011). Sex differences in intelligence. In R. J. Sternberg & S. B. Kaufman (Eds.), *The Cambridge handbook of intelligence* (pp. 253–272). Cambridge, MA: Cambridge University Press.

Hoffman, M., Gneezy, U., & List, J. (2011). Nurture affects gender differences in spatial abilities. *Proceedings of the National Academy of Sciences of the United States of America, 108*(36), 14786–14788.

Honig, A. (2006). What infants, toddlers, and preschoolers learn from play. *Montessori Life, 18*(1), 16–21.

Hund, A., & Minarek, J. (2006). Getting from here to there: Spatial anxiety, wayfinding strategies, direction type, and wayfinding efficiency. *Spatial Cognition and Computation, 6*(3), 179–201.

Hyde, J. S. (2005). The gender similarities hypothesis. *American Psychologist, 60*, 581–592.

Hyde, J. S., & Lindberg, S. M. (2007). Facts and assumptions about the nature of gender differences and the implications for gender equity. In S. S. Klein (Ed.), *Handbook for achieving gender equity through education* (2nd ed., pp. 19–32). Mahwah, NJ: Erlbaum.

Iachini, T., Sergi, I., Ruggiero, G., & Gnisci, A. (2005). Gender differences in object location memory in a real three-dimensional environment. *Brain and Cognition, 59*, 52–59.

Inzlicht, M. & Mangels, J. (2007). An integrative approach to understanding how cultural stereotypes affect performance, learning and retention. *Psychophysiology, 1*(44), S13–S14.

Jackson, C., Wilhelm, J. A., Lamar, M., & Cole, M. (2015). Gender and racial differences: Development of sixth-grade students' geometric spatial visualization within an Earth/space unit. *School Science & Mathematics, 115*(7), 330–343.

Jahoda, G. (1980). Sex and ethnic differences on a spatial-perceptual task: Some hypotheses tested. *British Journal of Psychology, 71,* 425–431.

Jones, C., Braithwaite, V., & Healy, S. D. (2003). The evolution of sex differences in spatial ability. *Behavioral Neuroscience, 117*(3), 403–411.

Kim, H., Rendon, L. I., & Valadez, J. (1998). Student characteristics, school characteristics, and educational aspirations of six Asian American ethnic groups. *Journal of Multicultural Counseling & Development, 26,* 166–176.

Kerns, K., & Berenbaum, S. (1991). Sex differences in spatial ability in children. *Behavior Genetics, 21,* 383–396.

Lawton, C., & Kallai, J. (2002). Gender differences in wayfinding strategies and anxiety about wayfinding: A cross-cultural comparison. *Sex Roles, 47,* 389–401.

Leng, X., & Shaw, G. L. (1991), Toward a neural theory of higher brain function using music as a window, *Concepts in Neuroscience, 2,* 229–258.

Leslie, L. L., McClure, G. T., & Oaxaca, R. L. (1998). Women and minorities in science and engineering—A life sequence analysis. *Journal of Higher Education, 69*(3), 239–276.

Livingston, R. W., Rosette, A. S., & Washington, E. F. (2012). Can an agentic Black woman get ahead? The impact of race and interpersonal dominance on perceptions of female leaders. *Psychological Science, 23,*354–358.

MacCorquodale, P. (1988). Mexican American women and mathematics: Participation, aspirations, and achievement. In R.R. Cocking & J.P. Mestre (Eds.), *Linguistic and cultural influences on learning mathematics* (pp. 137–160). Hillsdale, NJ: Erlbaum.

Mann, V. A., Sasanuma, S., Sakuma, N., & Masaki, S. (1990). Sex differences in cognitive abilities: A cross-cultural perspective. *Neuropsychologia, 28,* 1063–1077.

McGlone, M. S., & Aronson, J. (2006). Stereotype threat, identity salience, and spatial reasoning. *Journal of Applied Developmental Psychology, 27,* 486–493.

McGuinness, D. (1993). Gender differences in cognitive style: Implications for mathematics performance and achievement. In L. A. Penner, G. M. Batsche, H. M. Knoff & D. L. Nelson (Eds.), *The challenge in mathematics and science education: Psychology's response* (pp. 251–274). Washington, DC: American Psychological Association.

Moir, A., & Jessel, D. (1989). *Brain sex: The real difference between men and women.* New York, NY: Dell.

Muller, P. A., Stage, F. K., & Kinzie, J. (2001). Science achievement growth trajectories: Understanding factors related to gender and racial-ethnic differences in precollege science achievement. *American Educational Research Journal, 38,* 981–1012.

Murphy, J. S., Wynne, C. E., O'Rourke, E. M., Commins, S., & Roche, R. A. P., (2009). High-resolution ERP mapping of cortical activation related to implicit object location. *Memory, 82,* 234–245.

National Science Foundation. (2007). *Women, minorities and persons with disabilities in science and engineering.* Retrieved from http://www.nsf.gov/statistics/wmpd

Neisser, U. C., Boodoo, G., Bouchard, T. J., Jr., Boykin, A. W., Brody, N., & Ceci, S. J. (1996). Intelligence: Knowns and unknowns. *American Psychologist, 51,* 77–101.

Oakes, J. 1990. *Lost talent: The underparticipation of women, minorities, and disabled persons in science.* Santa Monica, CA: Rand.

Ostrosky, F., Ardila, A., & Rosselli, M. (1999). NEUROPSI: A brief neuropsychological test battery in Spanish. *Journal of the International Neuropsychological Society, 5*, 413–433.

Owen K, & Lynn R. (1993). Sex differences in primary cognitive abilities among Blacks, Indians, and Whites in South Africa. *Journal of Biosocial Science, 25*, 557–560.

Pinker, S. (2005). The science of gender and science. *Edge: The third culture* [Online serial]. Retrieved from https://www.edge.org/event/the-science-of-gender-and-science-pinker-vs-spelke-a-debate

Porteus, S. D. (1965). *Porteus maze test: Fifty years' application.* Palo Alto, CA: Pacific Books.

Rahman, Q., & Wilson, G. D. (2003). Large sexual-orientation-related differences in performance on mental rotation and judgment of line orientation tasks. *Neuropsychology, 17*(1), 25–31.

Rich, B. (2000). *The Dana brain daybook.* New York, NY: Charles A. Dana Foundation.

Robinson, N., Abbott, R., Berninger, V., & Busse, J. (1996). The structure of abilities in math-precocious young children: Gender similarities and differences. *Journal of Educational Psychology, 88*(2), 341–352.

Shih, M., Pittinsky, T., & Ambady, N. (1999). Stereotype susceptibility: Identity salience and shifts in quantitative performance. *Psychological Science, 10*(1), 80–83.

Shih, M., Pittinsky, T. L., & Trahan, A. (2006). Domain specific effects of stereotypes on performance. *Self and Identity, 5*, 1–14.

Silverman, I. Choi, J., & Peters, M. (2007). The hunter-gatherer theory of sex differences in spatial abilities: Data from 40 countries. *Archives of Sexual Behavior, 36*, 261–268.

Silverman, I., Phillips, K., & Silverman, L. K. (1996). Homogeneity of effect sizes for sex across spatial tests and cultures: Implications for hormonal theories. *Brain and Cognition, 31*, 90–94.

Sorby, S. A. (2007). Developing 3-D spatial skills for engineering students. *Australasian Journal of Engineering Education, 13*(1), 1–11.

Spelke, E. (2005). Sex differences in intrinsic aptitude for mathematics and science? A critical review. *American Psychologist, 60*(9), 950–958.

Tsang, S. K. M., & Yip, F. Y. Y. (2007). Positive identity as a positive youth development construct: Conceptual bases and implications for curriculum development. In D. T. L. Shek, H. K. Ma, & J. Merrick, (Eds.), *Positive youth development: Development of a pioneering program in a Chinese context* (pp. 227–235). Tel Aviv, Israel: Freund.

Voyer, D., Voyer, S., & Bryden, M. P. (1995). Magnitude of sex differences in spatial abilities: A meta-analysis and consideration of critical variables. *Psychological Bulletin, 117*, 250–270.

Voyer, D. (1997). Scoring procedure, performance factors, and magnitude of sex differences in spatial performance. *American Journal of Psychology, 110*(2), 259–276.

Wallentin, M. (2009). Putative sex differences in verbal abilities and language cortex: A critical review. *Brain and Language, 108*, 175–183.

Wilhelm, J. (2009).Gender differences in lunar-related scientific and mathematical understandings. *International Journal of Science Education, 31,* 2105–2122.

Wraga, M., Helt, M., Jacobs, E., & Sullivan, K. (2007, March). Neural basis of stereotype-induced shifts in women's mental rotation performance. *Social, Cognitive and Affective Neuroscience, 2*(1), 12–19.

Wu, L., & Jing, W. (2011). Real numbers: Asian women in STEM careers: An invisible minority in a double bind. *Issues in Science and Technology.* Retrieved from http://issues.org/28-1/realnumbers-29/

CHAPTER 7

DIVERSITY IN STEM?

Challenges Influencing the Experiences of African American Female Engineers

Delores Rice

The intellectual capital produced by a country is linked to the innovation and advancements made in science, technology, engineering, and mathematics (STEM), as literature purports (e.g., Jackson, 2010; Science and Engineering Indicators, 2014). However, the United States trend in STEM has seen minimal peaks with deep valleys regarding students pursuing STEM careers. To address the issue, oftentimes the field examines the existing talent pool, as well as efforts to increase the pipeline for STEM occupations (National Academy of Sciences, 2007; NACME, 2008) particularly targeting underrepresented populations (Chubin, May, & Babco, 2005). Women of color, specifically African American women, are considerably underrepresented in engineering workplace organizations. The National Science Foundation reports that a mere 15% of the engineering workforce is characterized by underrepresented populations, namely Blacks, Hispanics, American Indian/Alaska Natives, and Pacific Islanders (NSF, 2010b). Women as a group represent 14.6% of the engineering workforce. However,

Women of Color in STEM, pages 157–180
Copyright © 2017 by Information Age Publishing
All rights of reproduction in any form reserved.

African American women only account for 5% of the total number of women employed in professional engineering functions (NSF, 2010c).

Though a small representative sample of women have made entry into engineering and found success in the engineering profession, little information exists on these women and the factors that contribute to their experiences in the field. Additionally, there is a scarcity of research and literature examining the experiences of African American female engineers (e.g., Rice & Alfred, 2014). Therefore, the purpose of this study was to examine the experiences of African American female engineers and, thereby, explore the personal and structural factors that served as challenges for their career progression. This study was part of a larger study that also examined systems of support for African American female engineers (Rice, 2016; Rice & Alfred, 2014).

THEORETICAL FRAMEWORK

The theoretical framework for this study was Cook, Heppner, and O'Brien's (2002) adaptation of Bronfenbrenner's (1977) ecological model. The ecological perspective, as presented by Cook, Heppner, and O'Brien (2002, 2005) is grounded in Bronfenbrenner's work on environmental systems and the dynamic interaction that occurs between the person and the environment. He classified four environmental systems—microsystem, mesosystem, exosystem, and macrosystem—as key elements in human development. Cook, Heppner, and O'Brien propose the ecological model to frame career experiences for all women, and especially for women of color, because it creates space to recognize the gender and racial/ethnic factors that impact one's career. They stress that the macro and micro system experiences, due to race/ethnicity and gender, have a direct relationship to career intentions, pursuits, and experiences. Thus, the ecological system framed this research study by focusing on the interaction between the macro (e.g., environment, stereotypical images, political systems, and the institutional structure) and micro (e.g., individual self-efficacy, values, and interests) subsystems to examine the career experiences of African American female engineers.

RELATED LITERATURE

Typically, one can find a small body of research addressing one of the three distinct identities represented by the participants in this research study, namely, research on African Americans, women, or engineers. However, research examining the intersection of these three identities is relatively nonexistent. Furthermore, framing these identities within the context of career experiences or career development continues to limit the scope of available literature.

Therefore, in examining the literature on the topic at hand, which is also contextually framed in the works addressing career experiences, research was found that addressed the career experiences of African American engineers and the career experiences of women engineers.

However, the majority of the information focused on the experiences of White female engineers. The literature on Blacks and other underrepresented racial groups is often included in the works focusing on the experiences of White women (Berry, Cox, & Main, 2014; Richie, 1992; Stanley, 2006), as if the experiences are equivalent. Yet, there are distinct differences, as highlighted in the Catalyst (2004) report and noted by other researchers (e.g., O'Brien, Blodorn, Adams, Garcia, & Hammer, 2015; Obiomon, Tickles, Wowo, & Holland-Hunt, 2007). Those differences include grappling with issues associated with stereotypical images based on race, biculturalism, and representing lower socioeconomic class status. Nonetheless, there remains a deficit in the literature with African American female engineers at the center (Ossola, 2014; Rice & Alfred, 2014). Thus, the literature presented in the next section is focused on underrepresented groups in STEM based on gender or race/ethnicity. Moreover, the two key areas for this body of work target the engineering pipeline and the engineering workplace.

Engineering Pipeline

Based on the *Gathering Storm Report*, published by the National Academy of Sciences (2007), the pipeline is negatively impacted by inadequate science and mathematics training in the K-12 education system, and minimal interest in those same disciplines in undergraduate programs and as professional careers. Reports continue to show that the number of African American students majoring in science and engineering programs remains stagnant or is declining (Science and Engineering Indicators, 2014). Blacks represent 4.57% of all undergraduate engineering degrees earned (Engineering Workforce Commission, 2010) and Black women's representation has decreased (NSF, 2010a).

The engineering pipeline, specifically getting young students interested in math and science at an early age, is a standard component in the engineering discussion or equation (NACME, 2008; Science and Engineering Indicators, 2014) and is often reduced to an input/output function. That is to say, an increase in students interested in math and science on the front end is equal to an increase in students pursuing math and science careers on the back end. Therefore, it is not surprising that the majority of the research in this area is dedicated to factors that impact career choice (Burlew, 1982; Johnson, Stone, & Phillips, 2008; Lopez & Ann-Yi, 2006; McCowan & Alston, 1998; Moore, 2006; Perna et al., 2009; Sadler, Sonnert, Hazari, & Tai, 2012). These researchers examined the correlation between self-efficacy, barriers, parental influence, cultural identity, role of the institution, and factors for specific groups, such as African American males in career choice. While the research and literature centered on developing students for the engineering pipeline is a critical component in the STEM discussion, focusing solely on the pipeline is short sighted in examining the bigger issue.

Engineering Workplace

Much of the literature reviewed on women in STEM careers is dedicated to retention issues for women in professional engineering arenas and focused primarily on challenges and barriers. The limited number of women and people of color in the field make it problematic, in some cases, when entering predominantly White male organizations. Rosser (2003) posited that a significant number of challenges for women engineers are a direct result of the limited representation of women in the engineering profession. Sukumaran and Jahan (n.d.) shared a similar perspective regarding the issues women face in the workplace. They reported:

> Very few women are attracted to engineering because of gender stereotyping and discriminatory practices in the engineering workplace. The engineering profession has always been a male-dominated one; hence, the pervasive work culture continues to be fundamentally masculine. (p. 1)

Additionally, Sukumaran and Jahan noted factors such as a lack of training, lack of mentors, lack of advancement or promotion, family planning issues, and sexual harassment contribute to the factors that negatively impact women in engineering. Similarly, in the Catalyst (2004) report the impact of "stereotypes, visibility, and scrutiny; questioning of authority and credibility; lack of 'fit' in the workplace; double outsider status; and exclusion from informal networks" was emphasized (p. 3) as barriers in the engineering workplace. Roberts and Ayre (2002) also noted the detrimental effects associated with the predominantly male environment and reported findings similar to the Catalyst (1992) report, which addressed exclusion and isolation. As a result of the challenges and barriers that women engineers face, it is not alarming that some women voluntarily leave the field, which is reported by Hill, Corbett, and St. Rose (2011). The barriers explaining why women leave the engineering field provide a direct relationship to the problem of retaining women of color in the engineering workplace.

METHODOLOGY

The purpose of this study was to examine the factors that served as challenges and barriers for the African American women in their pursuit of engineering careers. The underlying paradigm guiding the research was interpretive inquiry, which allowed an exploration of the participant's lifespan and interpretations of their lived experiences. Complementing the interpretive research design, life history examinations (Cole & Knowles, 2001) were employed to obtain rich data from the participants. By delving into the participant's life story, we were able to address factors at the microsystem and macrosystem levels that contributed to their career progression.

Participant Selection

This research study targeted Black female engineers, working in an engineering capacity, in an engineering specific organization. The participants needed to have at least 10 years of work experience as an engineer and at least one promotion, or equivalent, from an entry-level position. The aforementioned tenure and promotion conditions provided a sample with experience navigating the engineering culture.

Initial participants were identified utilizing professional engineering networks. Additional participants were found via engineering workplace organizations directly and using snowball sampling (Goodman, 1961). Due to the specific parameters of the study, this method was effective in securing participants. The participants represented chemical (4), mechanical (3), and electrical engineering (2) as their undergraduate majors. Six women attended predominantly White institutions and three women attended an HBCU for their undergraduate degrees. Additionally, four participants had earned graduate degrees. Refer to Rice and Alfred (2014) for a summary profile of each participant. Each participant was given or provided a pseudonym.

Data Collection and Analysis

Data were obtained using in-depth interviewing employing a general interview guide approach (Patton, 2002). The general interview guide approach provided some structure to ensure that specific content was addressed during each interview; however, there was freedom in the sequence of the questions, which allowed for a more conversational design, resembling Cole and Knowles (2001) description of a guided conversation.

The data were analyzed in three phases: first, a case story was created; second, a thematic analysis was conducted for each case; and third, cross-case analyses were studied for common themes. Data trustworthiness was ensured using member checking, peer debriefing, and thick descriptions.

FINDINGS

The research question that guided the study was: What, if any, were the macrosystem and microsystem challenges influencing the career experiences of African American female engineers? The macrosystem addresses the structural factors and the microsystem highlights the personal factors for the participants. The findings were grouped into two key areas: the college experience and the professional workplace setting.

College Experience

Within the college environment, the participants shared experiences that further segmented their challenges into two distinct spaces: individual factors and characteristics at the collegiate level, and the university atmosphere.

Individual Factors

The women reflected on their collegiate experiences and shared the following individual factors that served as challenges during their collegiate career: (a) lacking discipline and focus, (b) difficulty seeking assistance, and (c) adjusting to the program rigor.

Lacking discipline and focus. Whether it was getting involved in a sorority or being too involved in outside classroom activities, the participants shared a similar sentiment when it came to a point in time during their college career when there was a lack of focus. Christine noted that coming into the university setting, she was not mentally ready for the amount of work required for success; she had not disciplined herself accordingly. She stated:

> I didn't make very good grades the first semester, but I put my scholarship in jeopardy and my mom was like, "Well, did you really do your best?" And my answer was, "No, not really," and she knows me . . . And I really wasn't studying. I thought it was enough, but I would miss class, and so I just was not very disciplined going in.

Similarly, Monica highlighted a lack of focus during her sophomore year of college. She stated, "My biggest challenge was probably just my own focus and you could get off track.... (Because) if I focused and put my mind to it, then I could do it." Monica knew that she was capable of doing the work, however she needed to remain disciplined. The independence and freedom as a college student, lack of focus, difficulty balancing school and outside activities, were all factors that negatively impacted their college experiences.

Difficulty seeking assistance. In their previous learning environments, the women were successful in their academic pursuits. Therefore, learning to ask for help was an attribute that developed in order for the women to be successful in their academic career. Tiffany shared,

> I actually had to apply myself more and seek out help where needed. That was new for me, too... to come out of my shell and ask the TA. [To admit] that I need[ed] help on something or ask other students where there were study sessions or something like that, you know, "Hey let's get together and study." ... I think that took a different maturity, and ... I grew into that eventually, but it was an experience.

Likewise, Jasmine shared her perspective regarding learning how to seek assistance. Initially, she told herself, "What do I need a tutor for? You know, I should be able to do this on my own." Toni's perspective was in the same vein regarding seeking assistance. However, it was directed toward working in a group. Toni often felt like she was the only person who did not understand the material and, therefore, did not want to seek assistance with a study group. She rationalized,

> I didn't want to slow down their progress. So if they had to continuously stop and tell me this is how you do it... I didn't want to be a hindrance to their study group. So, I was like, I will figure it out on my own.

For these women, this was the first time where they struggled to learn material and felt challenged academically.

Adjusting to the program rigor. Although, the women largely participated in honors and/or advanced placement courses in addition to attending, in some cases, private or magnet high schools, they still felt that they were not prepared for the college engineering curriculum. Toni noted her struggles with the early college coursework and the frustration that occurred from easily mastering the material in high school. She shared,

> Coming from high school, being an "A" student and graduating two in my class, it was a wakeup call. I was like, I'm not used to this, not being able to get it! And so, it was a big struggle!

Monica concurred by sharing how the coursework was progressively more difficult for her to comprehend. She added, "That was hard for me to deal with just because I had never really experienced that. Even like if I would study, I still didn't get it."

Adjusting to the rigor of the program was challenging for these women because, in most cases, this was their first experience with not knowing the answers, with not being able to grasp the information easily and quickly, and with learning how to ask for assistance from others. These individual factors, however, only presented one area of challenge; colleges and universities provided environmental or institutional challenges for the participants, as well.

Institutional Factors

As African American females, the participants recalled significant challenges that resulted from the campus climate. The majority of the participants attended a predominantly White institution (PWI) for their undergraduate engineering degree. However, even for the participants who attended a historically Black college or university (HBCU) for their undergraduate degree, they attended a PWI for their graduate degree and shared similar experiences as the others. The factors presented as challenges at the institutional level included: (a) limited African American female representation, (b) uncaring and unsupportive professors, and (c) an unwelcoming peer network.

Limited African American female representation. The participants often noted the lack of diversity in the engineering programs in their college or university. The women stated there was a limited number of women and people of color overall and specifically the minimal numbers representing African Americans and African American women in their engineering programs. Lisa shared that her classmates were typically international students or White males in the electrical engineering program at her large, private PWI; therefore, she was often the only female and only Black student in the class. Josephine, who majored in engineering at an elite PWI added, "I was the only Black the whole time I was there, and I was there four years. In that department I was the only Black, male or female there." Jasmine shared experiences similar to the others and also noted the transition from being in a minority-majority secondary education system to a completely different experience in terms of gender and racial representation. In regards to the sheer number of students of color and/or women in her engineering program, she commented,

> You didn't see you present, and so who do you talk to? Who do you communicate with? Your instructors are not you, your instructors are not even mostly Caucasian, they're maybe Indian, Asian, and I guess it goes back to your de-

mographics. If you're surrounded in an area where it's always been you and then you come to this whole place and it's like a melting pot, and now my instructors are people who I can't identify with, you know, some people were having real issues with that.

The limited representation, from a gender and racial perspective, had a strong impact on the participant's experience within the environment.

Uncaring and unsupportive professors. Regardless of institution type, PWI or HBCU, the participants perceived that professors were uncaring and unsupportive of their success in the engineering program. Furthermore, they were asked a follow-up question, which addressed if their professor's reaction was applicable to all students, or reserved for students of color, women, or some other factor of exclusion/inclusion.

One participant, Lisa, felt that the engineering professors were not particularly caring toward students in general in the engineering program. She stated, "I think that was a general feeling against all students. However, I also feel like if someone fit a certain profile, I'm sure the professor probably would, you know, maybe give that person a little bit more attention." As a follow-up question, she was asked to describe the profile that she felt generated interest from professors, and she stated,

Profile being, maybe, the son of someone who is important. Maybe someone who, internships are really big, and, so, maybe someone who had a certain internship with a certain company. That's a way in for [some professors] and I didn't know that at the time, but that's a way in for the professor to maybe get funding for some kind of project that they have. And so those types of connections, you know, I didn't have because my parents were not in oil and gas or a part of anything like that, to where they would have any particular interest.

Therefore, being connected with specific industry networks provided access and privilege for some students.

Monica attended a large PWI and she also felt that her engineering professors did not care about her success as a student. When asked if that was the treatment for all students regardless of race, gender, or other social constructs, she replied,

Well at the time, I thought it was [the same treatment for everyone], but now at work, I work with people that graduated from (the university) around the same time that I did and they're all, like, "Oh yea, professor so and so ... and he did this and you know we, we used to hang out with him," and I'm like "What!" I had no idea. So now as I look back on it I think that other people had a different experience than I did.

Moreover, she noted that all of her engineering professors were White men except one professor who was Asian.

Unwelcoming peer network. Due to their racial identity as African American, and their gender identity as women, the participants felt that they were often excluded or not invited into certain spaces by their peers. This dynamic manifested during classes when the students had to form study groups and oftentimes, as Black females, they felt isolated and excluded. This dynamic also occurred outside of the class setting, which is why the participants largely preferred joining the racially/ethnically affiliated and communal engineering organizations like the National Society of Black Engineers versus the typically predominantly White professional student engineering organizations for their particular major (e.g., Institute of Electrical and Electronics Engineers-IEEE).

Josephine used the word "hostile" to describe how she felt when her peers did not welcome her into the academic environment. She declared,

> It was hostile. I don't use that word lightly, but for me, the environment at (the elite White institution) was hostile. Let me give you an example:...most of the coursework you had to work in teams, so it was a team of people, you worked together on a project, which was a significant part of your grade. And so, every class I took, that required work in teams, which was just about every class. The first day of class is when you, at the end of class, you get together and form your team. And so the first quarter after every class I had people who...I would come to them and have a conversation you know to see if I could be a part of their team. They would look at me from head to toe and shake their head no, including the women.

Josephine's experience notes the rejection she felt by her peers in the classroom and by her peers overall. It was challenging for her to connect with the majority population: White students, male and female. However, this feeling was not limited to the classroom, it was also experienced in the student organizations.

Jasmine described the professional engineering organizations as all-White male organizations, and for that reason, organizations where she didn't belong. She noted,

> AICHE (American Institute of Chemical Engineers) was a good-old-boy social network and...when you go, everything was about a party and...they're doing things that's not me, my culture. I just couldn't relate to an entire group. I didn't feel a part of it.

Also, the predominantly White student organizations seemed to have access to additional resources that the Black organizations did not have the same access. Nicole highlighted the discrepancy between the predominantly White professional student organizations and the Black students as:

> They have this thing they called the bible for (the PWI) where it's basically a whole bunch of old tests from professors. And that's what the White kids have always had. That's what all the fraternities do; they have all those old tests.

Therefore, being excluded from the majority White peer network meant that one was also excluded from privileged resources.

Lisa attended a large PWI and described her perspective on the impact of stereotypes in the engineering college classroom. This viewpoint could provide the backdrop for the hostile environment as described by Josephine and a rationale for the limited resources as described by Nicole. Lisa shared:

> If you look at the stereotypes, when you get into the class, first day of the class and you look around, the Black female is probably not the person that people are gonna say, "Oh she's probably very smart and she is going to do well in this class." The Hispanic guy, you know, people are not gonna look at him and say, "Oh yeah, I'm gonna be his study partner." People were looking for, at that time, the Asian students, and partly because the Asian students seem to have camaraderie; they seem to have a community about themselves to where you knew that student had previous notes from somebody else who had taken the class. . . . Their group was a group that supported each other and helped one another. And I think the Black students . . . did that as well but . . . we were such a small group that, in some cases, there may simply have been no one who took your class within the past couple of years to where they could really offer stuff that would be relevant to you.

The African American women felt unplugged from and unable to access the resources given to and shared by the majority population. In addition to the challenges in the college environment, once the women completed their undergraduate degree and found employment in high profile organizations, they began their professional careers and the corresponding challenges.

Professional Workplace

The participants shared significant challenges as African American female engineers in predominantly White male engineering workplace organizations. The dominant subthemes emergent as challenges within this category include: (a) the lack of diversity within engineering organizations, and (b) the impact of the participants' age, race, and gender on their career experiences. The later ideally would be presented as three independent sections: age, race, and gender however, for the most part, the participants shared narratives that included all three components. There were limited cases where one of the variables—age, race, or gender—was presented as the dominant identifiable challenge and those cases are presented accordingly.

Lack of Diversity in the Organization

The participants noted that they were extremely aware of their identity because there were so few Blacks and women represented in the field and specifically within their engineering organization. Courtney described the distribution of African American female engineers in her company. She stated, "First of all, there were two of us . . . There were probably 400 in the entire company . . . at least 200 were architects, the other 200 may have been engineers; there were two of *us.*" Courtney's description of the architectural and design organization and her lived experience, representing one of two African American female engineers, served as a frequent reminder of her minority status in the workplace setting.

Jasmine shared related experiences working in predominantly White male organizations in the oil and gas industry. She highlighted, "For both of the companies I worked for, to be in the engineering field, there were no African Americans. In the refinery, the African Americans were typically operators or they worked in the personnel group." Being the only African American female engineer in the refinery meant that she had to learn quickly how to navigate the workplace with professional White males, as well as with paraprofessional Black males. Josephine provided an additional perspective regarding the limited number of females in the corporate research sector of her high-tech company. She stated, "Now I can also say that I was in research for 12 years and in those 12 years there was no other Black woman research staff member." Therefore, Josephine served as the only female engineer of color for her organization during her entire tenure in research and development. Consequently, when she left that sector of the organization for a temporary assignment in another area, she never returned.

Not only did participants note the lack of racial and gender diversity at their level within the organization, they also noted that there was limited diversity or representation of women and people of color in high-level leadership positions. Monica described what she noticed while working for an international company in the oil and gas industry. She shared:

> They did not have any diversity programs, and I actually told them this when I left. The uncertainty was the main reason that I left but . . . they were just doing, like, a diversity survey. They had not done anything on diversity, they didn't have any goals around diversity, [and] there were no women in leadership.

Due to a lack of racial and gender diversity in the engineering profession, the participants quickly understood that they would not see many, if any, people in their organization who looked like them. As Jasmine stated, "I think [one thing] we still continue to face, is not enough females, and it's definitely not enough African American females."

Participant's Age, Race, and Gender

The participants shared challenges associated with their identity based on their age, race, or gender, and a combination of all three identifiers. They experienced difficult encounters with managers, nonengineering support personnel, and their colleagues. In most cases, the interactions of all three variables was presented; however, in the descriptions that follow, the participant's age was the dominant factor.

Impact of age.   Transitioning from a recent college graduate to a professional engineer provided challenges for the women as they entered organizations with older engineering professionals. Lisa shared the complication of being a young engineer when she graduated from college and entered her first professional job in an oil and gas company. She highlighted one of her challenging experiences.

> Definitely good-old-boy system there, and not until I started having management type of responsibility did I really get push back. Previous to that, it was kind of, like, yeah, we'll help you and that type thing, but when it became a situation where a young twenty-something was a manager and had authority over them, then that's when there were issues.

Toni also worked in the oil and gas industry and felt similar challenges as a result of her age. She stated, "I think some people tend to say, well you are young... so, for people who have been operating in the plant for 40 years [they say], 'Who are you, young buck?'" Jasmine stated her challenges regarding age, specifically having to look a certain age to be credible and taken seriously in the workplace environment. She declared,

> And so when we come to the table, sometimes we're not taken as seriously... because there's such a huge age gap... and so they figure, how can you speak when you don't have enough experience? You know, "When did you come in?" You know, "What do you know?" So when I come to the table... first thing people think is, "Oh, she's in personnel." Or, some people thought, "Oh, I thought you were an administrative assistant." Because... they think most women, that's where they come from. And when you sit back and you tell them, "No, I come from operations. I've been working for this long." First thing (they typically say is), "You don't look that old." And I'm like, "How old am I supposed to look?"

The participants were challenged by their age in the engineering workplace and as young professional engineers they felt that they had to prove themselves, their engineering capabilities, and learn how to stand firm. They were not seen as credible because of the view that age is synonymous with knowledge and experience and therefore not viewed as competent.

Impact of gender.   Oftentimes, the African American female engineers stated that their gender was a more significant challenge than their race, in terms of opposition. Furthermore, they shared feelings as if they were not connected to the male network or that they were excluded from the network. When asked about situations where she felt excluded or challenged, Courtney stated, "I think it was primarily because I was female. Nobody said anything out of the way to me about race, so I can't attribute it to being Black female, but definitely because I was female." Likewise, Jasmine recalled a situation where the person in charge of an oil rig did not want her there simply because she was a woman, and he did not want women contaminating his all-male workplace environment. She described:

> And so at the time, because I was female, I go on location and the guy didn't have a problem with me being Black; he had a problem with . . . (as he stated), "[Jasmine] I don't want you to do work on my job," and I said, "Why?" He said, "Because women are a distraction to me and my men on the rigs. And I don't have women working on my rigs."

Ultimately, Jasmine began and completed the project on the rig while the client sought a male engineer for the job. After she finished the assignment, the client was pleased with her work and requested her for additional jobs, which she declined. The participants' gender, in some cases, had stronger negative consequences and implications than their race/ethnicity in the workplace.

Impact of age, race, and gender.   Several participants described organizational workplaces as unreceptive, hostile, and/or challenging environments. Christine learned about her organization's culture during an internship experience in the aerospace industry. She received firsthand experience of the unwelcoming environment for Black women. She recalled:

> You have these older men in engineering who . . . weren't very used to seeing women in engineering, let alone Black women. And, I could see that was an issue; that's not something that they were accustomed to . . . A few of them would make comments like "Yeah, you know, I don't know if you are going to make it."

As a result of the limited numbers of Blacks, females, or both identifiers represented in professional positions in engineering organizations, the participants often had to address or deal with assumptions from colleagues on a regular basis. Working in the research industry, Nicole recalled assumptions she had dealt with during a cross-functional team meeting.

> Challenge wise, it's really being able to break that barrier...we still have a glass barrier for African Americans and in particular for African American women...So that's the barrier that I've had to break and I've gotten there now because now people know who I am, they know the level of education that I have, they know the level of experience that I have, so they know when I come in, I'm an engineer...But before...when they saw me, they automatically assumed that I was the person that was going to be capturing the notes from the meeting minutes...Nope, wrong person...and it's like that because I'm usually the only African American sitting in the room. Every now and then there may be an African American male, but the females—African American technical females in the labs—are very low.

In addition to the experiences in team meetings and other office interactions, sometimes the unwelcoming working environment was manifested during social activities after work. These informal incidences and networks often excluded the Black female engineers. As Lisa shared,

> Our particular entity is very small and so the good-old-boy system is at play and even more so on the social side with dinner or drinks after work. Or, you know, one guy is from the East Coast and he has a beach home and he invited the guy to come with him for the weekend. They were going to go fishing or whatever. So, again that's not something that I would be able to participate in, right? So, it's not so much that I would say that guy excluded me from doing it, but it wouldn't be something that would be appropriate for me to spend the weekend with him fishing.

These often overlooked systems of exclusion served as challenges for the participants, particularly as they sought to develop networks to advance their careers. On the other hand, unfortunately, there were also occasions where the participants shared stories of blatant racism and sexism. Jasmine recalled an experience as a young Black female chemical engineer where she went to remote locations and worked in small rural areas in the United States. She stated,

> I just couldn't even believe they're people who still exist in the U.S. who act like this. And my operator who worked for me, he was just so bitter and he was like, "Only reason you got your job cause you," he said, "because you're a woman." Not only that, "You're a nigger woman and that's why you work here and you gone still be working here when I probably don't got no job because you're a nigger woman." I said, "Really?" you know, so I'm taken aback, and that really kind of hurt my feelings, and I remember I went home and cried.... So every day he had something just rude to say.

This situation was shocking to Jasmine, because the racism was blatant as compared to the subtle forms of racism and discrimination shared by women of color in other organizations. Due to this situation, Jasmine wanted to leave the company and the engineering field altogether.

The impact of age, race, and gender provided significant challenges in the engineering workplace. Josephine worked in a research environment for a global technology company and noted the similarities in the industry research environment and general hostility as well. She stated, "They challenge your thoughts, they challenge what you do, and in many instances for engineering because it's all male or overwhelmingly male at that time, they do it in a hostile way." Although her experience and description specifically addressed the corporate research culture, many of the participants shared similar perspectives, regardless of the industry type.

DISCUSSION

The purpose of the study was to investigate the challenges impacting the career experiences of African American female engineers. The themes that emerged from the data were categorized into two primary areas for the participants: their collegiate experiences and their experiences in the professional engineering workplace.

Individual Challenges to Career Development

Microsystem factors included a lack of discipline and focus, difficulty seeking assistance, and adjusting to the program rigor. The participants shared difficult transitions from high school to college as young Black women aspiring to become engineering professionals. In the literature, two of the subthemes—lacking discipline and focus, and adjusting to the program rigor—appeared to connect. For example, students entered undergraduate engineering programs with a high degree of self-confidence and unrealistic expectations of the required workload. This reality check, in turn, caused the students to conduct a self-evaluation. Consequently, if the student persisted, then they became focused and established a more disciplined academic lifestyle. Etzkowitz, Kemelgo, and Uzzi (2000) noted:

> Most women enter college in the U.S. at a peak of self-confidence, based on good high school performances, good scores in their Scholastic Aptitude Tests, and a great deal of encouragement and praise from teachers, family and friends. Soon after entry into college, women who felt intelligent, were confident in their abilities and prior performance level, and took their sense of identity for granted, began to feel isolated, insecure, intimidated, to ques-

tion whether they "belonged" in the sciences at all, and whether they were good enough to continue. (p. 59)

The African American women in the study were no different. Similarly, Goodman et al. (2002) noted that women left engineering because they could not handle the academic environment in engineering. Moreover, they reported that female engineers typically struggled with the engineering demands in academia because they often experienced this challenge for the first time as an undergraduate college student. Although the participants in the study had similar experiences in terms of their grades being negatively impacted at some point during their college career, they were determined to be successful and their academic goals were not disrupted. The participants knew that they could perform better scholastically than a semester or two with low grades and eventually proved it to themselves.

One factor that served to be significant in terms of navigating the academic requirements for engineering was learning to seek assistance. Although Brainard and Carlin (1997) reported that women who learn to work independently were more likely to persist in engineering programs, Goodman et al. (2002) stressed the importance of students working together, in study groups, for academic assistance and success. The participants in the study represented both sides of the pendulum. Toni shared her desire to work alone because she did not want to slow down the group's progress. Therefore, she found it easier to work independently or seek individual assistance from the teaching assistant. Other participants in the study eventually learned that they studied best with a group of students, typically other African American engineering students who provided support and challenged them at the same time.

Examining interpersonal traits without including the impact and climate of the environment presents a one-sided view of the system. That is to say, the environment may have provided barriers for the participants' difficulty seeking assistance.

Collegiate Challenges to Career Development

The engineering environment at the college/university level severely lacked racial and gender diversity. This meant that they were keenly aware of their status as the only person of color and/or woman in the engineering classroom, in their area of specialization, or in other spaces focused on core engineering. This finding was consistent with Goodman et al.'s (2002) report, which stated that women take notice of the lack of females in engineering programs as faculty, and as professional engineers in the workplace.

To address the lack of women and racial minorities, Busch-Vishniac and Jarosz (2004) suggest that one area that has not been addressed or significantly researched, but that can provide a space to explore and make gains in getting more diversity in the field, is in the content or engineering curriculum. The authors propose that by making changes to the curriculum, such as including the people tied to the concepts in engineering, including a social component that addresses the communities represented by women and people of color, and by adding explicit multicultural and diversity material in the classroom, engineering programs will gain more diversity. Busch-Vishniac and Jarosz assert that curricular changes in engineering need to occur, which are currently designed with a bias toward White males. However, curricular changes are not changed in a vacuum; in order to impact change in engineering content, one has to address the additional challenge presented by those who teach in the engineering classroom.

The African American female participants shared a common experience in the classroom: they felt that the professors did not take an interest in their success as a student. The uncaring and unsupportive professors served as a challenge for the participants. Perhaps the challenge is due to the difference in gender, as the participants noted. As cited by Farrell (2002), the typical engineering faculty member is male, representing 95% of the faculty population. Complementary to gender difference, Astin and Astin (1993) reported that faculty in major universities tend to focus on research more than teaching. These faculty members classically use teaching-centered pedagogical techniques (e.g., lecturing) instead of student-centered approaches. Combining this method of teaching with inequitable treatment in the classroom (Colbeck, Cabrera, & Terenzini, 2001) led the participants to feel that professors were uncaring and unsupportive of their learning and success. Therefore, a limited approach to teaching combined with an emphasis on research negatively impacts the classroom and college environment for all students, and especially for the African American female students who have other negative factors contributing to the environment and adding to the unwelcoming setting.

Colbeck, Cabrera, and Terenzini (2001) found in their research on faculty teaching and classroom environment that the underlying perception was that male students typically responded to and treated females differently than males. Similarly, Etzkowitz, Kemelgo, and Uzzi (2000) determined that, "Many men are well aware that they or their peers often exclude the women in their classes from their working or social groups solely because they are women" (p. 60). Consequently, although Goodman et al. (2002) reported how study groups were valuable and almost a needed resource in engineering college programs, the unwelcoming milieu makes it even more difficult for the African American women in class to connect and form alliances with classmates who are not interested in working with women and people of color. The participants experienced firsthand the feeling of being treated differently due to their gender and race.

In addition to the hostile environment, which resulted from gender differences in the classroom, the African American women also had to deal with issues based on race. According to the College Board (1999),

> Because White students are still a large majority on most campuses, the negative views of some Whites can contribute to a perception that minorities are "unwelcome." Although hard to measure, this "lack of hospitality," as one member of the Task Force puts it, appears to undermine the academic performance of many minority students. (p. 16)

While the participants did not directly state that the environment impacted their academic performance, they did note how the unwelcoming peer environment presented challenges and obstacles in supporting their success. As a result of the varying factors at different times in the academic lifespan, it is important to examine the interaction of elements in a common thread. Therefore, the discussion on challenges impacting the career experiences of African American females has to include the professional workplace setting and the macrosystem factors at that level.

Workplace Challenges to Career Development

Analogous to the challenges due to limited African American female representation in the collegiate environment, the same lack of diversity carried over into the workplace setting. It makes sense that a lack of diversity in the pipeline would extend to a lack of diversity in the professional workplace setting. The engineering community continues to note the unsatisfactory numbers for minorities in the field, yet as Watson and Froyd (2007) noted, diversity goals remain unmet. Although literature (e.g., Rosser, 2003; Sukumaran & Jahan, n.d.) in the field includes a multitude of challenges such as few mentors, balance of work and family, and sexual harassment, to name a few, the participants primarily shared challenges related to gender and the intersection of gender, race, and age.

There is limited research on the challenges in the engineering workplace associated with age, whether younger or older, and the intersection of this factor with race and gender (Gill, Sharp, Mills, & Franzway, 2008; Roberts & Ayre, 2002). Moreover, literature in the field often highlights the experiences of White women, but the challenges incurred by women of color are often overlooked (Richie, 1992). The experiences by White women and women of color are not synonymous, as noted in the Catalyst (2004) report. One distinguishing factor highlighted in the report stated, "Whereas White women frequently reference the 'glass ceiling' as blocking their advancement up the career ladder, women of color often characterize the barriers they encounter as comprising a 'concrete ceiling'—one that is more dense and less easily shattered" (p.3). One participant explicitly referenced the glass ceiling as a barrier in the workplace, and the others were aware that there were few, if any, African American women in positions that matched their career goals specifically and in leadership positions overall.

The Catalyst (2004) report also noted how African American women felt excluded from the professional network, due to their race and gender, which was consistent with the findings from the study. Miller's (2004) research on women engineers in the oil industry highlighted the importance of informal networks to the career progression for women in engineering. That is why the limited access to networks in the male-dominated structure was problematic for the women of color. McIlwee and Robinson (1992) researched the impact of gender in the workplace and found that men respond negatively to professional women in the workplace culture and especially those in male-dominated fields. They stated:

> As a result, men feel threatened, invaded, and uncomfortable. They react with hostility, subtle or overt, and try to reassert their superiority. They tease, belittle, insult, ignore. They respond with skepticism to women's contributions, or patronize them as "cute little things" who need their help. They assign them tasks that fit their own images of "women's work." They exclude women from casual conversations around the coffee machine, at lunch, or after work. At worst, they engage in outright harassment, sexual or otherwise. (p. 95)

Challenges presented by the participants included exclusion, racism, sexism, and general harsh treatment as defined by the participant. These factors parallel findings presented in research and literature, which addresses barriers and challenges for women (e.g., Gill, Sharp, Mills, & Franzway, 2008; Miller, 2004; Roberts & Ayre, 2002) and provide several points to address for workplace organizations seeking to retain African American female engineers.

The underlying assumption felt in predominantly male engineering organizations is, "To be taken as an engineer is to look like an engineer, talk like an engineer, and act like an engineer. In most workplaces this means looking, talking, and acting male" (Robinson & McIlwee, 1991, p. 406). The African American female engineers shared feelings related to this assumption and noted the challenges associated with confronting this norm and expectation.

CONCLUSION

African American female engineers shared challenging factors in the microsystem and macrosystem. It was imperative to note the participants' interactions with the environment, specifically focusing on gendered and racial experiences. The findings in this study provide such an analysis with a critical eye toward the interaction component of the systems in the environment. That is to say, it is difficult to analyze the microsystem components, which served as challenges for the women, without considering the larger context (i.e., macrosystem). Therefore, the influence and impact of the structural systems served as an umbrella of challenges for the individual personal experiences.

In analyzing the individual (microsystem) and environmental (macrosystem) challenges for these Black women engineers, one may recognize experiences commonly shared by White women and in some cases Black men. However, Black women are marginalized by race and gender, whereas the aforementioned groups encounter one or the other. Therefore, the interaction within the system, should it allow privilege at any given time, grants it to Black women engineers at the lowest level. Their struggles with racism, sexism, and ageism in addition to intrapersonal conflict and peer isolation are uniquely shared as Black women. What we learn from this group is the dynamic interaction between these Black female engineers and the environment, which provides insight into the variables of consideration. Moreover, any significant attempt by Black women to increase representation in STEM will need to consider the interrelationship of the system versus a compartmentalized approach.

This research adds pertinent data to understanding the career experiences of African American females and the challenges faced on their journey. Moreover, it is important to study African American women as an individual group because, "Women of color (African-American, Latinas, and Asian women) are clearly not a monolithic group. The personal and professional profiles of the African-American women research participants are quite different from those of Latinas and Asian women" (Catalyst, 2004, p. 3). There are opportunities for change to occur in the system, which could positively impact the career—academic and professional workplace— experiences of African American female engineers. As stated by John Brooks Slaughter, president and CEO of NACME, "We must pursue an agenda for change that removes barriers and builds bridges to opportunities for underrepresented minorities" (NACME, 2008, p. 7). For if we in the engineering community do not take this charge as an important action item on our agenda, then we are failing the future global leaders in engineering and technology.

REFERENCES

Astin, A., & Astin, H. (1993). *Undergraduate science education: The impact of different college environments on the educational pipeline in the sciences.* Los Angeles, CA: Higher Education Research Institute.

Berry, C., Cox, M., & Main, J. (2014). *Women on color engineering faculty: An examination of the experiences and the numbers.* Proceedings of the 121st ASEE Annual Conference & Exposition, Indianapolis, IN.

Brainard, S., & Carlin, L. (1997). A longitudinal study of undergraduate women in engineering and science. *1997 Frontiers in Education Conference, Session T2A, 1,* 134–143.

Bronfenbrenner, U. (1977). Toward an experimental ecology of human development. *American Psychologist, 32,* 513–531. doi: 10.1037/0003-066X.32.7.513

Burlew, A. (1982). The experiences of Black females in traditional and nontraditional professions. *Psychology of Women Quarterly, 6*(3), 312–327. doi: 10.1111/j.1471-6402.1982.tb00034.x

Busch-Vishniac, I., & Jarosz, J. (2004). Can diversity in the undergraduate engineering population be enhanced through curricular change? *Journal of Women and Minorities in Science and Engineering, 10,* 255–281. doi: 10.1615/JWomenMinorScienEng.v10.i3.50

Catalyst, Inc. (1992). *Women in engineering: An untapped resource.* Retrieved from www.catalyst.org/system/files/women_in_engineering_an_untapped_resource.pdf

Catalyst, Inc. (2004). *Advancing African American women in the workplace: What managers need to know.* Retrieved from http://www.catalyst.org/publication/20/advancing-african-american-women-in-the-workplace-what-managers-need-to-know

Chubin, D., May, G., & Babco, E. (2005). Diversifying the engineering workforce. *Journal of Engineering Education, 94*(1), 73–86. doi: 10.1002/j.2168-9830.2005.tb00830.x

Colbeck, C., Cabrera, A., & Terenzini, P. (2001). Learning professional confidence: Linking teaching practices, students' self-perceptions, and gender. *The Review of Higher Education, 24*(2), 173–191. doi: 10.1353/rhe.2000.0028

Cole, A., & Knowles, J. (Eds.). (2001). *Lives in context: The art of life history research.* Lanham, MD: AltaMira Press.

College Board. (1999). *Reaching the top: A report of the national task force on minority high achievement.* New York, NY: College Board Publications.

Cook, E., Heppner, M., & O'Brien, K. (2002). Career development of women of color and white women: Assumptions, conceptualization, and interventions from an ecological perspective. *The Career Development Quarterly, 50,* 291–305. doi: 10.1002/j.2161-0045.2002.tb00574.x

Cook, E., Heppner, M., & O'Brien, K. (2005). Multicultural and gender influences in women's career development: An ecological perspective. *Journal of Multicultural Counseling and Development, 33*(3), 165–179. doi: 10.1002/j.2161-1912.2005.tb00014.x

Engineering Workforce Commission. (2010). *Data for degrees.* Retrieved from http://www.ewc-online.org/

Etzkowitz, H., Kemelgor, C., & Uzzi, B. (2000). *Athena unbound: The advancement of women in science and technology.* Cambridge, England: Cambridge University Press.

Farrell, E. (2002). Engineering a warmer welcome for female students. *Leadership and Management in Engineering, 2*(4), 19–22. doi: 10.1061/(ASCE)1532-6748(2002)2:4(19)

Gill, J., Sharp, R., Mills, J., & Franzway, S. (2008). I *still* wanna be an engineer! Women, education and the engineering profession. *European Journal of Engineering Education, 33*(4), 391–402. doi: 10.1080/03043790802253459

Goodman, L. A. (1961). Snowball sampling. *The Annals of Mathematical Statistics, 32*(1), 148–170.

Goodman, I., Cunningham, C., Lachapelle, C., Thompson, M., Bittinger, K., Brennam, R., & Delchi, M. (2002). *Final report of the women's experiences in college engineering project.* Cambridge, England: Goodman Research Group.

Hill, C., Corbett, C., & St. Rose, A. (2010). *Why so few? Women in science, technology, engineering, and mathematics.* Washington, DC: American Association of University Women.

Jackson, S. (2010). *The quiet crisis: Engineering education in the 21st century.* Retrieved from http://www.rpi.edu/homepage/quietcrisis/ps101103-swe.html

Johnson, R. D., Stone, D. L., & Phillips, T. N. (2008). Relations among ethnicity, gender, beliefs, attitudes, and intention to pursue a career in information technology. *Journal of Applied Social Psychology, 38*(4), 999–1022. doi: 10.1111/j.1559-1816.2008.00336.x

Lopez, F., & Ann-Yi, S. (2006). Predictors of career indecision in three racial/ethnic groups of college women. *Journal of Career Development, 33*(1), 29–46. doi: 10.1177/0894845306287341

McCowan, C. J., & Alston, R. J. (1998). Racial identity, African self-consciousness, and career decision making in African American college women. *Journal of Multicultural Counseling and Development, 26*(1), 28–38. doi: 10.1002/j.2161-1912.1998.tb00181.x

McIlwee, J., & Robinson, J. (1992). *Women in engineering: Gender, power, and workplace culture.* Albany, NY: State University of New York Press.

Miller, G. (2004). Frontier masculinity in the oil industry: The experience of women engineers. *Gender, Work and Organization, 11*(1), 47–73. doi: 10.1111/j.1468-0432.2004.00220.x

Moore, J. L. (2006). A qualitative investigation of African American males' career trajectory in engineering: Implications for teachers, school counselors, and parents. *Teachers College Record, 108*(2), 246–266.

National Academy of Sciences. (2007). *Rising above the gathering storm: Energizing and employing America for a brighter economic future.* Washington DC: National Academies Press. Retrieved from http://www.nap.edu/catalog/11463.html

National Action Council for Minorities in Engineering (NACME). (2008). *Confronting the "new" American dilemma, underrepresented minorities in engineering: A data-based look at diversity.* Retrieved from http://nacme.org/user/docs/NACME%2008%20ResearchReport.pdf

NSF/Division of Science Resources Statistics. (2010a). *Table 5-4. Bachelor's degrees awarded to women, by field, citizenship, and race/ethnicity: 2001–2010.* Retrieved from http://www.nsf.gov/statistics/wmpd/2013/pdf/tab5-4.pdf

NSF/Division of Science Resources Statistics. (2010b). *Women, minorities, and persons with disabilities in science and engineering: Table 9-6. Employed scientists and engineers, by occupation, highest degree level, ethnicity and race: 2010.* Retrieved from http://www.nsf.gov/statistics/wmpd/2013/pdf/tab9-6_updated_2013_11.pdf

NSF/Division of Science Resources Statistics. (2010c). *Women, minorities, and persons with disabilities in science and engineering: Table 9-7. Employed scientists and engineers, by occupation, highest degree level, race/ethnicity, and sex: 2010.* Retrieved, from http://www.nsf.gov/statistics/wmpd/2013/pdf/tab9-7_updated_2013_11.pdf

O'Brien, L., Blodorn, A., Adams, G., Garcia, D., & Hammer, E. (2015). Ethnic variation in gender-STEM stereotypes and STEM participation: An intersectional approach. *Cultural Diversity and Ethnic Minority Psychology, 21*(2), 169–180.

Obiomon, P., Tickles, V., Wowo, A., & Holland-Hunt, S. (2007). Advancement of women of color in science, technology, engineering, and math (STEM) disciplines. *Faculty Resource Network, NYU.* Retrieved from https://www.nyu.edu/frn/publications/advancing.women/Adv.%20Women%20in%20Stem%20Tickles.html

Ossola, A. (2014). The different ways Black and White women see stereotypes in STEM. *The Atlantic.* Retrieved from http://www.theatlantic.com/education/archive/2014/11/black-girls-stand-a-better-chance-in-stem/383094/

Patton, M. (2002). *Qualitative evaluation and research methods* (3rd ed.). Thousand Oaks, CA: Sage.

Perna, L., Lundy-Wagner, V., Drezner, N. D., Gasman, M., Yoon, S., Bose, E., & Gary, S. (2009). The contribution of HBCUs to the preparation of African American women for STEM careers: A case study. *Research in Higher Education, 50*(1), 1–23. doi: 10.1007/s11162-008-9110-y

Rice, D. (2016). The STEM pipeline: Recruiting and retaining African American female engineers. *Journal of Research Initiatives, 2*(1), Article 5.

Rice, D., & Alfred, M. (2014). Personal and structural elements of support for African American female engineers. *Journal of STEM Education, 15*(2), 40–49.

Richie, B. (1992). Coping with work: Interventions with African American women. *Women & Therapy, 12,* 97–111. doi: 10.1300/J015V12N01_08

Roberts, P., & Ayre, M. (2002). Did she jump or was she pushed? A study of women's retention in the engineering workforce. *International Journal of Engineering Education, 18*(4), 415–421.

Robinson, J., & McIlwee, J. (1991). Men, women, and the culture of engineering. *The Sociological Quarterly, 32*(3), 403–421. doi: 10.1111/j.1533-8525.1991.tb00166.x

Rosser, S. (2003). Attracting and retaining women in science and engineering. *Academe Online, 89*(4), 24–28.

Sadler, P., Sonnert, G., Hazari, Z., & Tai, R. (2012). Stability and volatility of STEM career interest in high school: A gender study. *Science Education, 96,* 411–427.

Science and engineering indicators. (2014). Retrieved from http://www.nsf.gov/statistics/seind14/index.cfm/overview

Stanley, C. (Ed.). (2006). *Faculty of color: Teaching in predominantly White colleges and universities.* Bolton, MA: Anker.

Sukumaran, B., & Jahan, K. (n.d.). *The engineering workplace: Is it conducive to women?* Retrieved from http://users.rowan.edu/~sukumaran/personal/publications/asee-wash.pdf

Watson, K., & Froyd, J. (2007). Diversifying the US engineering workforce: A new model. *Journal of Engineering Education, 96*(1), 19–32.

CHAPTER 8

PRESENT BUT NOT ACCOUNTED FOR

Examining How Intersectional Identities Create a Double Bind for and Affect Leadership of Women of Color in Educational Settings

Adrienne R. Carter-Sowell, Danielle D. Dickens,
Gabe H. Miller, and Carla A. Zimmerman

Increasing and leveraging diversity in the science, technology, engineering, and math (STEM) fields is one of our nation's most pressing economic imperatives. To achieve this goal, we must increase the number of underrepresented racial and ethnic minority (URM) graduate students in STEM doctoral degree programs. STEM fields have significantly lacked representation of URM students both historically and presently (NSF, 2011). This underrepresentation is detrimental because diversity is beneficial to organizations by providing unique perspectives that enhance the goals of science, and also because the demographic makeup of a field is self-sustaining: seeing similar others as leaders in a field encourages young adults to follow the

Women of Color in STEM, pages 181–201
Copyright © 2017 by Information Age Publishing
181

same path, and provides mentors to early career scientists and researchers. Furthermore, cultural stereotypes are built upon representation; the lack of representation of underrepresented racial and ethnic minority students in STEM fields perpetuates cultural expectations of what these students both can and should accomplish.

In addition, intellect alone will not guarantee a successful ascent from graduate education to the professorate. Race and ethnicity are important when comparing rates of program completion by graduate students. Underrepresented racial and ethnic minorities do not complete doctoral programs in STEM fields at the same rate as majority students. For example, in 2002 the 7-year graduation rate for minority students in STEM doctoral programs was 39% compared to 48% for majority students and 62% for international students (Council of Graduate Schools, 2008). This trend is surprisingly stubborn given the persistent priority, extensive resources, and service hours that university leaders and professional societies dedicate to diversity programs. Since this problem has yet to abate, it is important to consider how professional and social interactions (and the lack thereof) across the educational system can impair efforts in the STEM fields to retain competent, motivated, and talented graduate students from underrepresented racial groups.

Similarly, the pace of recruiting and retaining women, especially women of color, for visible and influential leadership roles at U.S. colleges and universities remains stagnate. The umbrella term, women of color, refers to females who are descendants from Africa/African diasporas, plus women of Hispanic/Latin American, Native American, and Asian/Pacific Islander heritages (Yoo, 2013). The *Chronicle of Higher Education* (2010) reported the statistics in faculty hiring practices. The results indicated a systematic and pervasive gender and leadership gap existing in the academic labor markets. For instance, of all full-time, instructional faculty in degree-granting postsecondary institutions as of fall 2013, 6% were Black female faculty members, 5% were Hispanic female faculty members, and 7% were Asian/Pacific Islander female faculty members (Catalyst, 2015). Hence, the total women of color faculty representation at top U.S. universities was approximately half the 35% total of White female faculty and minimal to the 43% majority total for White male faculty on college campuses (IPEDS, 2013).

Additionally, the modest progress made in promoting qualified people of color into tenured and administrative positions lost ground from 14% to 13% between 2006 and 2011 (Cook, 2012). Predictably, these disparities in racial/ethnic diversity of academic positions in the United States highlight a similar global problem. For example in Australia and Canada, compared to their White faculty peers, the faculty of indigenous or aboriginal ancestry (67%) work mostly in nonacademic positions (Australian Government, Department of Education and Training, 2014) or experience higher rates of unemployment as university teachers (Canadian Association of University Teachers, 2010). Altogether, this information on underrepresented minority (URM) faculty reveals a trend that persists over time, as well as across national borders.

Traditionally, women of color on most U.S. college campuses are employed primarily in custodial work, hospitality jobs, and food service positions rather than as professional staff, faculty, or administrators (U.S. Census Bureau, 2013). Historically, women of color have been underrepresented and unnoticed, compared to White women, for high status and high profile collegiate occupations (Cocchiara, Bell, & Berry, 2006). Furthermore, women of color tend to earn less in salary than men of color, as well as their White male and White female counterparts (Potamites, 2007). Altogether, racialized sexism (e.g., sexism shaped by racism and racial stereotyping) can serve as a barrier for the advancement of women of color into the tenured faculty ranks and prestigious administrative appointments (Bell & Nkomo, 2001; Ospino & Foldy, 2009). Due to the double marginalization of experiencing racial and gender discrimination in the work environment, women of color are faced with the dual challenge of overcoming stereotypical beliefs while competing for leadership opportunities (Bell, 1990). Despite these disparities in the workplace, little research has been conducted to examine how gender and race (for some a double bind dilemma) interact in influencing leadership experiences in educational settings (Chin, Lott, Rice, & Sanchez-Hucles, 2008; Sanchez-Hucles & Davis, 2010).

Inevitably, the double bind dilemmas that female faculty of color face in their academic careers mirror the gender diversity obstacles found within Fortune 1000 firms (Carter, Simkins, & Simpson, 2003). According to Eagly and Carli (2007), gender discrimination in leadership positions exists because men are more commonly associated with masculine, agentic traits such as dominance, while women are more commonly associated with feminine, communal traits such as compassion. Consequently, these expectations create a double bind for women seeking positions of authority and influence in the business sector. Likewise, a growing number of studies publicize the similar double bind dilemmas occurring for women of color from diverse academic disciplines. For example, Malcolm, Hall, & Brown (1976) concluded that double bind dilemmas were an unavoidable circumstance for minority women working in the science fields. More recently, Ong, Wright, Espinosa, and Orfield (2011) provided a synthesis of the literature covering 40 years of scholarship and surveying 116 cross-disciplinary studies, to examine how hostile workplace climates have fostered complicated double bind experiences for women of color in STEM fields. Turner, González, and Wong (Lau) (2011) explored the historical, cultural, and social factors that have shaped double bind experiences for faculty women of color across three disciplinary areas: the STEM fields, humanities and arts, and SBE (social, behavioral, and economic sciences). In 2013, the Institute for Women's Policy and Research (IWPR) convened nearly fifty experts who reported that double bind experiences for faculty women of color in the STEM fields are instrumental to differences found in institutional account-ability, funding awards, and an individual's career progress (Hhess, Hess, Gault, & Yi, 2013). In this chapter, we will address the ways in which women faculty of color navigate their double bind dilemmas in order to prevail as leaders in the academy.

INFLUENCES OF GENDER AND RACE ON LEADERSHIP ROLES IN EDUCATIONAL SETTINGS

A meta-analysis (Eagly & Carli, 2003) indicated that women leaders adopt a people-focused leadership style, which suits societal expectations of women to be supportive and friendly. Evaluations of agentic women have demon-strated that female workers who violate prescriptions of feminine niceness are susceptible to backlash or hostile discrimination, as a penalty for be-ing perceived as socially deficient. In a set of three studies, Heilman and Okimoto (2007) provided evidence that women who are successful in male gender-typed domains are more disliked, more interpersonally derogated, and are less desired as supervisors. Heilman's (1983) lack of fit model ad-dressed the incongruity between female stereotypes and perceptions of the attributes needed for leadership positions. This model suggested that the greater the lack of fit, the more negative the expectations of women's per-formance were and the more bias a woman worker was likely to experience. Hence, the negative reactions to successful women in traditionally male domains are due to this perception that these particular women have vio-lated stereotype based prescriptions, or "oughts" about how women should behave (Heilman, Wallen, Fuchs, & Tamkins, 2004).

Women must carefully manage their demeanor as leaders to appear both competent and communal (Heilman, Wallen, Fuchs, & Tamkins, 2004). If women adopt stereotypically communal behaviors (i.e., warm, kind, sensi-tive, thoughtful), these women are liked by coworkers, but not respected as leaders. If women act nonstereotypically and portray noncommunal (i.e., direct, task oriented, and assertive) behaviors, these women are viewed by coworkers as competent, but not entrusted to lead. Additionally, women, compared to men, are more likely to receive high-risk work responsibili-ties that can lead to high profile failures. This situational exposure, termed the glass cliff, makes women compared to men in similar roles more to blame for mistakes, as well as the target for social repercussions by cowork-ers (Haslam & Ryan, 2008). Furthermore, researchers find that women, and especially women of color, are more likely to report feeling isolated in senior level positions, less likely to have others to turn to for advice, and less effective in getting help during challenging periods (Heilman, 2001; Rudman, Moss-Racusin, Phelan, & Nauts (2012). Overall, the perceived lack of fit for women leaders demonstrates how simultaneous identities of race/ethnicity and gender intersect to produce distinct workplace experiences for women of color. Time and again women, especially women of color, are bypassed as leaders due to gender role expectations. The missing link between recognized merit and career success in educational settings is intersectional invisibility (Purdie-Vaughns & Eibach, 2008).

BLACK WOMEN: PRESENT IN THE WORKPLACE, BUT NOT ACCOUNTED FOR IN LEADERSHIP ROLES

Settles (2006) found that for Black women, the intersected Black-woman identity was more important than either of the individual identities of Black person and woman. "Double jeopardy" describes the frustration of both racism and sexism faced by women of color (Beale, 1970). For example, Black women in the United States were supporters and followers of the Civil Rights Movement and then soon realized that the oppression of sexism existed both within the broader society and within the Black community (Reid, 1984). Settles (2006) argues that the distinctive experiences of Black women in the United States may lead them to be more conscious of their racial and gender identities in relation to their other important identities (e.g., class, age, and sexual orientation). Scholars (e.g., Freeman, 2007) often assume the relationship between these identities is independent. In reality, many Black women may live double lives and shift more often and more consistently than any other racial/gender group in America (Jones & Shorter-Gooden, 2004).

W. E. B. Du Bois (1903) argued that Blacks experience double consciousness of their African identity and American identity that allows the navigation of survival between two cultures: White and Black. In other words, Blacks must retain their Black culture and identity while living in a dominant White society that pressures them to assimilate. This pressure to assimilate has an impact on Black women's understanding of their race and gender identities, all of which they navigate in the process of assimilation or resistance. Unfortunately, the double consciousness of Black people living in a predominantly White society produces a difficult set of social roles and standards to follow, which results in adaptations and negotiations by Black people to societal norms (King, 1988). Black feminists suggest that trio and systematic discriminations of racism, classism, and sexism remain prevalent within our society (e.g., King, 1988; Sesko & Biernat, 2010).

Previous literature supports the notion that identity negotiation among women of color is multidimensional and has significance because it occurs in their daily lives (e.g., Jackson, 2004; Jones & Shorter-Gooden, 2004). Identities of women of color are negotiated when cultural differences are present and calling for individuals to consciously shift their worldviews/cultural behaviors. The cultural contracts paradigm (Jackson, 2002) involves an individual choosing between three contract typologies. For example, a Black women may have the following contract typology options: (a) a ready to sign contract (e.g., assimilation to the dominant White culture), (b) a quasi-completed contract (e.g., adaptation to the White and Black cultural environments), and (c) a cocreated contract (e.g., mutual valuation and appreciation for one's marginalized cultural values). A cocreated cultural contract involves an understanding and acceptance of the minority culture by the dominant culture (Jackson, 2010). Thomas & Hollenshead (2001) conducted research on identity negotiation among Black women who were already established in their careers. However, few studies have explored how Black women's identities are negotiated and shaped by their early career experiences. Furthermore, not all women of color perceive identity negotiation as a negative experience. The theory of intersectionality is an approach used to understand the intertwining oppressions of race and gender (Cole, 2009; Crenshaw, 1991; May, 2015). Next, we discuss possible coping responses to being ignored and excluded by others.

REACTIONS TO WOMEN OF COLOR IN LEADERSHIP ROLES IN EDUCATIONAL SETTINGS

Jobs as ghost writer and silent partner imply that no negative consequences accompany being an "invisible" worker. In a study examining the challenges that women leaders face, researchers find that women report feeling "socially invisible," and that they feel greater pressure to conform and to make fewer mistakes. These women also report greater isolation and difficulty being perceived as credible (Turner, 2002). Inclusive environments provide a feeling of recognition and empowerment, which enables individuals to be engaged in group decision-making processes and have access to critical group resources and information (Mor Barak, Cherin, & Berkman, 1998). Ostracism, that is being excluded and ignored by individuals and groups, causes the targets of this treatment to feel pain and distress (Williams, 2009). Individuals can experience ostracism at least once a day in their daily lives—sometimes minimally and other times in more meaningful social experiences (Nezlek, Wesselmann, Wheeler, & Williams, 2012).

Additionally, perceptions of isolation can occur from a form of partial ostracism; for example, being "out of the loop" or being unaware of information mutually known by others (Jones, Carter-Sowell, Kelly, & Williams, 2009). Both experiences are commonly reported occurrences that potentially elicit anger and sadness (Williams, 2009). Ostracism can be considered a "social death" because historically it severs social connections that would have been necessary for evolutionary survival (Williams, 2009).

Because leadership and identity are closely linked, one's social identities play an important part in perceptions of one's role as a leader (Knippenberg, Knippenberg, De Cremer, & Hogg, 2005). *Presumed Incompetent* (Gutiérrez y Muhs, Niemann, González, & Harris, 2012) is an edited collection of first-hand accounts of the path-breaking experiences of women of color faculty working in academia. *Sisters in Science: Conversations with Black Women Scientists on Race, Gender, and Their Passion for Science* (Jordan, 2007) allows Black women scientists to tell their professional stories in their own way. Given this challenge, women in some educational settings warrant special incentives to pursue leadership positions (Lips & Keener, 2007). For example, to overcome institutional barriers in promotion and recognition, top colleges and research institutions, such as the University of Michigan, provide leadership training programs to female faculty members in their colleges of medicine, sciences, and engineering (Stewart & LaVaque-Manty, 2008).

Workplace ostracism—being ignored and excluded by others in an organizational setting—has gained attention as a pervasive job stressor that has detrimental effects on its targets, including greater psychological distress, decreased job satisfaction, and higher turnover intentions (Ferris, Brown, Berry, & Lian, 2008). This experience can take a variety of forms, including being uninformed of information mutually known by others, known as being out-of-the-loop (Jones, Carter-Sowell, Kelly, & Williams, 2009). Purdie-Vaughns (2015) offered commentary on why so few Black women are senior managers in 2015:

> Based on interviews and a survey of women professionals, Black women's contributions go unrecognized. The Center for Talent Innovations (2015) reports that 26% of Black women feel their talents aren't recognized by their superiors, compared to 17% of White women. Additionally, while Black, female professionals are more likely to seek top leadership roles, they are treated as virtually invisible.

Individuals who face chronic ostracism are at risk for depression, are more likely to perceive their value to others as low, and engage in attempts to avoid further painful rejection.

According to social identity theory, when one's social identity is threatened, individuals will either attempt to dissociate themselves from their existing group, or attempt to make the group positively distinct (Tajfel & Turner, 1986). If an environment is extremely hostile to one's social group, it might be nearly impossible for individuals to overcome hostility and ultimately reduce their level of identity threat (Shelton et al., 2005). The extent to which women feel threatened depends on their construal of whether and how the stereotype will be applied to the self (Branscombbe, Schmitt, & Harvey, 1999). In educational settings, bullying and uncivil behaviors take an enormous toll on individuals, can cost colleges and universities billions of dollars, and occur at an even higher rate in higher education (Hollis, 2015).

Chronic conditions of a devalued social identity may promote the widespread adoption of individual mobility strategies or further disidentification with women and leadership roles (Tajfel & Turner, 1986). Beliefs that others will perceive them according to gendered stereotypes can result in a threat to one's identity and self-esteem on a personal and group level (Branscombe et al., 1999). The discriminatory experiences that women have faced in their own career advancement experiences can create reluctance for them to continue on, or feel as if their gender is not valued in the workplace. Concerns that their performance could confirm associated stereotypes increases the likelihood that these women will engage in avoidance motivations in hopes of neutralizing the threats to their self-esteem.

One manner of avoidance minority women may take is via directly *opting out* of leadership roles altogether. Instead of directly confronting discrimination in the workplace, women chose to either weaken their alignment with their identities, or opt out of leadership positions because they feel a lack of value and personal fit within male-dominated organizations (Ellemers, 2014). Additionally, another route of avoidance involves *identity dissociation*. Past research has focused on how stereotypical gender expectations in organizations can cause women in leadership roles to distance themselves, or opt out, from their gender identity at work (Ellemers, Rink, Derks, & Ryan, 2012). Rather than directly dealing with the threat, minority women aspiring to leadership positions may negatively cope with ostracism experiences by positioning themselves further away from any association with their gender or ethnicity. However, this may have implications for collective self-esteem, or feelings that their identities are valued in that organization. How can research help to shed light on ways to expand the number of women and women of color in leadership positions?

Next, a qualitative interviewing technique is employed to uncover how individuals may navigate their careers on campus given the double marginalization of their race and gender identities.

STUDY OVERVIEW

Data were collected using semi-structured interviews, via video chat throughout different regions within the United States, between October 2013 and January 2014. Data from the interviews were classified through identified themes, and interpretative phenomenological analysis. Common narratives derived from the data include: (a) the complexity of the intersectionalities of race, gender, and class identities; (b) negotiation of identities in predominantly White social and work environments; (c) negotiation of identities in a predominantly Black environments; (d) triggers for the negotiations of race, class, and gender identities; and (e) conflicted anxieties toward negotiating identities. All participants were treated in accordance with APA guidelines and ethics and the institutional review board through the university approved the study.

METHOD

Participants

The nonrandom sample was identified through emails to professional and personal networks and contacts, posts on social media websites (e.g., Facebook), and through the snowball technique, in which an identified respondent who is eligible to participate in the study was asked to identify and recommend another eligible participant. The sample consisted of 10 academically successful Black women who were 5 years out of their undergraduate education. To be eligible to participate in this study, coresearchers must have met the following criteria: (a) self-identified as a Black/African American woman, (b) obtained a bachelor's degree within the past 5 years, (c) currently worked in a predominantly White environment, and (d) lived in a majority Black urban area (see Appendix 8A for the participants' information).

All of the participants self-identified as Black/African American women and had an average age of 25.2 years, ranging from 22 to 28 years of age. All of the women reported that their biological parents identified as Black/African American and as part of the middle or working class. All participants worked in a predominantly White workspace and resided in cities where the percentage of the Black population ranged from 29% to 53%, which is an average of 41%. Six out of 10 of the participants had master's or doctoral degrees. One out of 10 of the women were married and all identified as heterosexual.

Procedure

Interviews ranged from 40 minutes to 91 minutes in length and were based on a semistructured protocol with 30 questions. Participants were encouraged to speak about their perspectives on the following: how they describe their identities, their interpersonal and professional interactions, their self-concepts, and their identity negotiation in work and social environments. In addition, respondents were asked general questions regarding their construction of race and gender identities. The contextual coding themes were constructed from answers to these questions. All interviews were tape-recorded and transcribed for coding.

Coding and Analysis Strategy

Qualitative coding of interview data was conducted using a method commonly referred to as interpretative phenomenological analysis (IPA). The interpretative phenomenological approach uses systematic procedures to explore the meanings of everyday lived experiences. The systematic nature of this analytic method and inclusion of detailed descriptions of the analytic process exemplifies that this method has become an attractive method for psychologists (Willig, 2008). IPA aims to use a fairly homogeneous sample by finding a similar and closely operationally defined group for whom the research question is significant (Smith & Osborn, 2003). This process consists of collecting data with individuals who have experienced a particular phenomenon by conducting interviews with 5 to 25 participants (Creswell, 1998). In the recent past, researchers have recommended that researchers consult at least five or six participants because IPA researchers want to find a considerably homogeneous sample (Smith & Osborn, 2003). Thus, 10 participants were recruited to participate in the current study.

IPA is utilized initially by openly coding one transcript and by adding comments in the left-hand margin regarding the meaning of the particular sections of the transcript relative to the language and similarities, differences, amplifications, and any contradictions in what the participants described (Langdridge, 2007). Initial notes were grouped into emerging themes, this process continued through the entire transcript. The notes were then transformed into emerging themes on the right-hand side of the margin, providing broader levels of meaning for each section of the transcript texts. The themes were then listed separately in another Microsoft Word document. Next, the researcher identified common links between the themes and grouped similar themes. After a list of 10 themes was created, a color-coding scheme was used for each theme and then the researcher went back to the transcript to check the emerging themes with specific quotes from the text. This step was repeated until the themes were distinct and completely representative of the text by checking the themes against the text with three transcripts.

Next, the transcriptions were triangulated with a research assistant, who identified as a Black woman, for final coding to make sure that the coding categories were reliable. The second coder first blindly coded two transcripts with the generated themes. Then the two coders talked through their coded transcripts in order to reconcile any differences in coding, and the second coder went over the primary researcher's eight coded transcripts and made notes and comments where discrepancies arose between the researcher and the second coder's coding choices. Deciding which themes to focus on was dependent upon not only the frequency of each theme, but also the richness and explicit negotiations of intersectional identities of particular passages that highlighted the themes. In addition, how the themes illuminated other aspects of identity negotiation was taken into account when selecting the final themes (Smith & Osborn, 2003). The themes were narrowed down by the highest number of prevalent topics among the cosearchers; committee members assisted with narrowing down the number of themes. Consistent with Creswell and Clark (2007), it is suggested that narrowing down to at least five to seven themes is sufficient.

RESULTS

The following section critically explores constructed themes from the interviews with these women. These themes describe and relate to the experiences associated with the long overdue recognition of identity negotiation of race and gender among early career Black women. The two themes constructed from the data include: (a) perceived race and gender identities among career-oriented Black women, and (b) triggers for negotiation of identities in predominantly White environments. Each of the emergent themes identified during the coding process was applied to the following research question: How do academically successful Black women describe their race and gender identities?

The two constructed themes focused on common narratives (e.g., themes had to appear four or more times) of each interview and/or important data that emerged. These benchmarks were relevant to better understanding each participants' experiences of negotiating their race, class, and gender identities in social, familial, and professional environments. After the themes were finalized, the first author reviewed each transcript again, using the themes and subthemes to synthesize common data elements.

THEME A: PERCEIVED RACE AND GENDER IDENTITIES AMONG CAREER-ORIENTED BLACK WOMEN

The identity theme captured the true essence of the importance of race and gender identities for each participant. Intersectionality serves as an illumination of the ways multiple oppressed identities are experienced and how they influence one another. The critical theory of intersectionality is best suited to understanding the interlocking oppressions of race and gender (Crenshaw, 1991). The Black women in their early career in the study conveyed the significance of their race and gender identities in shaping their worldview and daily life experiences within their career and personal lives. Some participants explored the unique struggles of Black womanhood; for example, Jessica described the double marginalization of being both Black and a female.

> So you are not only overcoming the female piece and wanting to get respect that you deserve and the respect that you should be getting, even though you are a woman. Then with the Black piece, you have to overcome the piece where it's, like, you want to be respected and you know you have to overcome some people's thoughts of you are not as good or you're not talented. I think having those two things can make it hard in some instances, because you have to overcome two sets of obstacles as versus one or the other.

THEME B: TRIGGERS FOR NEGOTIATION OF IDENTITIES IN PREDOMINANTLY WHITE ENVIRONMENTS

The theme of the negotiation of race and gender identities serves as the central theme for the current study, focusing on identity negotiation in predominantly White workplaces and social environments. This theme was assembled through the direct review of transcripts based on participants' responses to experiences of racism or discrimination on the job. The subthemes constructed by the primary investigator from the data included the following: managing professionalism, managing interpersonal rejection, the stillness effect, and linguistic negotiating.

Brittany discussed how the stereotypes of Black women affected her and increased the pressure she felt to act professional.

> It has affected me and made me more aware of how to conduct myself in a professional setting; and even sometimes in my personal life, I found that when I want to be taken seriously I have to get in that mindset, like, okay, be serious right now.

In essence, Brittany described that she had to act a particular way in professional settings among majority Whites in order to be taken seriously. Along those same lines, Brittany made a historical reference to racialized gender stereotypes of Black women and the transition of Black women into the workforce. "Our image was very overly sexualized, and now we are women who are heading businesses, doctors, and lawyers."

Also, in many discussions about professionalism that were raised, being professional was characterized as "acting White" due to the various ways that Black women felt pressured to assimilate to the White workplace culture. Acting White is analogous to a standard etiquette and way of speaking in professional settings. This pressure to appear professional applied outside the workplace as well. For instance, Brittany discussed how she was in a clothing store and one of the employees seemed annoyed when she asked her question and assumed that she wasn't going to buy anything. In the face of experiencing discrimination in a social environment, she shifted her language to a "professional voice."

> I kind of just put on my professional voice. I was not just, like, relaxed, I became professional, like, "Oh yes ma'am, can you please get me this, or oh yes, I would like this," like I asserted myself.

The dynamics involved with identity negotiation in predominantly White environments consists of being professional even in the face of confronting racism and negative stereotypes associated with Black women. There is a workplace identity that Black women have to negotiate in their workspaces to be taken seriously.

DISCUSSION

Findings from this study provide insight into factors that may influence Black women's participation in the negotiation of their race and gender identities, and the unique experiences of early career Black women in the United States. In particular, there is a perception that the United States is currently a "post racial" society because the United States has their first Black president, Barack Obama. But that is far from the reality. Although there are increased enrollments of Black women in higher education and increased employment of Black women, they still experience both blatant and subtle forms of racism and discrimination (Reynolds-Dobbs, Thomas, & Harrison, 2012). Accordingly, the Millennial population faces a difficult dilemma: they are perceived to live in a post-racial society, but simultaneously they are required to confront long-standing stereotypes and prejudices, which require the shifting and negotiation of their identities.

Participants also consistently discussed their combined racial and gender identity, where they do not see their race and gender identities as separate, but instead identify as a Black woman. This perspective is consistent with the literature suggesting that Black women place equal importance on their race and gender, where the Black-woman identity is often more significant than either the Black or woman identities separately (Settles,

2006). Participants also discussed the pride of being a Black woman, yet were aware of the extremely negative and extremely positive stereotypes that plague Black women, such as being the domineering sapphire or the strong, independent Black woman. Thus, there is a unique intersection of race and gender among Black women, and they come to see themselves in terms of the combined identity (Settles, 2006). Research argues that Black Americans code their experiences with White Americans and with social institutions in terms of race, not class or gender (Ogbu, 2004). However in the current study, the participants conceptually could not tease apart their racial and gender identities, which speaks to the importance of grasping how these identities interlock and that these Black women exemplify Settles's statement.

Another important theme that came up was "the triggers for negotiation of identities." Participants cited several reasons for negotiating race, class, and gender including: assimilating in the face of White power structures, confronting and refuting stereotypes of Black women, model Black citizenship, building and maintaining relationships, and avoiding being labeled the Black elite. These factors were a result of how the participants were perceived by others.

Some of the participants discussed perceptions of being a representative on behalf of the Black race, and more specifically for Black women. This is also consistent with the out-group homogeneity effect (Quattrone & Jones, 1980), which argues that the dominant culture may have a misperception that underrepresented groups are more similar to one another than people who are part of the dominant group. As a result, out-group members—in this case Black women—are at risk of being seen as interchangeable or expendable, and thus are more likely to be stereotyped. Because of being stereotyped, this can affect their chances of getting promotions on jobs or moving up in the career due to the unfortunate stereotypes of Black women being unreliable and not having credibility.

Another prominent finding mentioned in the face of experiencing racial and gender microaggressions in predominantly White environments was the *frozen effect*. After experiencing discriminatory situations, some participants discussed becoming silent and mentally paralyzed by mentally "checking out" in conversations. This was consistent with the literature exploring the invisibility syndrome among marginalized populations. According to Franklin (1999), invisibility is described as an inner struggle with the feeling that one's abilities and talents are not valued or are ignored because of prejudice and racism. In particular, the invisibility syndrome (Franklin, 1999) is a conceptual model to understand the factors determining adaptive responses to racism and invisibility (e.g., lack of recognition, no gratification from encounter, and self-doubt). As a result of racism, coresearchers discussed how they began to "shut down" and remove themselves from certain situations and conversations to avoid the internalized effect of racism. As a result, their coworkers may have adopted the perception that Black women were not motivated or content in their current jobs, without having the knowledge of the societal stigma and experiences of racial and gender microaggressions that these women were facing. Thus, this could have risked potential job promotions, and budding professional and personal relationships.

IMPLICATIONS

One of the most prominent discussions among the participants concerned the act of confronting and disputing stereotypes of Black women. The implications of this study also suggest that identity negotiation can take a psychological toll on the psyche of Black women because it can be a very stressful process to engage in. Past studies have found that there is an association between racial or gender discrimination and health outcomes among Black women. For instance, a study conducted by Taylor et al. (2007) found that perceived experiences of racism are associated with increased rates of breast cancer, particularly among younger Black women in the United States. Other studies have suggested that the prevalence of health issues among Black women is associated with the psychological stressors associated with perceived discrimination (e.g., Bowen-Reid & Harrell, 2002). This research can inform policymakers, stakeholders, and advocates for institutional changes of the daily stress and exhaustion associated with identity negotiation among Black women, to better understand their experiences and the potential physical and psychological effects of stress associated with negotiation on other outcomes.

PRACTICAL IMPLICATIONS AND FUTURE RESEARCH

Enrollment rates are growing for women of color seeking higher education. The diversity of groups entering the academic career pipeline is increasing, yet the rates of recruiting and retaining women of color faculty is stagnant. Several studies have discussed the mentoring dilemmas for junior faculty women due to the lack of access to senior faculty women in certain sectors (e.g., Blake, 1999). The pain and frustration associated with unrecognized leadership abilities remains a constant challenge to the prosperity of women of color in educational settings (Harris, 2007). Devoting research to understanding the complexities of identity negotiation for women of color is critical to diversifying leadership that differs from the status quo at today's colleges and universities.

APPENDIX 8.A Summary of Demographic Characteristics of Participants				
Name	Age	Marital status	Level of education	Professional status
Jasmine	28	Single	Bachelor's	Student affairs
Levi	27	Single	Master's	Case management
Kara	26	Single	Master's	Student affairs
Jessica	26	Married	Master's	Student affairs
Angie	26	Single	Master's	Family services
Nicole	26	Single	Master's	Program associate
Claire	26	Single	Doctorate	Physical therapist
Brittany	24	Single	Bachelor's	Educator
Nicki	22	Single	Bachelor's	Health care researcher
Harriett	23	Single	Bachelor's	Educator

REFERENCES

Australian Government, Department of Education and Training. (2014). Table 3.2: Number of full-time and fractional full-time indigenous staff by state, higher education institution, function, gender and current duties classification. *Selected Higher Education Statistics-2014 Staff Data, 2014 Staff Indigenous.* Retrieved from https://docs.education.gov.au/node/36255

Beale, I. L. (1970). The effects of amount of training per reversal on successive reversals of color discrimination. *Journal of the Experimental Analysis of Behavior, 14*(3/1), 345–352.

Bell, E. L. (1990). The bicultural life experience of career-oriented Black women. *Journal of Organizational Behavior, 11,* 459–477.

Bell, E. J. & Nkomo, S. M. (2001). *Our separate ways: Black and White women and the struggle for professional identity.* Boston, MA: Harvard Business School Press.

Blake, S. (1999). At the crossroads of race and gender: Lessons from the mentoring experiences of professional Black women. *Mentoring dilemmas: Developmental relationships within multicultural organizations, 83,* 104.

Bowen-Reid, T. L., & Harrell, J. P. (2002). Racist experiences and health outcomes: An examination of spirituality as a buffer. *Journal of Black Psychology, 28,* 18–36.

Branscombe, N. R., Schmitt, M. T., & Harvey, R. D. (1999). Perceiving pervasive discrimination among African-Americans: Implications for group identification and well-being. *Journal of Personality and Social Psychology, 77,* 135–149.

Canadian Association of University Teachers. (2010, January). The changing academy? A portrait of Canada's university teachers. *CAUT Education Review, 12.* Retrieved from http://www.caut.ca/docs/education-review/the-changing-academy-a-portrait-of-canada-rsquo-s-university-teachers-%28jan-2010%29.pdf?sfvrsn=14

Carter, D. A., Simkins, B. J., & Simpson, W. G. (2003). Corporate governance, board diversity, and firm value. *Financial Review, 38,* 33–53.

Catalyst. (2015, July 9). *Women in academia: In Australia, women hold fewer senior faculty positions than men.* Retrieved from http://www.catalyst.org/knowledge/women-academia#footnote36_u1eabua

Chin, J. L., Lott, B., Rice, J., & Sanchez-Hucles, J. (Eds.). (2008). *Women and leadership: Transforming visions and diverse voices.* Hoboken, NJ: Wiley.

Cochiara, F., Bell, M., & Berry, D. P. (2006). Latinas and Black women: Key factors for a growing proportion of the U.S. workforce. *Equal Opportunities International, 25,* 272–284.

Cole, E. R. (2009). Intersectionality and research in psychology. *The American Psychologist, 64,* 170–180. doi: 10.1037/a0014564

Cook, B. J. (2012). The American college president study: Key findings and takeaways. *American Council on Education, Spring Supplement.* Retrieved from http://www.acenet.edu/the-presidency/columns-and-features/Pages/The-American-College-President-Study.aspx

Council of Graduate Schools. (2008). *PhD completion and attrition: Analysis of baseline program data from the PhD completion project.* Washington, DC: Author.

Crenshaw, K. (1991). Mapping the margins: Intersectionality, identity politics, and violence against women of color. *Stanford Law Review,* 43(6), 1241–1299.

Creswell, J. W. (1998). *Five qualitative traditions of inquiry: Qualitative inquiry and research design.* Thousand Oaks, CA: Sage.

Creswell, J. W. (2009). *Research design: Qualitative and mixed methods approaches.* Thousand Oaks, CA: Sage

Du Bois, W. E. B. (1903). *The souls of Black folk.* Oxford, England: Oxford University Press.

Eagly, A. H., & Carli, L. L. (2003). Finding gender advantage and disadvantage: Systematic research integration is the solution. *The Leadership Quarterly, 14,* 851–859.

Eagly, A. H., & Carli, L. C. (2007). *Through the labyrinth: The truth about how women become leaders.* Boston, MA: Harvard Business School Press.

Ellemers, N. (2014). Women at work: How organizational features impact career development. *Policy Insights From the Behavioral and Brain Sciences, 1,* 46–54.

Ellemers, N., Rink, F., Derks, B., & Ryan, M. (2012). Women in high places: When and why promoting women into top positions can harm them individually or as a group (and how to prevent this). *Research in Organizational Behavior, 32,* 163–187.

Ferris, D. L., Brown, D. J., Berry, J. W., & Lian, H. (2008). The development and validation of the Workplace Ostracism Scale. *Journal of Applied Psychology, 93,* 1348–1366. doi: 10.1037/a0012743

Franklin, A. J. (1999). Invisibility syndrome and racial identity development in psychotherapy and counseling African American men. *The Counseling Psychologist, 27,* 761–793.

Freedman, E. (2007). *No turning back: The history of feminism and the future of women.* New York, NY: Random House.

Gutiérrez y Muhs, G., Niemann, Y. F., González, C. G., & Harris, A. P. (Eds.). (2012). *Presumed incompetent: The intersections of race and class for women in academia.* Logan, UT; Utah State University Press.

Harris, T. M. (2007). Black feminist thought and cultural contracts: Understanding the intersection and negotiation of racial, gendered, and professional identities in the academy. *New Directions for Teaching and Learning, 110,* 55–64.

Haslam, S. A., & Ryan, M. K. (2008). The road to the glass cliff: Differences in the perceived suitability of men and women for leadership positions in succeeding and failing organizations. *The Leadership Quarterly, 19,* 530–546.

Heilman, M. E. (1983). Sex bias in work settings: The lack of fit model. *Research in Organizational Behavior, 5,* 269–298.

Heilman, M. E. (2001). Description and prescription: How gender stereotypes prevent women's ascent up the organizational ladder. *Journal of Social Issues, 57,* 657. doi:10.1111/ 0022-4537.00234.

Heilman, M. E., & Okimoto, T. G. (2007). Why are women penalized for success at male tasks? The implied communality deficit. *Journal of Applied Psychology, 92,* 81–92.

Heilman, M. E., Wallen, A. S., Fuchs, D., & Tamkins, M. M. (2004). Penalties for success: reactions to women who succeed at male gender-typed tasks. *Journal of Applied Psychology, 89,* 416–427.

Hess, C., Gault, B., & Yi, Y. (2013, November). Accelerating change for women faculty of color in STEM: Policy, action, and collaboration. *Institute for Women's Policy Research (IWPR).* Retrieved from http://www.iwpr.org/publications/ pubs/accelerating-change-for-women-faculty-of-color-in-stem-policy-action-and-collaboration

Hollis, L. P. (2015, June). Bully university? The cost of workplace bullying and employee disengagement in American higher education. *Sage Open, 5*(2), doi: 10.1177/2158244015589997

Integrated Postsecondary Education Data Systems. (2012). Full-time instructional staff, by faculty and tenure status, academic rank, race/ethnicity, and gender (Degree-granting institutions): Fall 2012. *National Center for Education Statistics Fall Staff 2012 Survey.* Retrieved from http://nces.ed.gov/ipeds/datacenter/ Default.aspx

Jackson, R. L. (2002). Cultural contracts theory: Toward an understanding of identity negotiation. *Communication Quarterly, 50,* 359–367.

Jackson R. L. (2004). Negotiating and mediating constructions of racial identities. *Review of Communication, 4,* 6–15.

Jackson, R. L. (2010). Exploring African American identity negotiation in the academy: Toward a transformative vision of African American communication scholarship. *Howard Journal of Communications, 13,* 43–57.

Jones, C., & Shorter-Gooden, K. (2004). *Shifting: The doubles lives of Black women.* New York, NY: Harper Perennial.

Jones, E. E., Carter-Sowell, A. R., Kelly, J. R., & Williams, K. D. (2009). "I'm out of the loop": Ostracism through information exclusion. *Group Processes & Intergroup Relations, 12,* 157–174.

Jordan, D. (2007). *Sisters in science: Conversations with Black women scientists about race, gender, and their passion for science.* West Lafayette, IN: Purdue University Press.

King, D. (1988). Multiple jeopardy, multiple consciousness: The context of a Black feminist ideology. *Signs, 14,* 42–72.

Langdridge, D. (2007). *Phenomenological psychology: Theory, research and method.* Upper Saddle River, NJ: Pearson Education.

Lips, H. M., & Keener, E. (2007). Effects of gender and dominance on leadership emergence: Incentives make a difference. *Sex Roles, 56,* 563–571.

Malcom, S. M., Hall, P. Q., & Brown, J. W. (1976). *The double bind: The price of being a minority woman in science.* Washington, DC: American Association for the Advancement of Science.

May, V. M. (2015). *Pursuing intersectionality, unsettling dominant imaginaries.* New York, NY: Routledge.

Mor Barak, M. E., Cherin, D. A., & Berkman, S. (1998). Organizational and personal dimensions in diversity climate: Ethnic and gender differences in employee diversity perceptions. *Journal of Applied Behavioral Sciences, 34,* 82–104.

National Science Foundation (NSF), National Center for Education Statistics. (2011). *Graduate students and postdoctorates in science and engineering: Fall 2009. Table 30. Graduate students in science, engineering, and health fields in all institutions, by field, citizenship, and race/ethnicity of U.S. citizens and permanent residents: 2003–2009.* Retrieved from http://www.nsf.gov/statistics/nsf12300/pdf/nsf12300.pdf

Nezlek, J. B., Wesselmann, E. D., Wheeler, L., & Williams, K. D. (2012). Ostracism in everyday life. *Group Dynamics: Theory, Research, and Practice, 16,* 91–104.

Ogbu, J. U. (2004). Collective identity and the burden of "acting White" in Black history, community, and education. *The Urban Review, 36,* 1–35.

Ong, M., Wright, C., Espinosa, L., & Orfield, G. (2011). Inside the double bind: A synthesis of empirical research on undergraduate and graduate women of color in science, technology, engineering, and mathematics. *Harvard Educational Review, 81,* 172–209.

Ospina, S., & Foldy, E. G. (2009). A critical review of race and ethnicity in the leadership literature: Surfacing context, power and the collective dimensions of leadership. *Leadership Quarterly, 20,* 876–896.

Potamites, E. (2007). *Why do Black women work more? A comparison of White and Black married women's labor supply.* (Working paper.) New York University, New York, NY.

Purdie-Vaughns, V. (2015, April). Why so few Black women are senior managers in 2015. *Fortune.* Retrieved from http://fortune.com/author/valerie-purdie-vaughns/

Purdie-Vaughns, V., & Eibach, R. P. (2008). Intersectional invisibility: The distinctive advantages and disadvantages of multiple subordinate-group identities. *Sex Roles, 59,* 377–391. doi: 10.1007/s11199-008-9424-4

Quattrone, G. A., & Jones, E. E. (1980). The perception of variability within in-groups and out-groups: Implications for the law of small numbers. *Journal of Personality and Social Psychology, 38,* 141.

Reid, P. T. (1984). Feminism versus minority group identity: Not for Black woman only. *Sex Roles, 10,* 247–255.

Reynolds-Dobbs, W., Thomas, K., & Harrison, M. (2008). From mammy to super-woman: Images that hinder Black women's career development. *Journal of Career Development, 35*, 129–150.

Rudman, L. A., Moss-Racusin, C. A., Phelan, J. E., & Nauts, S. (2012). Status in-congruity and backlash effects: Defending the gender hierarchy motivates prejudice against female leaders. *Journal of Experimental Social Psychology, 48*, 165–179.

Sanchez-Hucles, J. V., & Davis, D. D. (2010). Women and women of color in leader-ship: Complexity, identity, and intersectionality. *American Psychologist, 65*, 171.

Sesko, A. K., & Biernat, M. (2010). Prototypes of race and gender: The invisibility of Black women. *Journal of Experimental Social Psychology, 46*, 356–360.

Settles, I. H. (2006). Use of an intersectional framework to understand Black wom-en's racial and gender identities. *Sex Roles, 54*, 589–601.

Shelton, J. N., Yip, T., Eccles, J. S., Chatman, C. M., Fuligni, A., & Wong, C. (2005). Ethnic identity as a buffer of psychological adjustment to stress. In G. Downey, J. S. Eccles, & C. M. Chatman (Eds.), *Navigating the future: Social identity, coping and life tasks* (pp. 96–115). New York, NY: Russell Sage Foundation.

Smith, J. A., & Osborn, M. (2003). Interpretative phenomenological analysis. In J. A. Smith (Ed.), *Qualitative psychology: A practical guide to research methods* (pp. 51–80). London, England: Sage.

Stewart, A. & LaVaque-Manty, D. (2008). Advancing women in science and engi-neering: Overcoming institutional barriers. In H. M. Watt & J. S. Eccles (Eds.), *Gender and occupational outcomes: Longitudinal assessments of individual, social, and cultural influences* (pp. 299–322). Washington, DC: American Psy-chological Association.

Taylor, T. R., Williams, C. D., Makambi, K. H., Mouton, C., Harrell, J. P., Cozier, Y., . . . Adams–Campbell, L. L. (2007). Racial discrimination and breast cancer incidence in U. S. Black women: The Black women's health study. *American Journal of Epidemiology, 166*, 46–54.

Tajfel, H., & Turner, J. C. (1986). The social identity theory of inter-group behavior. In S. Worchel & W. G. Austin (Eds.), *The psychology of intergroup relations* (2nd ed.; pp. 7–24). Chicago IL: Nelson-Hall.

The Chronicle of Higher Education. (2010). Almanac of higher education 2010–2011. *The Chronicle of Higher Education, 57*, 20.

Thomas, G. D., & Hollenshead, C. (2001, July). Resisting from the margins: The coping strategies of Black women and other women of color faculty members at a research university. *Journal of Negro Education*, 166–175.

Turner, C. S. V. (2002). Women of color in academe: Living with multiple marginal-ity. *The Journal of Higher Education, 73*, 74–93.

Turner, C. S. V., & González, J. C. & Wong (Lau), K. (2011). Faculty women of color: The critical nexus of race and gender. *Journal of Diversity in Higher Education, 4*, 199–211.

U.S. Census Bureau (2013). *Table B24010B. Sex by occupation for the civilian employed population 16 years and over (Black or African American alone).* Retrieved from http://factfinder.census.gov/faces/tableservices/jsf/pages/productview. xhtml?pid=ACS_13_1YR_B24010B&prodType=table

Van Knippenberg, B., Van Knippenberg, D., De Cremer, D. & Hogg, M. A. (2005). Research in leadership, self, and identity: A sample of the present and a glimpse of the future. *The Leadership Quarterly, 16,* 495–499.

Williams, K. D. (2009). Ostracism: A temporal need-threat model. In M. Zanna (Ed.) *Advances in Experimental Social Psychology* (Vol. 41; pp. 275–314). New York, NY: Academic Press.

Willig, C. (2008). A phenomenological investigation of the experience of taking part in extreme sports. *Journal of Health Psychology, 13,* 690–702.

Yoo, L. (2013). *Feminism and race: Just who counts as a 'woman of color'?* Retrieved from http://www.npr.org/sections/codeswitch/2013/09/12/221469077/feminism-and-race-just-who-counts-as-a-woman-of-color

ABOUT THE EDITORS

Julia Ballenger, PhD, is a professor at Texas A&M University-Commerce. She teaches in the Masters in Educational Administration and the Doctoral in Educational Leadership Programs. Dr. Ballenger has been a member of the Research on Women and Education (RWE) SIG for 14 years. She has served on the RWE Executive Committee as the co-chair, program co-chair, membership chair, and on several committees. She currently serves as treasurer-elect. Dr. Ballenger recently received the 2015 Information Age Author Legacy Award.

Dr. Ballenger's research agenda consists of culturally relevant pedagogy, leadership for social justice, educational leadership, global competence, and mentoring women administrators in higher education. Dr. Ballenger has presented her research at the state, national, and internationally levels. She has presented research on leadership for social justice at the Oxford Roundtable in London, and research on mentoring women in higher education at the World Education Conference in Athens, Greece.

Dr. Ballenger has published more than 60 peer-reviewed articles and book chapters. She is the coauthor of six books. Dr. Ballenger's most recent co-edited research entitled, *The Fiery Melting Pot: Immigrant Women and Girls in Pursuit of Social Justice*, was published in the 2016 special issue of the NCPEA Education Leadership Review Journal. This special issue includes discourse that challenge and counter media, legislative policy, and access issues for immigrant women and girls. Dr. Ballenger's professional career spans more than 40 years. Prior to entering academe, she served as regional director at the Texas Education Agency, Central Office Administration, and as a teacher, consultant, counselor, and principal in several public school districts.

Women of Color in STEM, pages 203–204
Copyright © 2017 by Information Age Publishing
203

Dr. Beverly J. Irby, EdD, is professor and chair of educational administration in the Department of Educational Administration and Human Resource Development at Texas A&M University, College Station, Texas. She earned her doctorate from the University of Mississippi in 1983. She has earned the reputation as an excellent professor and her mentored students have garnered numerous research awards. Dr. Irby's research focus is that of social responsibility for instructional leadership; theory development/validation; women's leadership; gender equity; early childhood, bilingual/ESL, gifted, and science education; online learning; reflective practice portfolios; international leadership; principal and teacher evaluation/professional development; program evaluation; and various research techniques, including bricolage. A national/international speaker, she and her research group have developed studies and garnered more than $35 million in grant funding. She developed the Hispanic Bilingual Gifted Screening Instrument and the Synergistic Leadership Theory. Dr. Irby, who has held the Texas State University System Regents Professor since 2009, has several awards and honors among which are Bilingual Research Journal Senior Reviewer 2012, AERA Educational Researcher Reviewer 2010, AERA Research on Women and Education Information Age Publishing Legacy Award 2012, Editor of Mentoring and Tutoring Journal, Board of Reviewers for ELCC, and AERA Willystine Goodsell Award 2005.

Barbara Polnick, Ed. DED, is a professor and instructional leadership coordinator in the Educational Leadership Department at Sam Houston State University, Huntsville, Texas. Her expertise lies in writing and evaluating grants; leading school improvement initiatives; and conducting research on gender and social justice issues, women in leadership, teacher leadership in mathematics, early childhood, and mathematics learning. Dr. Polnick's scholarship contributions include more than 70 national presentations, 30 peer-reviewed articles, eight book chapters, two edited books, and one textbook. Dr. Polnick is currently serving as coeditor of the *Advancement of Women in Leadership* online journal and was a recent recipient of the Outstanding College of Education and Human Resources Alumni Award from Texas A&M University, and the Research on Women and Education AERA SIG Information Age Publishing Legacy Award. She holds leadership roles in several local and national organizations and currently serves on the AERA SIG Research on Women and Education Board as past chair. She has more than 26 years of experience in public education as a teacher, regional consultant, instructional supervisor, assistant principal, and district curriculum director.

ABOUT THE CONTRIBUTORS

Lindsay Brown is currently a doctoral student in the industrial-organizational psychology program at the University of Georgia (UGA). Lindsay is also a graduate research fellow at the J. W. Fanning Institute for Leadership Development at UGA. Lindsay earned her BS in psychology from the University of Houston and her MS in industrial-organizational psychology from UGA. Her work involves understanding underrepresented or stigmatized identities in the workplace, prejudice and discrimination, career development, and occupational segregation.

Lisa Brown is a professor at Sam Houston State University. She teaches in the Curriculum and Instruction Department and serves as the Secondary Education Program coordinator. She began her teaching career as a classroom teacher teaching science to at-risk middle and high school students in the Houston area. Dr. Brown worked with NASA in the Aerospace Education Services Project where she was responsible for conducting workshops for teachers and administrators in schools, colleges, and universities.

Adrienne R. Carter-Sowell, PhD, is a jointly appointed assistant professor in the Psychology Department and Africana Studies Program at Texas A&M University. Dr. Carter-Sowell is leading an interdisciplinary research program addressing the costs of being "socially invisible" (see http://www.diversitysciences.org). Dr. Carter-Sowell purposely seeks pathways to recruit, educate, and mentor individuals in the academic community, as well as cultivate outreach opportunities with organizations that share her mission to promote diversity science research. Dr. Carter-Sowell is a co-principal

Women of Color in STEM, pages 205–208
Copyright © 2017 by Information Age Publishing

investigator on the NSF TAMUS AGEP–Transformation Grant: Advancing Interdisciplinary STEM Graduate Education.

Danielle Dickens, PhD, is an assistant professor of psychology at Spelman College. Dr. Dickens received her MS and PhD in applied social and health psychology from Colorado State University and her BA degree from Spelman College. Her research uses an interdisciplinary approach to examine the intersection of socially constructed identities and their implications for health behaviors, academic performance, and psychological well-being. Specifically, her research explores the role of identity negotiation on psychological health and self-perception.

Torri A. Draganov is a senior doctoral student in the Higher Education Leadership Department at Texas A&M University in Commerce, Texas, and an assistant chemistry professor at Cypress College, California. Her research interests, under the direction of her faculty adviser Dr. JoHyun Kim, fall in STEM student retention at the community college level. For her dissertation, Torri intends to focus on the influence of the STEM support program on STEM student outcomes at Cypress College. Draganov provided editorial support for this book.

Andrea Foster's STEM education career has spanned decades. She has taught in K–12 public schools and higher education. A 1994 recipient of the Presidential Award for Excellence in Science Teaching, Dr. Foster was recently honored with the Howard Hughes Medical Association Skoog Cup for her contributions to the development of quality science education programs. She is an associate professor in the Curriculum and Instruction Department at Sam Houston State University.

Dr. Samina Hadi-Tabassum, EdD, is an assistant professor at Northern Illinois University in the Literacy and Elementary Education Department. She teaches courses in the Bilingual and ESL Program. Her teaching career began in 1993 when she was recruited by Teach for America to teach in Houston as a middle school bilingual science teacher. After 10 years in the K–8 classroom, she obtained a doctorate from Teachers College at Columbia University, in curriculum studies. Her first book, *Language, Space and Power*, focuses on dual language education.

Lindsay N. Johnson is an assistant professor in the Department of Psychology, Organizational Leadership & MAP Program at the University of Cincinnati. Johnson's research focuses on workplace phenomenon including culture & bias, social identity, discrimination, and incivility towards women and other underrepresented groups. She received her PhD and Masters in Industrial-Organizational Psychology from the University of Georgia.

Nicole M. Joseph is an assistant professor of mathematics education at Vanderbilt University. Recently a National Academy of Education Spencer Postdoctoral Fellow, she is currently examining the origin and development of STEM education for Blacks attending historically Black colleges and universities during the late 19th century. She uses critical frameworks to ground this work to illuminate problems and possibilities in the evolution of race work in STEM including structural, pedagogical, and environmental spaces.

Jacqueline Leonard is the director of the Science and Mathematics Teaching Center and professor of mathematics education at the University of Wyoming where she has served since August 2012. Her research interests include computational thinking, culturally specific pedagogy, and place-based education. She has published numerous articles; one book, *Culturally Specific Pedagogy* (2008); and one coedited volume, *The Brilliance of Children in Mathematics*.

Gabe Miller is a doctoral student in the Department of Sociology at Texas A&M University. Under the direction of his adviser, Dr. Joe Feagin, Miller's main research area is race and ethnicity, focusing on racism and whiteness in the United States. He works as a research assistant for the Race and Ethnic Studies Institute (RESI) with Dr. Verna Keith, and he is a graduate student worker with Dr. A. R. Carter-Sowell on the NSF TAMUS AGEP–Transformation Grant Project.

Cailisha L. Petty, PhD, is the teacher education coordinator in the Department of Biology at North Carolina A&T State University. In 1999, her teaching career began as a 7th-grade science and math teacher. She obtained a master's degree in biology education in 2004. In 2006, she began full-time teaching in higher education at North Carolina A&T State University. In 2015, she obtained a doctorate from the University of North Carolina at Greensboro in teacher education with a focus on science education. Her research focus is equity in science education.

Barbara Polnick's involvement in STEM, specifically mathematics, spans more than 40 years. From high school mathematics teacher, mathematics and curriculum specialist, curriculum director, and now professor at Sam Houston State University she has focused much of her work on improving teaching and learning in mathematics as it relates to gender, leadership, and early childhood. The author of more than 40 peer-reviewed publications (articles and book chapters) and one textbook, she holds an EdD in educational administration from Texas A&M University.

Delores Rice is an assistant professor in the Department of Higher Education and Learning Technologies, College of Education and Human Services at Texas A&M University-Commerce. In addition to teaching and supporting the university, Dr. Rice conducts research in STEM (science, technology, engineering, and mathematics), with a passion for engineering education and social justice. Having earned a bachelor of science in mechanical engineering, her research focuses on African American female engineers and other underrepresented groups in the STEM disciplines.

Kecia M. Thomas is a professor of I/O Psychology and African American Studies at the University of Georgia, where she also serves as an Associate Dean in the Franklin College of Arts and Sciences. Thomas' research focuses on the psychology of workplace diversity with an emphasis on understanding and supporting the careers of women of color. She is a graduate of Bucknell and Penn State, and an elected Fellow of both the SIOP and APA.

Catherine Dinitra White, associate professor of biology at North Carolina A&T State University, obtained a PhD in microbiology and immunology from Wayne State University in 2002, and completed postdoctoral training at the University of North Carolina at Chapel Hill in 2006. She teaches several biology classes and maintains an active microbial pathogenesis research laboratory. As director of the North Carolina A&T Pre-Professional Scholars Program, she assists minority students in their pursuit of professional and graduate careers.

Erica N. Walker is professor of mathematics education at Teachers College, Columbia University. Her research focuses on the social and cultural factors that facilitate mathematics engagement, learning, and performance, especially for underserved students. Dr. Walker is the author of numerous journal articles as well as two books: *Building Mathematics Learning Communities: Improving Outcomes in Urban High Schools* (2012), and *Beyond Banneker: Black Mathematicians and the Paths to Excellence* (2014).

Carla A. Zimmerman is a senior doctoral student in the Psychology Department at Texas A&M University in College Station, Texas. Her research interests, under the direction of her faculty adviser, Dr. A. R. Carter-Sowell, fall in the intersection between social exclusion and stigmatization research. Specifically, Zimmerman is interested in ostracism resulting from stereotyping and discrimination. For her dissertation, she intends to focus on the influence of gender and gender-based stereotypes on perceived experiences of ostracism.

CPSIA information can be obtained
at www.ICGtesting.com
Printed in the USA
LVHW081731290621
691473LV00004B/304